The Science of Fiction
and the Fiction of Science

CRITICAL EXPLORATIONS IN SCIENCE FICTION AND FANTASY
(a series edited by Donald E. Palumbo and C.W. Sullivan III)

1. *Worlds Apart? Dualism and Transgression in Contemporary Female Dystopias* (Dunja M. Mohr, 2005)

2. *Tolkien and Shakespeare: Essays on Shared Themes and Language* (edited by Janet Brennan Croft, 2007)

3. *Culture, Identities and Technology in the* Star Wars *Films: Essays on the Two Trilogies* (edited by Carl Silvio and Tony M. Vinci, 2007)

4. *The Influence of* Star Trek *on Television, Film and Culture* (edited by Lincoln Geraghty, 2007)

5. *Hugo Gernsback and the Century of Science Fiction* (Gary Westfahl, 2007)

6. *One Earth, One People: The Mythopoeic Fantasy Series of Ursula K. Le Guin, Lloyd Alexander, Madeleine L'Engle and Orson Scott Card* (Marek Oziewicz, 2008)

7. *The Evolution of Tolkien's Mythology: A Study of the History of Middle-earth* (Elizabeth A. Whittingham, 2008)

8. *H. Beam Piper: A Biography* (John F. Carr, 2008)

9. *Dreams and Nightmares: Science and Technology in Myth and Fiction* (Mordecai Roshwald, 2008)

10. Lilith *in a New Light: Essays on the George MacDonald Fantasy Novel* (edited by Lucas H. Harriman, 2008)

11. *Feminist Narrative and the Supernatural: The Function of Fantastic Devices in Seven Recent Novels* (Katherine J. Weese, 2008)

12. *The Science of Fiction and the Fiction of Science: Collected Essays on SF Storytelling and the Gnostic Imagination* (Frank McConnell, 2009)

The Science of Fiction and the Fiction of Science

Collected Essays on SF Storytelling
and the Gnostic Imagination

FRANK MCCONNELL

Edited by GARY WESTFAHL
Foreword by NEIL GAIMAN

CRITICAL EXPLORATIONS IN
SCIENCE FICTION AND FANTASY, 12
Donald E. Palumbo *and* C.W. Sullivan III, *series editors*

McFarland & Company, Inc., Publishers
Jefferson, North Carolina, and London

LIBRARY OF CONGRESS CATALOGUING-IN-PUBLICATION DATA

McConnell, Frank, 1942–1999.
    The science of fiction and the fiction of science : collected essays on sf storytelling and the gnostic imagination / Frank McConnell ; edited by Gary Westfahl ; foreword by Neil Gaiman.
        p.   cm. — (Critical explorations in science fiction and fantasy ; 12)
    Includes bibliographical references and index.

    ISBN 978-0-7864-3722-1
    softcover : 50# alkaline paper ∞

    1. Science fiction — History and criticism. 2. Storytelling in literature. 3. Gnosticism in literature. I. Westfahl, Gary. II. Title.
    PN3448.S45M35   2009
    809.3'8762 — dc22   2008046162

British Library cataloguing data are available

Copyright ©2009 Celeste McConnell Barber and Gary Westfahl. All rights reserved

No part of this book may be reproduced or transmitted in any form or by any means, electronic or mechanical, including photocopying or recording, or by any information storage and retrieval system, without permission in writing from the publisher.

Cover image ©2009 Photodisc

Manufactured in the United States of America

McFarland & Company, Inc., Publishers
  Box 611, Jefferson, North Carolina 28640
    www.mcfarlandpub.com

To Eaton.
And the 16 years that followed.
—Celeste McConnell Barber

Acknowledgments

The first, and most important, person to acknowledge is Frank McConnell's widow, Celeste McConnell Barber, who from the very start has been unfailingly helpful and supportive in getting this volume into print, making helpful suggestions, and providing important information. Without her, this volume could not have been completed. I also heartily thank Neil Gaiman and the other distinguished individuals who happily agreed to contribute their comments on Frank McConnell to this volume without receiving any compensation.

I must also thank the following persons and institutions for permission to republish the writings of Frank McConnell:

Stacey Hayes (permissions) of the University of Georgia Press, for permission to republish "Alimentary, My Dear Watson: Food and Eating in Scientific and Mystery Fiction," originally published in *Foods of the Gods: Eating and the Eaten in Fantasy and Science Fiction,* edited by Gary Westfahl, George Slusser, and Eric S. Rabkin (Athens, Georgia: University of Georgia Press, 1996); "'Turn That Shit Down!' Or, How to Market an Underground," originally published in *Science Fiction and Market Realities,* edited by Gary Westfahl, George Slusser, and Eric S. Rabkin (Athens, Georgia: University of Georgia Press, 1996); and "You Bet Your Life: Death and the Storyteller," originally published in *Immortal Engines: Life Extension and Immortality in Science Fiction and Fantasy,* edited by George Slusser, Gary Westfahl, and Eric S. Rabkin (Athens, Georgia: University of Georgia Press, 1996).

Angela Moore-Swafford, permissions agent of Southern Illinois University Press, for permission to republish "Boring Dates: Reflections on the Apocalypse Game," pp. 232–238 by Frank McConnell; originally published in *Storm Warnings: Science Fiction Confronts the Future*, edited by Slusser, Greenland, and Rabkin ©1987 by the Board of Trustees, Southern Illinois University; "Born in Fire: The Ontology of the Monster," pp. 231–238 by Frank

McConnell; originally published in *Shadows of the Magic Lamp*, edited by Slusser and Rabkin ©1985 by the Board of Trustees, Southern Illinois University; "Frames in Search of a Genre," pp. 119–130 by Frank McConnell; originally published in *Intersections: Fantasy and Science Fiction* edited by Slusser and Rabkin ©1987 by the Board of Trustees, Southern Illinois University; "From Astarte to Barbie and Beyond: The Serious History of Dolls," pp. 199–207 by Frank McConnell; originally published in *Aliens: The Anthropology of Science Fiction* edited by Slusser and Rabkin ©1987 by the Board of Trustees, Southern Illinois University; "The Playing Fields of Eden," pp. 78–87 by Frank McConnell; originally published in *Mindscapes: The Geographies of Imagined Worlds* edited by Slusser and Rabkin ©1989 by the Board of Trustees, Southern Illinois University Press; and "Sturgeon's Law: First Corollary," pp. 14–23 by Frank McConnell; originally published in *Hard Science Fiction* edited by Slusser and Rabkin ©1989 by the Board of Trustees, Southern Illinois University.

James Carman, managing editor of *The Wilson Quarterly*, for permission to republish "H.G. Wells: Utopia and Doomsday," reprinted with permission from *The Wilson Quarterly*, Summer 1980. copyright ©1980 by The Woodrow Wilson International Center for Scholars. All rights reserved.

Karl Kvitko, editor of Xenos Press, for permission to republish "It's Only a Paper Moon: Fantasy and the Professors," originally published in *Genre at the Crossroads: The Challenge of Fantasy*, edited by George Slusser and Jean-Pierre Barricelli (Riverside, California: Xenos, 2003).

Suzanne Paris (rights and permissions) of Greenwood Press for permission to republish "The Missionary Physician, from Asclepius to Kervorkian," originally published in *No Cure for the Future: Disease and Medicine in Science Fiction and Fantasy*, edited by Gary Westfahl and George Slusser. Copyright 2002 by Gary Westfahl and George Slusser. Reproduced with permission of Greenwood Publishing Group, Inc. Westport, CT; and "Seven Types of Chopped Liver: My Adventures in the Genre Wars," originally published in *Science Fiction, Canonization, Marginalization, and the Academy*, edited by Gary Westfahl and George Slusser. Copyright 2002 by Gary Westfahl and George Slusser. Reproduced with permission of Greenwood Publishing Group, Inc. Westport, CT.

Marsha Grove, director of the Champaign (Illinois) Public Library and Information Center, for permission to republish "Realist of the Fantastic: H.G. Wells about/in/on the Movies," originally published in *H.G. Wells: Reality and Beyond: A Collection of Critical Essays Prepared in Conjunction with the Exhibition and Symposium on H.G. Wells.* edited by Michael Mullin (Champaign, Illinois: Champaign Public Library and Information Center, 1986).

Jennifer Dunbar Dorn, senior editor of *Sniper Logic*, for permission to republish "The Science of Fiction and the Fiction of Science: A Storytelling Animal in an Inhospitable World," originally published in *Sniper Logic*, 7 (Winter-Fall 1999), pp. 113–120, and Bruce Kawin's "Frank McConnell, May 20, 1942–Jan. 17, 1999," originally published in *Sniper Logic*, 7 (Winter-Fall, 1999), pp. 118–119.

Mary Jane Winokur, permissions manager of Heldreth Publications, for permission to republish "Song of Innocence: *The Creature from the Black Lagoon*" originally published in *Journal of Popular Film*, 2 (1973), pp. 15–28. Reprinted with permission of the Helen Dwight Reid Educational Foundation. Published by Heldref Publications, 1319 18th Street, NW, Washington, DC 20036-1802. www.heldref.org. Copyright@1973.

The process of preparing a complete, authoritative bibliography of the innumerable works of Frank McConnell demanded the expert assistance of several individuals, including the staff of the Interlibrary Loan Department of the University of California, Riverside's Tomás Rivera Library: Janet Moores, Maria Mendoza, Esther Sanchez, and Kimberly Noon; Lisa Yaszek and Joshua Cuneo of the Georgia Institute of Technology; and Donna Haraway and Scout Calvert of the University of California, Santa Cruz.

Finally, I thank Donald E. Palumbo who capably helped to get this volume into print.

Table of Contents

Acknowledgments   vii
Foreword by Neil Gaiman   1
Introduction by Gary Westfahl   5

I. Frank McConnell B.C.E. (Before Coming to Eaton)   9
  1. Born in Fire: The Ontology of the Monster   11
  2. Song of Innocence: *The Creature from the Black Lagoon*   18
  3. H.G. Wells: Utopia and Doomsday   29
  4. Realist of the Fantastic: H.G. Wells about/in/on the Movies   37

II. Slouching Toward Bedlam: The Early Eaton Essays   47
  5. Sturgeon's Law: First Corollary   48
  6. Boring Dates: Reflections on the Apocalypse Game   57
  7. Frames in Search of a Genre   63
  8. From Astarte to Barbie and Beyond: The Serious History of Dolls   74
  9. The Playing Fields of Eden   82
 10. It's Only a Paper Moon: Fantasy and the Professors   91
 11. "Turn That Shit Down!" Or, How to Market an Underground   102

III. Gnostic Lunch: The Later Eaton Essays   111
 12. Alimentary, My Dear Watson: Food and Eating in Scientific and Mystery Fiction   112

13.	You Bet Your Life: Death and the Storyteller	124
14.	Seven Types of Chopped Liver: My Adventures in the Genre Wars	132
15.	The Missionary Physician, from Asclepius to Kervorkian	146
16.	The Science of Fiction and the Fiction of Science: A Storytelling Animal in an Inhospitable World	155

Epilogue: Memories of Frank — 164
    Paul Alkon — 164
    Gregory Benford — 166
    Harold Bloom — 167
    Sheila Finch — 167
    Carl Freedman — 168
    Howard V. Hendrix — 169
    Bruce Kawin — 172
    Joseph D. Miller — 173
    Eric S. Rabkin — 175
    Mark Rose — 177
    George Slusser — 178

Chapter Notes — 181
A Bibliography of the Works of Frank McConnell — 187
A Bibliography of Primary and Secondary Works Cited in the Text — 201
Index — 213

Foreword
by Neil Gaiman

Frank McConnell entered my life in February 1992 with a review he had written of *Sandman*, the story sequence I was writing in comics form, for *Commonweal*. This was early in the history of *Sandman*, early enough that he was pretty much the first person to write about *Sandman* in a serious, non-comics-related forum, early enough that he was pretty much the first person to notice that I was writing a story about stories.

And then, a year later, he was the first professor ever to bring me in to talk to a university. I addressed his English class, which had been studying *Sandman*. (When, in 1996, an art department brought me in to a university in St Louis, I was told the English department was boycotting the event because people who write comics weren't real writers, and I thought of Frank, and I smiled.) Ten years after Frank's first invitation, it became fashionable for English departments to invite me to come and talk to them, and graphic novels were hip and cutting edge. But Frank McConnell was the first. He listened when his students told him things.

Which I mention partly because it makes me happy and mostly because it demonstrates that Frank was an iconoclast, and always way ahead of the curve. Also, because somewhere between the publication of the article and the end of the first talk in Santa Barbara, we became friends. I don't remember how we first started talking. Did he write to me mentioning the review and invite me to come and speak? I think so. I think that was where it began.

So. Meeting Frank for the first time — in my head he has cigarette ash spilled down the bulging front of his suit and a glass of whisky in his hand (although I am sure the whisky came later, after the talk and the signing) and he is whisking me through the English department as all around him people explain that it's "no smoking, except for Frank, of course." And everywhere he goes, he is swearing. Swearing better than anyone I've ever heard, and I once worked on a building site, obscenities deployed like hand grenades in the conversation — for emphasis, for punctuation, for effect, for ammunition or covering fire, forcing you to hear the rest of the words he was using too, swearing because he liked to swear and because he liked to shock and because he had tenure and he was damned well going to swear if he wanted to. Only Frank would never have said *damned* in that sentence.

After that first encounter, he phoned me, though, and I was charmed by him, as people who wanted to learn from him were charmed. Often I would be the one to phone. Mostly we talked about writing — he sent me his fiction books, which he dismissed as trivial moments before he confessed that they were the most important things to him, that in his heart he was a blocked mystery writer; he was part of the brotherhood of Mystery Writers that went back to Hammett and Chandler and before, and he was moonlighting as a professor, hoping that no one would catch on. That was what he'd say, between the words and around them, and I believed it.

I was soon an annual visitor to Santa Barbara. I was never entirely sure of the cause and effect — did he teach his students a book by me each year to give him an excuse to bring me in to talk, or did he bring me in because he was teaching them a book by me? I suspected the former. I know that I went to speak to his students mostly because before the event started, and once it was done, Frank and I would talk, face to face rather than on the phone. I loved to see how his students reacted to him. Once it turned out that an old friend of mine, who came along to see me talk, had studied under him in Chicago. He was the only professor she had cared for or remembered, over fifteen years earlier. I still get notes and messages from people Frank taught, who remembered. Frank was beloved. He touched people's minds and hearts.

We would talk long on the phone. Not as often as either of us would like, but each conversation turned into a marathon — we would talk about writing, about poetry, about detective fiction. We'd talk about Chesterton and Byron and H.G. Wells. I would recommend Gene Wolfe to him. I would try to chivvy him into writing fiction again, and sometimes I felt like I was succeeding. We'd talk about fiction and about life. He thought I was really smart, and I knew that he was, and we would talk and we would talk. He believed in writing, believed that we were imperfect beings who made good art.

I asked him to write the introduction to *Sandman: The Kindly Ones*, and he did, and I was pleased that he did it and he was pleased to be asked.

I was on a book-signing tour in 1999 when I heard that he had fallen and was in hospital and then, suddenly and shatteringly, that he had died. I still miss him — miss the phone calls, miss the cigarette ash and the whisky glass and the hugeness of heart and mind.

I had hoped that his pleasures would somehow conspire together to keep his death at bay. That he'd be one of the old, wise ones preserved by alcohol, dusted with ash, sharing his knowledge and his thoughts, inspiring students, finding more authors to champion ahead of the curve, writing detective novels, his conversation still crackling with expletives and obscenities and great and mighty swears.

But we can read what the man left us. It's not the same — it's never the same — but it's a start.

Introduction
by Gary Westfahl

If you were ever asked to introduce Frank McConnell at a conference, you always spoke briefly and rapidly, because you knew that the audience was anxious to hear Frank, not you, and because you knew that anything you could say to introduce Frank would never be as insightful or as funny as the things that Frank was about to say. In writing an introduction to a collection of Frank's essays, I will strive to follow the same policy.

I first met Frank at one of the annual J. Lloyd Eaton Conferences on Science Fiction and Fantasy Literature, sometime in the early 1980s, when I was still a young and awestruck spectator to, and not a participant in, the proceedings. I recall a conversation when the topic of favorite science fiction films came up, and I hesitantly confessed to having a special fondness for "giant insect movies." Frank immediately launched into a delightful anecdote about how he had first met his second wife, Celeste, while carrying on an animated conversation about their mutual fondness for the movie *Them!*, concluding with a perfect imitation of the eerie screeching sounds made by the giant ants in that movie. And that, coming from a professor of English at a major university who had published on William Wordsworth and Thomas Pynchon, essentially defined Frank. I have never known a man who had such an incredibly broad range of enthusiasms: he loved *King Lear*, he loved Wile E. Coyote, he loved Charlie Parker, he loved Mary Shelley's *Frankenstein*, he loved Wallace Stevens, and he loved *Seinfeld,* all with equal devotion, and he could effortlessly discern connections between such disparate texts to buttress his always surprising, and always persuasive, arguments. But I don't want to explain Frank's jokes; I want you to hear them, and I am trying to get you there as fast as I can.

During the two decades of the Eaton Conferences, it was fascinating to observe the evolution of Frank's essays. In the beginning, he brought to the conference the generally subdued and serious voice previously employed in his other scholarly publications. However, as Frank adjusted to the friendly confines of the Eaton Conference, he gradually adopted a new style of writing — more informal, more humorous, and more inclined to take breathtaking leaps from one disparate topic to another while unfolding what was actually a carefully structured analysis. In addition, while he dutifully addressed each of the increasingly specific themes of these annual conferences, he was visibly employing these topics to outline his own developing argument about science fiction.

Some aspects of this argument surfaced in his early Eaton essays like "Frames in Search of a Genre." He maintained that all genres and categories of literature were essentially arbitrary and artificial, and that it was better to consider all texts simply as examples of the art of storytelling, humanity's most ancient and evocative activity. And his focus on this point led to an accompanying contempt for some contemporary literary scholars who, in his view, were so obsessed with "critical theory" that they lost sight of the real reasons people create, and cherish, works of literature. These points allowed Frank to display his vast knowledge of literature, film, and music, to establish stimulating connections between apparently incongruous pairings of texts, and to amuse audiences with startling digressions and good-natured barbs at the critical establishment.

Still, as I believe Frank himself came to realize, this argument did have certain limitations; for surely, despite their overriding significance as stories, there had to be *some* reason other than random accident why certain texts had been universally identified as "science fiction" and embraced as such by readers, fans, publishers, and critics. And Frank eventually hit upon a satisfying explanation when he was asked to respond to one of the Eaton topics he had most bitterly criticized — "food in science fiction and fantasy." What on Earth can I say about *that*? he fumed to me when the topic was first announced, and his initial impatience with the task comes out clearly in the introduction to "Alimentary, My Dear Watson." And yet, forced to ponder why the food in detective fiction was so often sumptuous and elaborately described, while the food in science fiction was so often sterile and marginalized, he concluded that science fiction could be understood as a literary legacy of the ancient Christian heresy of Gnosticism, a belief system which emphasized knowledge and spirituality while disdaining the body and the physical world. While there had been a brief reference to Gnosticism during "Born in Fire," his early discussion of the Frankenstein monster, "Alimentary, My Dear Watson" served as the first extended version of the argument that science fiction was fundamentally a Gnostic literature; and this argument, he discovered, then enabled him to understand and explain many things about the genre: not only why the food in future worlds is so often terrible, but why science fiction writers are obsessed with transcending the body and achieving immortality, why there is a problematic relationship between science fiction and the academy, why science fiction displays a curious lack of interest in future advances in medicine, and why there is a perceived gap between the "two cultures" of literature and science. Frank was effectively demonstrating that, within the purportedly technological mindset of science fiction authors and readers, there lurked at the genre's core a basic spirituality — a host in the machine, so to speak. In sum, while never forgetting his fundamental insistence upon science fiction as storytelling, Frank had also laid the groundwork for a distinctive argument about the nature of science fiction which could have been cohesively supported in a scholarly monograph by means of a broad range of topics and texts; and I was by no means the only colleague of Frank who began urging him to revisit his Eaton essays and refashion them into this sort of unified text. Unfortunately, however, as he continued to focus on innumerable scattered assignments for various publications, he never took the time to craft such a book.

So it was that, immediately after Frank's shocking death in 1999, I wanted to put together a collection of his Eaton essays, which would necessarily have to serve as an ersatz substitute for the book he had never been able to write. I also believed that his brilliant writings merited a broader audience and would prove entertaining and enlightening even to readers without a strong interest in science fiction. However, I still had many other tasks to work on in 1999, and it was not until early 2006 that I finally could devote myself to the creation of this volume. But it is a tribute to the love and admiration that Frank had inspired throughout his career that the project came together with amazing speed: his widow, Celeste, immediately agreed to the project; despite a vow to stop writing introductions, Neil Gaiman agreed within hours to contribute a foreword; and virtually all of the friends and colleagues I contacted about providing some concluding reminiscences about Frank quickly promised to do so. All that was left to do was to retype or scan the essays compile a Frank McConnell bibliography, and, as Frank would probably put it, anal-retentively add scholarly footnotes to all of his myriad references and quotations. (As one of his quirks, Frank refused to provide footnotes, boldly asserting that his unfailing accuracy in citations rendered them unnecessary; in checking on his work, I found that he was indeed almost always accurate; and on those few occasions when he was not, I have generally chosen to silently correct the error.)

A few words about the contents of this book, and I will finally get out of Frank's way. It is mostly devoted to Frank's twelve Eaton papers, presented in chronological order as they were written; the McConnell bibliography includes information about the original dates of presentation. But there are also a few added attractions. Celeste suggested that a few other essays could be included: an early article on *The Creature from the Black Lagoon,* which could serve as a fitting complement to Frank's Eaton paper about *Frankenstein,* and two other essays about H.G. Wells, an author he had studied with special attentiveness. Finally, an essay written in 1988 for the first issue of George Slusser's proposed new journal, *Fantasy Studies,* seemed very much part of the continuum of analysis that Frank had provided for George's Eaton Conferences. Many other items — scholarly essays, book reviews, and his numerous columns for *Commonweal* magazine — might also have been included, but none of them, upon reflection, seemed to fit within this particular volume. However, in compiling the McConnell bibliography, I did strive to include the URLs for all items that are online, so that interested readers can examine more of his always rewarding works.

All right; the boring introduction has been completed as hastily as possible, and you are now free to enjoy the wit and wisdom of Frank McConnell. Please fasten your seat belts, and enjoy.

Part I
Frank McConnell B.C.E. *(Before Coming to Eaton)*

The first essay in this section, "Born in Fire: The Ontology of the Monster," is actually the first paper Frank McConnell ever presented at an Eaton Conference; but it was written, of course, before he had had the chance to experience an Eaton Conference, and so it does not yet display the characteristically colorful tone and style of his later Eaton essays. The essay is followed by three other essays from the 1970s and 1980s representing his work on the science fiction subjects that he specialized in before becoming an Eaton regular: horror films, and H.G. Wells.

1

Born in Fire

The Ontology of the Monster

He has never had a name. The unenlightened call him "Frankenstein," confusing him with his creator. The less-unenlightened call him "the monster," confusing him with his popular reception by the villagers and the local constabulary. But none of us knows, really, what to call him: knows, as it were, what name he would choose for himself, if he were given the choice.

And that is ironic, for perhaps no creature of the past two hundred years of imagination has been more intricately involved with, more spectacularly crucified upon, the cross of language, His discovery of speech — of the fact that we can convey meanings to one another — is perhaps the most important and certainly the most poignant episode in the novel that tells his story for the first time. And, over a hundred years later, nearly his first words on film — in *The Bride of Frankenstein* (1935) — "Friend good!" are almost an encapsulation of all his loneliness, all his panic, and all his profound connection with our own condition.

But, as I say, he has never had a name. Perhaps because he is so important to us, and so much a part of our own loneliness and uncertainty. He is dead matter become conscious, mere stuff that has learned a language and therefore has an illusion of possessing a soul. Mary Shelley's friend Byron, who was with her during the splendid summer of 1816 — the summer that produced *Frankenstein* (1818), *Mont Blanc* (1817), *Manfred* (1817), and so much more — described man, in *Don Juan*, as "fiery dust."[1] It is an image that incarnates a century and more of doubt about the real validity, the real nobility of human consciousness. It is also a perfect description of the Frankenstein monster.

Walton, the frame-narrator of Mary Shelley's novel, writes early in the book to his sister: "I shall commit my thoughts to paper, it is true; but that is a poor medium for the communication of feeling. I desire the company of a man who could sympathize with me; whose eyes would reply to mine."[2] This, of course, is the quintessential romantic search for the double, the romantic nostalgia for a human universe that would be a hall of mirrors, of perfect and perfectly responsive replicas of the self. And any number of commentators have remarked how Walton is fated to meet precisely that friend, that dreamt-of and dreaded double, in the person of Victor Frankenstein. But there is another double for Watson — in this tale which is a nest of doubles — the monster himself, the purely imaginative creature, whose "eyes would reply to mine,"[3] of necessity, since he is the sheer projection, the sheer self-consciousness, of language. Harold Bloom, in a brilliant brief essay on *Frankenstein,* has observed how the warfare of creator and creation in that novel is a reflection and inversion of the positive quest for the double in poems like Shelley's *Alastor* (1816) or Byron's *Childe Harold* (1812–1818).[4] And, building upon Bloom, we can observe that the monster's outraged and outrageous status as mad mirror image of the questing Walton is an anticipation of such powerful sights as Charles Foster Kane, at the end of his life, trapped in loneliness and splendor among the infinite mirror images of the palace he has built for himself. What is monstrosity, after all, if not the image of ourselves we have searched for and which, having once gazed upon it, we cannot ever forget?

In film after film, reincarnation after reincarnation, what being has been so often immolated as Frankenstein's monster? The title of the 1969 Hammer film, *Frankenstein Must Be Destroyed,* is almost an epigraph for the whole myth of the monster. Frankenstein — or his creation — *must* be destroyed. In tale after tale, version after version. Like spectators at a Greek tragedy, we watch, waiting for the preordained conclusion, which does not surprise us at all, but fulfills us because it is what we came, after all, to see.

Like spectators at a Greek tragedy; or like participants at a Mass. For there is, after all, one other character in our collective consciousness who has been immolated and resurrected quite as often as the monster.

Let me observe a pun. It is one of those deep puns — those figures which "probe ancient fetid shafts and tunnels of truth," as Thomas Pynchon puts it[5] — implicit in the nature of the language, and therefore not willed by anyone but, indeed, preordained. The word, "monster," derives from the Latin *monere,* to warn; but *monere* itself probably derives from an Indo-European root which also generates the Latin word, "to show." The monster, in other words, is both a warning and a spectacle.

And a spectacle is also a *speculum,* a looking-glass. And a monster is also a *monstrance,* the elaborate golden vessel that holds and displays the Host on certain solemn occasions in the Roman Catholic Church. Another double:

for if the Host (itself doubling the doctrine of the Incarnation) is mere matter infused from above with divine life, the monster is its precise reversal, mere matter struggling up — or raised up — from below toward consciousness.

A *speculum:* a created image that gives back the image of its creator, or a mirror that — like all mirrors — can take on an eerie and threatening reality of its own, when gazed into too intently. Zosimus the Panopolitan, one of those alchemists who somehow lies behind the figure of Victor Frankenstein, observed that "He who looks in a mirror looks not at shadows, but at what shadows hint of, understanding reality through fictitious appearances."[6] This, again, is the benevolent version of the Gnostic quest to transcend the world of illusion by multiplying the complexities of illusion. And, again, the myth of the monster gives us the nightmare inversion of that quest. It is remarkable how often in the Frankenstein films, ever since James Whale's first recension, the monster is caught at a crucial moment looking at his reflection — in a pool, in a window, in a mirror — and recoiling in horror at what he sees. At such moments we invariably realize that his horror at his own monstrosity is a deflection and a purification of our own terror at meeting ourselves.

The very first film of *Frankenstein* was made in 1910 by the Edison Company. It is lost, but the scenario survives. And the last scene of this short film appears to have been a wonderfully inventive bit of filmmaking, and a wonderfully perceptive approach to the concerns we have been examining. After the monster has wreaked various bits of mayhem, to the horror of his creator, he finally invaded Frankenstein's bedchamber on the wedding night. And scene 25 reads, "Monster seeing his vision in glass disappears. Frankenstein's mind becomes peaceful."[7] The demonic incarnation of the self is destroyed, in other words, by the same process of mirroring of which it is a limiting expression.

I am not — please believe me — trying to work my way toward a reading of the Frankenstein myth as a Christian allegory; that would be entirely too Chestertonian. But I do think it important to get clear the fact that, in inventing her seminal modern myth of consciousness, Mary Shelley, either consciously or not, was led toward a story which parodies the determinative story of our culture. Karl Marx says that every event in history occurs twice, first as tragedy and then as farce. And we may remark that the event — so runs the tale — that occurred first on a starry night in Bethlehem is echoed and completed as bitter farce in the event of that dark and stormy night in Ingolstadt, two millennia later.

And to realize this is to realize something, I think, fairly important about the relationship between the two major manifestations of the Frankenstein story — the novel, that is, and the roughly two dozen major films "based on" the novel since 1931. It is also to realize something about the general relationship between film and literature as the central narrative modes of our time.

It is a truism of scriptural studies since Rudolf Bultmann that *kerygma* precedes myth. That is, in the history of religion, ritual invariably predates the *stories* that explain how the ritual came to be. This is particularly true in the history of Christianity. The earliest Christian texts, Paul's letters to the Thessalonians and the Galatians, are mainly concerned with ritual observance, and with the proper form of the Lord's Supper — the Mass, in other words. It was only some years later that the Gospels were written — Mark first, then Matthew, then after a while Luke, then after a *long* while John — to explain the story behind the cult, to elaborate the ritual into a founding-tale.

This all sounds harmless enough, except that the history of the Frankenstein myth exactly inverts this process, too, just as the image of the monster inverts the image of Christ the incarnate son of God. Remember the title of the Hammer film I mentioned before: Frankenstein *must* be destroyed. That is not really the title of a story, it is a formula for a ritual. In the history of the Frankenstein tales, in other words, myth precedes *kerygma*; narrative precedes ritual; story precedes the solidification of story into cult-observance. For that, to be blunt, is what the films of the Frankenstein cycle are: cult observances, inverted Masses whose conclusion is preordained and all of whose plot elements are as predictable as the *Lavabo* or the Offertory verse.

C.G. Jung, in his great essay on "Transformation Symbols in the Mass," observes that the ritual of the Mass is actually two rituals melded together, a communal meal and a sacrificial offering, *deipnon* and *thysia*, as Jung calls them.[8] In the Mass, the order is *thysia-deipnon:* the sacrifice of bread and wine precedes their transformation and sharing in a common meal, the Offertory precedes the Communion. Again, and by now predictably, this order is inverted in the rituals of the Frankenstein films. First the Communion: the monster attempts to enter human society in one way or another, only to be rejected again. Then the sacrifice: his inevitable, and preferably fiery, sacrifice. This rhythm is caught most slyly in *The Bride of Frankenstein*, where the monster shares his famous meal of bread and wine with the blind hermit, and where the appearance of the bride — a failed communion if there ever was one — is liturgically introduced by the grandiose, wicked and wickedly funny gesture of Doctor Praetorius (Ernest Thesiger).

But the same rhythm is also visible in almost every film version of the tale. Mel Brooks, in his attempt to finish the legend once and for all in *Young Frankenstein* (1974), builds upon it as subtly as did the early James Whale, carrying it all the way through, for once, to the monster's *acceptance* by the society that had earlier rejected him. Frankenstein *need not* be destroyed, says Brooks's very serious film; at least, not if we can think our way through to the inescapable point behind the ritual of the monster's endless resurrections and public burnings, the point being that he is the reflection — the *speculum,* the looking glass — of our own horror at having bodies.

How can we be gifted with speech, thought, the power of aspiration and longing when we know the full loathsomeness of our own physicality? It is a question that the myth of the incarnation tries to deny, and is the question that romanticism will not let us stop asking ourselves. Yeats was probably not thinking of Mary Shelley's creation when he wrote of his soul, "Fastened to a dying animal/It knows not what it is."[9] He didn't have to be.

Think about a more recent film than *Young Frankenstein*: *The Elephant Man* (1980). Why should John Merrick, congenitally and horribly deformed and yet articulate, sensitive, and gentle, have become the celebrity he was at precisely *that* time — the time of the Industrial Revolution, the Romantic Era, of the germination of Darwin's thought? David Lynch, the director of *The Elephant Man,* suggests that Merrick's monstrosity is part and parcel of the monstrosity of his age, of its increasing emphasis on the similarity between man and intricately organized machine; so that the Elephant Man's transcendent ugliness, his *unsuitability* for any but the least mechanical (most human?) of tasks is almost a guarantee of his spirituality. Lynch must have had the Universal Studios Frankenstein series in mind while making the film: his monster is too close in humanity and in essential dignity to the movie-made monster for it to have been otherwise. Life imitates art, in other words, and the art itself imitates the life on which the art could have been patterned.

A film like *The Elephant Man* or that other great monster movie, François Truffaut's *The Wild Child* (1970), helps us see precisely how the Frankenstein series itself is quintessential science fiction. For all these films remind us that science fiction is really *technological* fiction, and that the first of human technologies, the first artificial imposition humans make upon their environment, is language itself.

Are we human because we speak or do we speak because we are human? It may be the most critical question in anthropology and political theory since Rousseau. What is the origin of the Word? When Merrick in *The Elephant Man* first utters articulate sounds, we know his salvation is assured. And when Victor, the "wild child" of Truffaut's film, fails to learn speech, we know that he is doomed. It was René Descartes, in the *Discourse on Method* (1637), who established definitively, for our age, the equation of ability and humanity. We have not gotten over it yet.

Particularly, we have not gotten over it in the case of Frankenstein's monster. For it is speech, after all, which he desires more than anything else: speech to another being, speech with another being. And it is speech which he is most definitively denied.

Denied, that is, in the films; not in the novel. It has always struck me as one of the truly curious details of the myth that the monster, in Mary Shelley's novel, is so incredibly eloquent, while in the classic Frankenstein films he is, at worse, incapable of speech altogether and, at best, gifted with a mean baby talk that sounds like a demonic version of the Cookie Monster. Even in *The Ghost of Frankenstein* (1942), where the brain of the cretinous Igor (Bela Lugosi) is transplanted to the monster's body, the best he can manage is a slurred Transylvanian snarl.

Does this mean that we are dealing with two separate visions of the creature? I think not. I think it means we are dealing with two separate, and complementary, versions of the creature. It is by now a cliché of film-and-literature studies to say that while literature gives us a world of words, reaching out toward a perception of things, film gives us a throng of things, reaching in toward an understanding of language. The myth of the Frankenstein monster is the myth, disconcerting in the extreme, of an artificial creation that seems to possess life, and to possess it as fully as you and I. Naturally, in a novel, this should be the imagination of a creature who, for all his monstrosity, is nevertheless capable of learning language. And just as naturally, in film, this should be the image of a creature who, for all his evident humanity, is incapable of speaking. For the monster of film is already what Mary Shelley had to labor so hard and so brilliantly to envisage: an artificial construct, a make-up masterpiece, a triumph of special effects, that nevertheless seems to us to live.

To say this much is to say, in a serious way, that the myth of Frankenstein and his monster is also largely the myth of film itself. For film — the medium that presents the monster, and not solely the monster — is an artifice, a technology that imitates life so successfully it almost, at times, seems a larger and more capacious version of life. The monster is forever mute on film, perhaps, because film is the medium he was predestined for all along. All he needs to do is be there. And the unvoiced testimony of his presence is enough to remind us of the fragility of our own pretensions to specialty, to intelligence, to a soul.

I know of no more articulate or moving moment in the history of film than the first appearance, in the first film of *Frankenstein,* of Boris Karloff, moving his monstrously distorted face into the light: our first full view of the monster, and our first realization that the monster is made possible by precisely the techniques and technologies which also allow us to believe in the humanity of the other characters in the story. Where is, then, the distinction?

Nowhere, is the answer these quite grim films give us. The immensely affecting, sympathetic character of HAL in Stanley Kubrick's *2001: A Space Odyssey* (1968) is simply one of the mutated heirs of the monster. For if the monster is form without language, poor HAL is language without form — only that glaring red eye, and the most civilized discourse in Kubrick's *bitter* film. And a book like Douglas Hofstadter's *Gödel, Escher, Bach: An Eternal Golden Braid* (1979), which attempts to explain the evolution of an infinitely creative human consciousness from a mechanistic model of the operation of the brain, is in fact a distant, but still recognizable, heir to the problems invented by Mary Shelley in 1817, and thereafter perpetuated by the most effective storytelling method — film — civilization has yet devised.

In his excellent history of science fiction, *Billion Year Spree* (1973), Brian Aldiss identifies *Frankenstein, or the Modern Prometheus* as the first "true" novel of science fiction. It is perhaps one of the cleverest things anyone has observed about the form. But is also needs to be said that a true reading of *Frankenstein* shows us, not just that it is the first science fiction novel, but shows us also how much, and how desperately, science fiction is the distinctive genre of our own contemporary self-consciousness: and how much film itself, *the* art of the twentieth century, is itself an art that incarnates, even more than it expresses, the dominant concerns of science fiction. From the first, silent films, in which photographs of men and women and machines seemed to move, seemed suddenly and miraculously to become capable of a simulacrum of life itself, the myth of Mary Shelley's monster was realized: and it can be said that all subsequent film theory is really an attempt to come to terms with that central scandal, the scandal of life or soul created out of the most artificial, soulless of means. *Frankenstein,* in other words, can be taken as an encoded textbook for the exploration of film itself; can be taken as a kind of long, complex name for the art of film. And, if we cannot yet really name what film is, we can also realize that it shares that cosmic anonymity with the monster who is its symbol, its anticipation, and perhaps its most distinctive expression.

2

Song of Innocence
The Creature from the Black Lagoon

As the popular film, and popular culture generally, become more and more a subject of serious academic interest, we are likely to be treated to more and more thoughtful excurses upon those works which many of us enjoyed, years ago, in the cool unthinking darkness of Saturday afternoon. Not that this multi-leveled coming to light is at all a bad thing: on the contrary, it is one of the healthiest signs of the continuing life of our culture — and of the critical mind which depends so desperately for its own life *upon* that culture. And reading the criticism of a Leslie Fiedler or a Parker Tyler, or the brilliant "pop" fictions of a Thomas Pynchon (*The Crying of Lot 49* [1966]) or a Brock Brower (*The Late Great Creature* [1971]) is, for a generation trained to be abashed about enjoying films later than *Battleship Potemkin* (1925), itself a kind of liberation. But there is a danger in the meeting of academicism and pop culture: one implicit in the phrase, "pop," itself. The danger is, simply, that critics — and their readers and students — might too easily forget that pop culture is, after all, *culture*: that, on its own terms, it is no less serious, and potentially no less moving, than the culture which produced an Ovid or a George Herbert. Those Saturday afternoons — how could we deny it? — were wonderful. But we cannot, should not, go back there; and a criticism which tries to, which turns a serious appreciation of their films into an excuse for returning there, is actually ducking the duties of the more complex and dangerous fun of which, at their best, they were a prophecy.

The film I wish to discuss is, in its way, a parable of this problem, a fable for pop critics. In histories of the horror film, Jack Arnold's 1954 *The Creature from the Black Lagoon* is most often regarded as a late and degenerate variant of the Frankenstein motif, a fast-buck piece of sensationalism, a "B-picture" even by the standards of a B-picture genre. There is, certainly,

2. Song of Innocence

something ludicrously adventitious about the existence of the "gill-man": he is neither a monstrous threat to society (the scientists have to go to the Lagoon to be terrorized by him), nor an extra-terrestrial threat to the world at large (vulnerable, unlike his cousins Godzilla and Reptilicus, to bullets and spear guns). And the charge of silliness may well apply to Arnold's sequel to the first film, *Revenge of the Creature* (1955) and John Sherwood's *The Creature Walks Among Us* (1956), although those productions, too, are not without their delights for the horror aficionado.

The original *Creature*, though, is a far better — and far more important — film than has yet been recognized. Much more than such relatively celebrated efforts as Don Siegel's 1956 *Invasion of the Body Snatchers* or Howard Hawks's/Christian Nyby's 1951 *The Thing (from Another World)*, it is definitively a film of the fifties, that curious and psychotic decade of American life we seemed, in the seventies, to be rediscovering with an affectionate and horrified smile. In terms of his popular success — an index of quality frowned upon, sometimes with good reason, by serious film critics — the Creature has established himself along with Dracula, Frankenstein's monster, and the Wolfman as one of the staples of the national crop of fear. I refer, of course, to the series of plastic monster-models produced in the mid-sixties, with great success, by Aurora Plastics, Inc., which officiated the canonization of the Creature. And I also invoke the fact, unverifiable but obvious, that *any* moviegoer between twenty-five and thirty-five, while he may not recognize the provenance of the Man from Planet X, the Thing, or the phrase "seed-pod," will unquestionably know, upon sight, from what movies comes a photo of the gill-man. The Creature, against all odds of believability, official recognition, and even, possibly, artistic quality, has *made it*. It behooves us to ask why.

The tradition of horror in the cinema, as we are coming to realize, is one of the oldest and most continuous of cinematic genres. That this is so should really surprise no one with even a minimal acquaintance with the imaginative life of the West, since terrifying tales are among the most ancient and most persistent stories in our inheritance: perhaps, indeed, in the inheritance of the human subconscious. A psychic history of culture, in fact, could be written very efficiently from the morphology of its monsters: the history of those personifications of the void which successive generations have selected as their central nightmares. Roy Huss and T.J. Ross's anthology, *Focus on the Horror Film*, intelligently classifies "varieties" of horror into "Gothic Horror" (or supernatural), "Monster Terror" (mechanical men, zombies, etc.), and "Psychological Thriller" (the terrors of dementia).[1] It is a convincing catalogue for the history of film and, indeed, for the history of literature since the romantic era, developing from the Satanic villains of the Gothic tale, through the demonic puppets of Mary Shelley and Charles Dickens, into the frozen mental landscapes of Franz Kafka and Samuel Beckett. But these phases of horror are not *stages*, at least not in an evolutionary sense. According to the particular needs for fear of a given age, any one of the "later" phases of the monster may revert or collapse into a more primal incarnation of the unspeakable, though perhaps overlaid with the trappings of contemporary, "scientific" verisimilitude. Each era chooses the monster it deserves and projects: and all of them are, in their terribleness, blood brothers.

The Creature from the Black Lagoon is a significant case of this. For during the fifties, surely the most dominant form of the monster was the alien invader, the hyper-rational saucerman, or the sub-rational insect mutant, whose threat was not so much personal violence as an insidious, fiendishly cold undermining of the normally (i.e. bourgeois–American) human. I have already mentioned *Invasion of the Body Snatchers* and *The Thing*—both of which exploit the "undermining" of civilization by vegetable life. There are also such classics of fifties apocalyptism as *The Day the Earth Stood Still* (1951) and *The Man from Planet X* (1951)—in both of which the alien is, ambiguously, well-intentioned but stung to malevolence by human mistrust; *Them!* (1954), *Tarantula* (1956), and *The Beast from 20,000 Fathoms* (1953), where the alien is a fearful result of nuclear alchemy; and *This Island Earth* (1955), *Earth Versus the Flying Saucers* (1956), and *Not of This Earth* (1957), "true" types of the evil bug-eyed-invader movie.

Sociologists and psychoanalysts of the film have for a long time now been making clear the political paranoia underlying these movies: their deep connection with the McCarthyist fear of the subtle Red Menace, with the threat of a massive and nefarious Fifth Column infesting the entire fabric of American society, and (in the case of the gigantic reptilian or insect mutations), with the fear of The Bomb. Raymond Durgnat's splendid essay on *This Island Earth* in *Films and Feelings* may conveniently stand, as example and consummation, of such readings.[2]

But, valuable as these interpretations are, they do not explain the peculiar power of the Creature: and lead one to suspect, therefore, that the Creature himself might lead us to a more efficient insight into the life of the decade. He is, as I have said, neither alien invader nor atomic mutant: he is, as one of the scientists observes in the film, "an evolutionary dead-end," a manfish who has, simply and absurdly, survived the eons since his race was spawned. He survives, furthermore, *because* he is the Creature *from the Black Lagoon*— an out-of-the-way South American inlet where time has stood still. His very existence, in other words, is the origin of his peculiar horror. Unlike any other monster one can think of, he is the result of no cause, neither accident nor devilish science nor the supernatural: he simply *is*, primal and eldest, and the outrage he generates is the curse only of those unlucky enough to discover his existence. The story begins with the discovery, by an archaeologist, of a claw-fossil belonging to one of the Creature's ancient race. And the action of the film, then, is the story of what happens to those who seek out — and seek to capture — the primal secrets which are *there* all along in the innocence and blandness of their unharassed privacy.

In what, then, does the terror of the Creature's being there (almost exactly in the sense of Heideggerian *Dasein*) consist? To answer this is to analyze the tightly conceived plot of the film; and to realize, first of all, that within that plot itself the Creature is almost as adventitious as he is in the larger tradition of horror-monsters. For while most films in the genre involve some (usually sketchy) love-interest between the young scientist — evil or benign — and the horror's intended female victim, in *The Creature from the Black Lagoon*, unusually and brilliantly, the love-story all but displaces the horror element of the plot. This is for the very good reason, I shall suggest, that the love-story is *another version* of the horror plot.

After the discovery of the initial fossil, a team of scientists take a small boat to the remote Black Lagoon, hoping to locate more fossils and establish a definite date for their find. The team, besides the mandatory old sage and a pipe-smoking, middle-aged establishment figure, consists of Mark (Richard Denning), David (Richard Carlson), and Kay (Julie Adams). Mark is a brilliant and ambitious young archaeologist, already with a string of important discoveries behind him and anxious to consolidate his fame; David, his assistant, is a more reflective, sensitive, and as yet unproved man; and Kay, Mark's colleague and girlfriend from childhood, is beginning to fall in love with David — much to Mark's chagrin. It is in terms of this triangle — Kay's instincts, Mark's possessive jealousy, and David's uncertainty and self-doubt — that the action will develop. And as the Creature gradually emerges into the center of that action, we see him — perhaps subconsciously, but inevitably, crucially — as a strange symbol and projection of the murderous sexual tension. For *The Creature from the Black Lagoon* is a daemonic pastoral, and its titular monster is, if anything, an almost-allegorical vision of sexual terror.

I do not mean to identify the Creature as that shibboleth of critical oversimplification, a "phallic symbol": he is much more than a sublimation, he is a realization of the psychic violence of the phallus itself. He is a *gill man*, a man-fish, a dweller in the aboriginal bath of the world's youth, a rigid swimmer in the generative fluid. I have mentioned that he is one of the most recognizable, memorable of monsters. And surely part of the reason for this is that his make-up is exactly in tune with his deep-structure function in the plot: simply, his now famous head *looks* like a penis. And his behavior in the film, an ambiguous meld of canniness and sheerly instinctual reaction, is not a "symbol" as much as it is a hieroglyph, an icon for the infinitely variable but single-minded urging of the libido.

The Creature's identifying locale, furthermore, as is usual for pastoral, is central to his meaning. The "Black Lagoon," physically, at least, is hardly black at all. Only a few of the film's scenes take place at nighttime, and the Lagoon itself is, as both Kay and David note, lovely—deceptively deep, still waters. The Lagoon's blackness, then, is a matter of its depth—on the naturalistic level of the plot—or of the preconsciously "black," on the symbolic level of the film. For the "*Black* Lagoon," in this sense, invokes inevitable associations of the cloacal: which, as we now know, has strong implications—particularly in the maturely infantile world of the pastoral—with the genital. The very word, "Lagoon," in the popular mythology of American art, has an inevitable tinge of the exotic and erotic about it—*via* innumerable love songs and Dorothy Lamour; imagine the tonal difference in a Creature from the Black Lake, or the Black Estuary.

Two years after the Creature, Fred Wilcox's *Forbidden Planet* (1956) was to earn a justifiable but overblown reputation for its evocation, within a science-fiction context, of Shakespearian pastoral and "the monster from the Id," projected and finally abhorred by its physicist–Prospero. The great advantage of the *Creature*, both as art and as socio-political history, is that it represents a confrontation, not with a futuristic monster from the Id, but, in a timescape contemporary to the decade which spawned it, with the Id *itself.* If *Forbidden Planet* is, as many have insisted, Hollywood's *The Tempest, The Creature from the Black Lagoon* is its *As You Like It*: less perfect, less profound, even, in a sense—but ultimately richer, truer to generic form, and more humanely inclusive.

To go to the Black Lagoon, then, is to return to the primal sink, the nursery site and origin of the species' sexual jealousy. The Lagoon is a place, like all true pastoral places—Arcadia, Arden, Shangri-La—of clarification and terror. And, in this respect, the casting of the *Creature* is a marvel of subtlety and wit. For throughout the first part of the film, we simply do not know with whom our sympathies are to lie. Granted that the Creature himself is phallus-fascination and phallus-fear, *whose* fascination and fear is he? Richard Denning and Richard Carlson, Mark and David, are two of the most perennial starring leads of all fifties B-movies, and thus present a serious dubiety of identification to the viewer. If Mark is sometimes overbearing, David is sometimes too feckless: they even look alike, complicating their sexual contest with overtones of sibling rivalry, older brother against younger brother. And Julie Adams, as Kay, may also — though less predictably — emerge as the dominant member of the trio. Ms. Adams was, simply, one of the sexiest leading ladies that Hollywood managed to produce in the fifties, a tantalizing combination of chippie and girl-next-door (the raped schoolteacher in *The Blackboard Jungle* [1955], the standoffish school nurse in *The Private War of Major Benson* [1955]), at once statuesque and approachable. In *Creature*, as sexual motivation for both horror and psychodrama, she is usually photographed — with great good sense — from below and in a one-piece bathing suit.

David (Carlson) emerges at the end of the film as our agent of identification, but not without a good deal of vacillation on the part of the storyline. Even before that, though, the film establishes itself as what we might today call a "sexist" tale, that is, a tale about the warfare for Kay, which never, however, takes into account Kay's own emotions in the matter. Bound to Mark by nostalgia and loyalty, she is bound to David by the stronger tie of love. And, in fact, once she admits this tie, the central action of the film can begin. For her function is simply *to love*: and the problem facing Mark and David is how to come to terms with the promise and threat to their masculinity of her decision.

After the characters enter the Lagoon, their rivalry and mutual tension become increasingly explicit; that, after all, is what pastoral landscapes are there for. The culmination of the first (non-monstrous) part of the film is, surely, the scene — almost absurdly obvious for a generation of Freudian cineastes — where David and Kay, pledging their love on the deck of the ship, are interrupted by Mark, preparing to dive for gill-man fossils armed with flippers, oxygen mask, and spear-gun. Mark makes a pointed demonstration of the spear-gun's power by firing it into the ship's mast, and then gruffly commands David to prepare for their dive. He has become, visually and psychologically, a mirror-image of the archaic monster who will destroy him.

This scene is terribly important, since it establishes for us the nature of the sexual warfare between David and Mark. Possession of Kay is, in reality, only a strategic objective in that war, since the real issue at stake is the nature of manhood itself. Who shall have, finally, the courage to appropriate to himself the energies and violences of the libido? To be, in other words, a *man* for the decade? Both David and Mark — siblings, twins, co-scientists — are good, job-oriented, middle-class rationalists exploring the cloacal-genetic Lagoon: and their contest is a *Kulturkampf*, a definition of what sort of "manhood" their culture will tolerate or sanction. Mark, as owner of the murderous phallic spear-gun, as "older brother," begins with the upper hand; but this itself is a tipoff since, at least in fiction, upper hands are always dealt to be called. So the Tale of the Monster will, among other things, chasten his individualism and ambition, leading us to recognize in gentle, self-effacing David the waited-for dragonmaster of the Eisenhower decade.

Immediately after the spear-gun scene comes the central — and surely the most famous — passage in the movie, Kay's swimming excursion in the Lagoon. As Kay swims at the surface of the water, the Creature, making his first extended appearance, swims only a few feet below her, his body exactly synchronized with hers, looking up at her. It is a wonderfully balletic sequence, and one of the most striking allegories of sexual desire in the history of the art. For the Creature certainly *does* desire Kay, and all the more intensely since he is, himself, a highly abstract, nearly "disembodied" projection of that desire in David and Mark. He is, to repeat, that force which men face only in the simplified world of the Lagoon, which civilization, indeed, refuses to let them face.

The great horror-film analogue for this situation, of course, is King Kong's lust for Fay Wray. But *King Kong* (1933) is a far more conventional, perhaps simpler, exploitation of erotic panic. The giant gorilla, after all, is not a projection of the psyches of the film's two male leads, the slick showman-entrepreneur and the rough-edged but human sea captain. He is, as innumerable commentators have pointed out, himself a pathetic, all-but-human victim of that rage for beauty which is man's cross and crown in this tradition of mythology. *Kong* assimilates, then, to the uncounted retellings of the Beauty and the Beast story, from James Whale and Jean Cocteau to Claude Chabrol's brilliant *Le Boucher* (1970). *The Creature*, however, as I have already suggested, belongs to the older, sterner archetype of the dragon and the dragon-slayer. In that archaic contest we recognize the ultimate stakes to be the recreation of the world, through control of the anti-human, instinctual chaos which the dragon incarnates — and which the hero must slay in himself before meeting his apocalyptic adversary.

As the film develops, the Creature manages to kill three of the crew and, escaping from momentary capture, to maim another. Mark, the assertive, sexual and intellectual bully, insists on staying to capture or kill the monster — insists, in other words, upon being the simple hero which the archetype demands, on *mastering* the penis-fear of the Creature and thus establishing his right to Kay. David, however, is kinder. He realizes that the Creature is himself an innocent monster, provoked only by human intrusion, as he realizes that his older-brother adversary, Mark, is the prey of emotions over which he has no control. After the last attack, though, supported by the remaining crew, David insists that the ship leave the Lagoon, for the safety of all. Nor can it be accidental that that last attack is the maiming of the middle-aged, establishment figure of the team (Whit Bissell), whose judicious yet still-productive place in the microcosmic society of the science-ship needs now to be filled.

It is the first time in the film David has usurped Mark's authority, and a decisive — though not a final — moment in his struggle for manhood. For *The Creature* is, psychosexually, a much subtler movie than many recent "serious" films in the same area (to take one among many, John Schlesinger's *Sunday, Bloody Sunday* [1971]). David's *public* assertion of control must be supported by a more difficult, privately won self-assurance. And the film, without ever suggesting the least dramatic agony in the character of David, brilliantly projects that struggle, with a tact almost like that of medieval allegory, in its final movement.

To a psychoanalyst, the young David's early, forced assertion of dominance might well lead to a kind of sexual paralysis, an uneasy standoff between the adult and the adolescent within him. In terms of the movie itself — and of a long tradition of Western allegory — it is not enough to escape from the phallic Creature and all he represents: he must be faced, and faced maturely. How appropriate, then, that as the ship, under David's command, begins to sail out of the Lagoon, the crew finds that the exit channel has been blocked *by the Creature*. Exit and entrance channel, one should say, since it is an exit from the clarified world of erotic drives in the Lagoon, and an entrance to the "real" world of grownup life: a real *limen*, a threshold, with all the associations Freud, Jung, and Jack Arnold are capable of giving that word.

"Crossing the threshold" is the traditional duty of initiates and, in our own culture, of bridegrooms about to take on the full rights of manhood. No less so for David. For to cross this threshold is at once to overcome the final terror of the Creature, to establish is professional/societal usurpation of Mark, and to win his intended bride, Kay. If the film, as a whole, has been on one level a parable of occlusions to sexual maturity, this last movement is beautifully (physically, *filmically*) its culmination and resolution.

In order to remove the blockade the Creature has placed across the channel, Mark and David once again go under water, but now with David directing operations. Once they are below, the Creature, predictably enough, attacks, grabbing Mark. And now David takes the spear-gun, already established as the emblem of Mark's self-confidence, to save his partner. The transfer of power, made socially on the deck of the ship, is now being ratified in the Lagoon-world. And it is important to note that David seizes the spear-gun, as he had seized power, out of a kind of higher selflessness, a primarily *corporate* sexuality and psychic maturity.

But this, too, is not enough. There has to follow the climactic test upon David, his confrontation with the Creature himself. In the well-known sequence that follows, the wounded Creature summons the strength to take Kay from the ship through his secret underground passage into his own subterranean lair. David, of course, follows: and by now, in this film, we are not surprised to see the re-emergence of such an archetypal motif as the night-journey through the labyrinth (cf. Theseus searching for the Minotaur, Aeneas in the Underworld, Leopold Bloom in Nighttown). To meet the Creature face-to-face is to meet, in a preternaturally violent atmosphere, the *full* terror of maturity; and it is thus a brilliant touch that the Creature wrests away from David his spear-gun, robbing him of any of the mechanical attributes of manhood in a terminal — sexually, an apocalyptic — crisis. But David, to the end, is a corporate hero. As he has sacrificed his own *rite de passage* to the good of society, so society intervenes to complete that rite for him. He stands his ground, facing the unspeakable gill-man. And in an ending that can only be called *civitas ex machina*, we find that the other crew-members have followed him through the labyrinth, and shoot — though they do not kill — the Creature, driving him away, back to the Lagoon so that they, David and Kay, may rejoin the daylight world to which all pastorals, ultimately, lead back.

A strange film, a strange blend of insight and inadvertence, of the archaic and the post-industrial. And, I suggest, a film, a work of art, which like all major works of art makes sense only by making sense of its age. *The Creature from the Black Lagoon* confronts, as frankly as fifties reticence will allow and more subtly, perhaps, than sixties and seventies frankness can manage, the tangled skein of sexual, social, and violent impulses out of which politics is made. It is a horror story whose true theme is the refusal of heroism, a story of battle against the monstrous almost without battle. And, as such, it makes deeper sense of those other fifties monster movies I have mentioned. For beyond the political, anti-communist implications of the seed-pods in *Invasion of the Body Snatchers* or the withered, dessicated saucer-men of *Earth Versus the Flying Saucers*, we glimpse in *The Creature* the central evasion of energy, the central fear of the life-force itself which underlay the witch-hunts and HUAC purges. Philip Wylie, in his celebrated attack on McCarthy in the revised *Generation of Vipers* (1955), identified the real power of the charismatic Senator as an extension of the timidity and protracted adolescence of "Mom-ism." *The Creature* helps us see — beautifully, in every sense of the word — how right Wylie was.

In a film of the year before *The Creature*, Samuel Fuller's 1953 *Pickup on South Street*, one can see the traditions of the thriller and the film noir undergoing a metamorphosis into the political shadings of the decade: the enemy has become The Enemy, the mysterious and incredibly resourceful Fifth Column, and the hero's battle against the crooks has become Richard Widmark's quest for the ability to love Jean Peters. Arnold's film gives us the same transformation, but from the other side of the spectrum. If the thriller was turning into sexually timid romance, the sexually timid romance of the horror film was also turning into political thriller, in a more subtle way. David's wetsuit in *The Creature*, at least symbolically, is made of grey flannel. Like Hugh Marlowe in *Earth Versus the Flying Saucers*, Rex Reason in *This Island Earth*, James Whitmore in *Them!*, and John Foster Dulles in the Suez crisis or Eisenhower in Vietnam, David fights only when provoked by the eruptive terror of the insidious, the anarchic, the asocial. And his fight, although it may seem an entry into maturity, is in reality a struggle to *maintain* the innocence, the happy consciousness of a man who knows his place in the system and comfortably functions therein. The threshold becomes a circle, the labyrinth a maze of a standardized I.Q. test.

This is what I mean by insisting that the Creature, unlike other and earlier versions of horror, is almost *not there*. He is *what threatens*: but it is an abyss glimpsed only in three-quarter profile. One is not surprised to discover that the horror film, after its late heyday in the mid-fifties, should take two quite different lines of development from anything that had gone before. The Roger Corman Poe-cycle, featuring Vincent Price, is almost a non-horror genre; Price is usually cast, not in the role of villain, but of perturbed and deranged *victim* of forces too awful and too complex to be even visualized (*House of Usher* [1960]; *The Haunted Palace* [1963]). It is as if he were at once David and the fearsome Creature. The nostalgic revivals of Dracula and Frankenstein produced by Hammer Films, on the other hand, represent a kind of vision of America from abroad that insists, like British rock of the sixties (the Beatles, the Who, the Rolling Stones), upon rediscovering, in a continental context, the true roots of the American vision of the abyss. Their great popularity in the States, like the successes of the rock groups, is in fact a testimony to the persistence of those dangerous visions, even throughout the relative doldrums of the Eisenhower and Kennedy years.

But to say this much is, perhaps, to read *The Creature* as a failure of the imagination: and that, definitely, it is not. The film, brilliant in its truth to its own form and era, is also a landmark in the psychic history of the horror film. Song of innocence it may well be, but in its final (unintentional?) implications it is not only an exploration, but a criticism of those monsters our younger selves found fit to tremble at. And in the sad, abandoned figure of the Creature himself we may read an equally powerful, maybe even more compelling, version of that insight into the tragedy of the human denial contained in Robert Lowell's 1956 song of experience, "Skunk Hour":

> a mother skunk with her column of kittens swills the garbage pail...
> and will not scare.[3]

It is what Saturday afternoon was really *about*, and its darkness is central to whatever of light we may have achieved since.

3

H.G. Wells
Utopia and Doomsday

"I grieved to think how brief the dream of the human intellect had been. It had committed suicide."[1]

Herbert George Wells made that melancholy observation in his first novel, *The Time Machine* (1895). He spent the rest of his life — and 200 books — trying to erase it.

He never succeeded; nor did the world succeed in entirely escaping the truth of what he said — Wells died in 1946, a year almost to the day after Hiroshima.

Historian Ernest Barker recalls meeting a sick, aging Wells in 1939. Wells had lost the audience that, during the 1920s and early 1930s, made him the most celebrated and influential English intellectual of his time. Europe was plummeting, again, into war — a war he had warned against for two decades. Barker asked Wells how he was. "Poorly, Barker, poorly," said Wells. "I am composing my epitaph." And what would that be? Asked Barker. "Quite short, just this — God damm you all: I told you so."[2]

It ought to be his epitaph, catching as it does so much of Wells's arrogance, bitter humor, passion for man's survival — and sadness.

From *The Time Machine* to his bleak last book, *Mind at the End of Its Tether* (1945), Wells journeyed from despair to despair. His books served as his public struggles against that despondency. Science fiction and realistic fiction, history, economic and political analysis — all offered Wells potential ways out of the trap, as he saw it, that evolutionary history had laid for man. His fellow novelist George Orwell doubted that any intelligent Englishman or American educated between the wars could have escaped Wells's influence.

Conspiracy of Silence

There is little doubt that Orwell was right, but it takes an effort to remember how right. For one of the most remarkable things about Wells's notable career is its eclipse.

Wells's great early science fiction novels — *The Time Machine, The Island of Dr. Moreau* (1896), *The Invisible Man* (1897), *The War of the Worlds* (1898), and *The First Men in the Moon* (1901) — remain in print. They are taught, with growing frequency, in colleges, although usually banished to that academic ghetto — the science fiction class.

The rest of Wells seems to have vanished without a trace. Who today is aware that Wells's imprint on his time was equal to or greater than that of D.H. Lawrence, Virginia Woolf, C.S. Lewis, or W.H. Auden? And yet it was — despite the recent conspiracy of silence.

Conspiracy, of course, is a harsh word. Yet, it is not unjustified. One of the reasons for Wells's continuing relevance also partially explains why he has not been — and probably cannot be — canonized by the literary establishment. His work represents a serious challenge to the principles of specialization and scholarly disinterest upon which academic culture is founded and thrives.

"I *hammer* at my main ideas," Wells insisted in *The Fate of Homo Sapiens* (1939) — with little respect for those to whom the "intellectual life" means the contemplation of compartmentalized intricacies.[3] Ideas mattered, and mattered passionately, to him because he believed they were the only things that might save the human race from extinction. But the comfortable niches in which we store our ideas — "science," "aesthetics," "economics," "sociology" — had to go.

Forging a New World

If the world did not make sense *altogether*, it could not long continue to make sense at all.

Science and socialism, argued Wells, would unite the world. But Wells's socialism was highly idiosyncratic. He enthusiastically joined the famed Fabian Society (dominated during the early 1900s by George Bernard Shaw and Beatrice and Sidney Webb) and later noisily broke away when he could not take command of the group.

Socialism for Wells, write his biographers Norman and Jeanne MacKenzie, "was essentially a state of mind rather than a set of practical policies."[4] He came to see the Fabians as a "bureaucratic regime of small-minded experts," as critic Van Wyck Brooks put it.[5] All forms of socialism were, for Wells, only partial steps toward the formation of a new World State.

Wells's semimystical utopia incorporated socialist programs (public ownership of energy sources and land; financial aid for the unemployed, the ill, and the aged) but was a benevolent dictatorship where "voluntary noblemen" would exercise a firm hand (controlling human procreation, for example). These scientifically trained new samurai — mechanics, engineers, doctors, teachers, writers — would rule mankind through a loose and informal worldwide cooperative organization unlike any previously existing government.

Wells was a "global thinker," who, for better or worse, took all contemporary knowledge for his province. It was for this that he was most often attacked, even during the days of his greatest fame. He does indeed display much of the eccentricity and intolerance associated with the self-educated genius. But he also displays all the humanizing passion of that breed.

There is a moment in *Kipps* (1905) that catches Wells's special tone. Near the end of that wonderfully comic novel, the working-class hero, Artie Kipps, and his wife, Ann, have earned a comfortable degree of wealth and a house in a neighborhood far above their station. They quarrel over their inability to behave properly among their upper-class neighbors. It is terribly funny, until the narrator suddenly interrupts himself:

> The stupid little tragedies of these clipped and limited lives! ... See what I can see! Above them, brooding over them, I tell you there is a monster, a lumpish monster, like some great, clumsy griffin thing, like the Crystal Palace labyrinthodon ... like pride, like indolence, like all that is darkening and heavy and obstructive in life. It is matter and darkness, it is the anti-soul, it is the ruling power of this land, Stupidity. My Kippses live in its shadow.[6]

This interruption is an aesthetic flaw, if you conceive of the novel as a disinterested, wholly pure narrative. The narrator is preaching here, and preaching at the top of his lungs — "See what I can see!" It is also a moment, however, in which we hear Wells's characteristic voice demanding that we understand the middle-class comedy of Kipps in its widest significance, and insisting that that significance be taken seriously.

Kipps, by the way, was one of Wells's last books to appear before the onset of his quarrel with Henry James. That feud, in its way, determined much of the 20th-century debate over the function and purpose of art. James (who admired *Kipps* for its "rawness") insisted that a novel should be an utterance like a lyric poem. Wells increasingly insisted that fiction should serve the purpose of mass education and social transformation. The only hope for mankind's survival, believed Wells, was knowledge; education was the road to that knowledge.

It was once assumed, by the mandarins of the London literary establishment, that James had won the quarrel. Recent experiments in fiction by Thomas Pynchon, Kurt Vonnegut, and Robert Coover call that decision into question.

Wells — in his urgency and prophetic fervor, in his insistence on taking the whole range of knowledge as his domain, and, particularly, in his utopianism — may be not only the characteristic writer of the early 20th century but (as he would have hoped) the characteristic writer of the century's end. Against the monster "Stupidity" that he describes in *Kipps*, he struggled his whole life. Even at his most "realistic," he was a science fiction writer. His two central beliefs lie at the heart of science fiction: Man is under universal sentence of death, but he has it within his power to cheat that cosmic doom.

His own life story seemed to portray this drama. Destined to be an intellectual bull, Wells was born in 1866, literally, in a china shop — a business his parents, a housekeeper and a professional cricketer, failed at. His mother's fondest wish for him had been that he might become a draper's assistant. At 14, he did — only to fail rapidly and totally. (He couldn't keep accounts straight.)

After a few years, he was again apprenticed to a draper. (He later said that his mother's belief in God was equaled only by her faith in drapers.) He also served as an apprentice to a druggist and, finally, to a grammar school teacher. His record of failure continued.

Free Love

Wells broke the habit — temporarily — when he won a national competition for a scholarship to the Normal School of Science (now the Royal College of Science) in 1883. It was a turning point. There he met Charles Darwin's staunch defender, biologist T.H. Huxley. Wells never forgot Huxley's lessons, but after three years he left without a degree.

In 1891, he married his cousin Isabell and was soon bored and unhappy. (A man of voracious sexual appetite, Wells openly advocated free love. It is likely that he never found a partner who met his expectations.) He was also very ill, with a lung ailment diagnosed as tubercular and terminal. Yet he insisted on controlling his life. He began to write witty sketches on the implications of modern science for man's self-image for London newspapers. In 1892, he was teaching biology at William Briggs's Tutorial College. Two years later he ran off with one of his students, Amy Catherine Robbins. He married her in 1895. She was probably the woman who understood him best — and forgave him most.

A sickly young man with little means of support and two families is not likely to be either happy or productive. Nevertheless, in 1895, Wells published *The Time Machine* to great acclaim.

During the next decade, he produced enough work to consolidate his position as one of the most popular writers of the age. From World War I until his death in 1946, he published at an astonishing rate. Through periods of depression and numerous disruptive and passionate love affairs (including a famous liaison with Rebecca West), he continued to write "for dear life."

It is worth noting that seven years before Wells's birth two books appeared that shaped the course of his intellectual life. The more immediately successful of the two was *Self-Help* (1859) by Samuel Smiles. Smiles, a Victorian clergyman and a dedicated "social worker," ardently contended that man's will and self-control could overcome any obstacle.

The other book was *On the Origin of Species* (1859). It took away everything Smiles's book seemed to promise. Man, in Charles Darwin's scheme, was not a specially created, specially gifted architect of his own salvation or damnation. He was, rather, the random side-effect of a blind, reasonless, and awesomely long process of evolution.

"Heads — Merely Heads"

It is not too much to say that a great deal of 20th-century intellectual debate has centered around the tensions between the visions of Smiles and Darwin. Are we condemned to be the playthings of forces over which we have no real control? Or are we the agents of a consciousness and a purpose beyond the mere physical dimensions of our world?

The plethora of recent American best sellers on self-help psychology, along with the equally large number of popular books on biological determinism, shows how persistent the debate remains.

Wells gave full expression to these ideas. His most deeply held convictions were Darwinian in origin. For all its splendid accomplishments, he believed, society was on the verge of overspecializing itself into extinction. This was Wells's point in *The War of the Worlds*. Those soulless Martian invaders are future versions of ourselves who have become "heads — merely heads," and who are pathetically prey to so simple a threat as the common cold.[7]

If Wells was moved to Darwinian despair, it was precisely through expressing it that he exemplified, in his own life, Samuel Smiles's (and, later Horatio Alger's) success fable. Through sheer will and application, he lifted himself from the bleakest of backgrounds to international fame.

Wells's career suggests a triumph of mind that his central ideas denied. Could man, through common sense, avert disaster? Wells had, and he always thought of himself as a "very ordinary brain." The prognosis for the human race was not good, but it was not altogether fatal. At least, he thought, not if the rest of mankind could be persuaded to act as H.G. Wells had.

Isaac Asimov, who ought to know, has written that science fiction is best understood as "ordinary," novelistic fiction, with one crucial difference: Its hero is no individual but the human race itself.

This is an accurate description of Wells's work—not only his science fiction but also his realistic novels and most of his historical and sociological writing. Wells was a very heroic man, and a very vain one. His permanent and preeminent concern was the fate of mankind, and his reference point for the fate of the human race was, always, himself.

These two outlooks are present in Wells's writings from the beginning.

In *The Time Machine*, the Time Traveller relates his tale of universal despair to an anonymous narrator. At the end of the book, after the Traveller has embarked again on his journey into time, the narrator reflects upon his curious friend. He "thought but cheerlessly of the Advancement of Mankind," observes the narrator, "and saw in the growing pile of civilization only a foolish heaping that must inevitably fall back upon and destroy its makers in the end." Here speaks the Darwinist, the calm and dispassionate analyst of the human condition against the absolute background of scientific truth. Yet, this voice does not have the last word. "If that is so," says the narrator, "it remains for us to live as though it were not so."[8]

"Living as though it were not so" is, indeed, the theme of most of Wells's writing after *The Time Machine*. The despairing, time-traveling hero and the willfully optimistic narrator continued their debate in his books for the next 50 years.

Optimism or Despair

To be sure, Wells gave an increasingly ample role to the hopeful narrator. By World War I, Wells's scientific romances had taken a distinctly positive turn. He was now writing utopian fiction. In it, he imagined that following the cataclysmic war to which mankind was surely doomed, a new golden age of rational organization and scientific progress would emerge.

This vision, too, was the projection of his own massive will to survive, his insistence that turmoil and disaster *must* be redeemable. It is the implicit argument of his massive survey of civilization, *The Outline of History* (1920), and also of his last great social prophecy, *The Shape of Things to Come* (1933).

Wells, however, was never a "utopian" in the pure sense of the word. He never, even at his most strenuously assertive, fully trusted his own optimism. The voice of the time traveler, with its message of a great darkness at the end of all striving, was never entirely stilled.

It was once fashionable to attack Wells for his optimism — to denigrate his boyish insistence that, if only the world could be handed over to the engineers and the scientists, they would produce a clean, sane, chromium and glass civilization.

This optimistic side of his vision is expressed most unabashedly in his one screenplay, *Things to Come* (1936). The Marxist critic of the 1930s, Christopher Caudwell, accused Wells of being irresponsibly "spiritual" in his hopes for the future.[9] C.S. Lewis, at almost the same time, accused Wells of being overly "materialistic."[10] But Wells's optimism was held, throughout his career, in a creative and humanizing tension with a deep pessimism and melancholy. The man who whistles loudest in the dark is likely to be the one who feels the darkness most. It is *this* Wells, the Wells of the dark places, who matters — or should matter — more and more for us.

We may be closer to the self-destruction Wells warned of in 1895 than we have ever been before. Critics have remarked how much recent American fiction — Saul Bellow in *Mr. Sammler's Planet* (1969), Thomas Pynchon in *Gravity's Rainbow* (1973), John Barth in *Letters* (1979) — makes serious use of themes and techniques once thought to be the province of pulp science fiction. Recent "explainers" of the human condition — from Robert Ardrey and Arthur Koestler to Carl Sagan — insist that we cannot fully understand or control our own fate until we begin to see it in the context of evolutionary history.

These writers are not Wells's "disciples." Wells was too idiosyncratic a thinker to have any real disciples. He would not have wanted any, anyway. As a *reactor*, a highly intelligent, extraordinarily sensitive, middle-class man who courageously confronted the central problems of his age, Wells has gained something more important than followers. He has found brothers.

All of Wells's writing is science fiction. It is (as the claim is often made by science fiction writers) important because it is prophetic. "Prophetic," not in the sense of accurate technological forecasting but as poet William Blake was. Wells understood how men come to feel in a world in which they are capable of unprecedented self-aggrandizement (we *can*, technologically, do almost anything we want) and total humiliation (we might kill ourselves doing it). In surveying such a world, he managed to be infinite in hope, yet sober in expectation.

Wells is cantankerous enough not to be readily admitted into the polite world of literary history. Scholars, however, have begun to examine his importance for the history of 20th-century thought and writing, and especially his relevance to the way we think and live today. Nevertheless, Wells is still best read and understood by those "ordinary brains" who were always his audience. Rediscovering Wells is not a matter of stumbling upon an interesting literary curio but rather of recognizing a powerful, immensely kind, and good-humored voice.

Perhaps Wells described himself best in *When the Sleeper Wakes* (1897). There, his revolutionary hero, Graham, is about to address the nations of the Earth and rid them of their slavery:

> He found the thing in his mind too vague for words. He paused momentarily, and broke into vague exhortations, and then a rush of speech came to him. Much that he said was but the humanitarian commonplace of a vanished age, but the conviction of his voice touched it to vitality.[11]

4
Realist of the Fantastic
H.G. Wells about/in/on the Movies

In 1895, several things presaging the twentieth century should have made people nervous. Gugliemo Marconi developed the radiotelegraph, ensuring for the first time in human history the instantaneous transfer of information. Wilhelm Roentgen discovered the X-ray, opening the world of human thought to the surrealistic vistas of quantum mechanics. Georges Sorel organized the first international trade union, heralding an age in which workers would increasingly assert their right to control the economy they sustained. Equally portentous, Auguste and Louis Lumière opened the first film theatre in an abandoned Paris restaurant. And a tubercular, faintly disreputable young man named Herbert George Wells published, after numerous journal serializations, a novel called *The Time Machine*. Science fiction had begun.

I

Born in the same year, science fiction and the movies continued as siblings throughout the century — sometimes uncomfortably. Here I refer to "the movies" (as opposed to the more highfalutin term "film" or "cinema") from Georges Méliès's 1902 *A Voyage to the Moon* through the Flash Gordon serials of the thirties and Wells's *Things to Come* (1936) to *Star Wars* (1977), *Close Encounters of the Third Kind* (1977), and *Cocoon* (1985). In fact, as film critics have suggested, the art of the film — a technological innovation that produces living, moving stories and parables — is itself a kind of science fiction, a fiction produced by science. As a wedding of science and storytelling, mechanism and mythmaking, it has been optimistic about the power of the human imagination, however dire may be its idea of the straits of the human species.

If this general observation about the meaning of the movies sounds suspiciously Wellsian, it is.

Think about the term "movies." The act of reading requires that you focus your eyes on the page; the messages are encoded in print. As you read this, you are doing exactly that right now. The movies force their reality on you if you look at them at all. The eye, as William Wordsworth says, cannot choose but see. That makes film perhaps the ultimate medium for propaganda, since for all its complexity of production, it is the simplest medium to absorb. Fascinated with the movies, Wells devised special effects in his prose that anticipated those in film. In a passage from *The Time Machine*, for instance, the Time Traveller describes his return from the distant future to the "present":

> I saw one little thing that seemed odd to me. I think I have told you that when I set out, before my velocity became very high, Mrs. Watchett had walked across the room, traveling, as it seemed to me, like a rocket. As I returned, I passed again across that minute when she traversed the laboratory. But now her every motion appeared to be the exact inversion of her previous ones.[1]

We recognize this, of course, as the phenomenon of film run in reverse at high speed. But in 1895 Wells could not have seen such a film, for no such film had been made. Merely by speculating on the idea of time travel, he visualized what would become a standard effect in filmmaking — it was a remarkable feat of imagination.

There is another connection between *The Time Machine* and the art of the film. Soon after the success of the book, Wells invested heavily in a "Time Machine" diorama where customers would sit in capsules displaying scenes from prehistory through their windows. Although some of the rides at Disneyland and other amusement parks show that it wasn't such a bad idea, the venture was a financial catastrophe. Nevertheless, it demonstrated how much Wells thought even of his earliest books as "cinematic." Other analogies between his early books and film abound. T.S. Eliot, certainly no friend to the Wellsian outlook, records that he remained throughout his life moved by the passage describing the miraculous growth of lunar vegetation in *The First Men in the Moon* (1901):

> As far as the eye could see over the enormous disorder of rocks that formed the crater floor the same bristling scrub that surrounded us was starting into life, diversified here and there by bulging masses of a cactus form, and scarlet and purple lichens that grew so fast they seemed to crawl over the rocks.[2]

We recognize this description as a "cinematic" event: the time-lapse sequences of flowers growing or landscape changing. But once again we see that, in the theater of his mind, Wells invented the technique before it was reinvented in the theater of the twentieth century movie house.

Not surprisingly, pioneer film director Georges Méliès followed Wells and used elements of Wells's *The First Men in the Moon* in his film *A Voyage to the Moon*. Méliès's space travelers go to the moon in a space gun a la Jules Verne's *From the Earth to the Moon*. But when they get there, the hostile insectoids they encounter are obvious counterparts to Wells's Selenites. Consciously or not, Wells returned the compliment in 1936, when in his screenplay for *Things to Come* the young astronauts (boy and girl — the new Adam and Eve) travel to the moon in a Vernesque capsule shot from a gigantic space gun.

The Invisible Man (1897) prompted Joseph Conrad, who had said he wanted to make his readers see, to describe Wells as the "realist of the fantastic!"[3] A man who cannot be seen becomes all the more visible, as Wells brilliantly realized. Indeed, the French film critic Christian Metz has suggested that the whole tradition of special effects in film can be traced to what he calls the "Invisible Man" syndrome: convincing us that what we see on the screen is what we do not see, or that what we do see is what cannot possibly be there. And, he goes on to say, this kind of special effect may be close to the heart of what film is all about in the first place. Yet Metz never gives Wells himself much credit for the effect that he names after Wells's novel. Consider for instance, this passage from *The Invisible Man* where Griffin, the title character, already half unwrapped from his clothing, finishes the job to escape the local constabulary:

> The stranger ran his arm down his waistcoat, and is if by a miracle the buttons to which his empty sleeve pointed became undone.[4]

It is no problem for us to visualize what is happening here, for we have seen it in any number of science fiction films. Think back to what it would have been like to be a reader in 1897. To appreciate what a stunning writer Wells was, think what it must have taken in 1897 to imagine a scene like this, to write it so clearly as to make it easy for the reader to imagine it. From the beginning of his career, Wells was, in a sense, a film pioneer — without making a film.

Why? Why did he so uncannily anticipate the technology of film, and why, afterwards, did he never engage himself more than diffidently in that technology? To answer those questions is to learn something else about this difficult, complex man.

Start with the Victorian novel. The Victorian novel may have been the last great moment in European culture when an art form could legitimately claim to be both great art and great popular communication. Thackeray, Dickens, even George Eliot, brought together a nation of readers. This is the idea of the novel on which Wells was raised. He had scant sympathy for a Henry

James, a Virginia Woolf, or a James Joyce who could write fiction for "the few" and believe that the acceptance of those few justified their work and their dedication to art. In a sense, Wells would naturally have been drawn to the idea of the movies as the successor to the Victorian novel in popular appeal and artistic possibility.

D.W. Griffith, by common consent the first great director in the history of the film, once observed that all he learned about the art of storytelling he learned from his reading of Dickens. Sergei Eisenstein, the second great director in the history of film, argued that he thought of film as a form of propaganda. Between Griffith and Eisenstein, I believe we can locate the center of Wells's own commitment to the art of storytelling. He wanted to write stories that would be powerful as stories and also change your mind: about your life, about your society, about everything. In the seminal science fiction of the nineties as well as in *Kipps* (1905), *Tono-Bungay* (1909), *Ann Veronica* (1909), and *The History of Mr. Polly* (1910), he tried to write novels that would have the same effect as the novels upon which he was raised, and the same effect as the evolving art of film that paralleled his own growth as a writer.

This may be, in fact, why, for all his fascination and affection for film, *Things to Come* is his only major screenplay. He thought of himself, above all else, as a writer, and he never could abandon the self-image. He was a man of artistic integrity. Rather than desert writing for the congenial art of film, he tried to write books which could have the same immediate impact as films. This "first modern man," in other words, is perhaps nowhere more modern than in his nostalgia for the lost community of the nineteenth-century novel.

In one of his splendid reviews for the *Spectator* in the thirties, Graham Greene says that what film has in common with the Victorian novel is that they both evoke the "Wembley roar": the massive communal response — "mass feeling, mass excitement"— bringing all levels of society together in a shared enthusiasm that otherwise may only occur at a football or baseball game.[5] Wells tried — and often succeeded — to achieve that community response in his fiction. No wonder that he had little tolerance for the experiments of Virginia Woolf or a James Joyce, who were turning the "serious" novel into a private communication between the author and a select group of properly cultured readers.

To be sure, Wells was not beyond narrative experiment — much of it cinematic in a general sense. In his introduction to *A Modern Utopia* (1905), Wells suggests that the book be read as if narrated by an anonymous voice offscreen, and that occasional scenes or slogans from his imagined future be thought of as projected onto a screen somehow "behind" the narrative itself.[6] It is all very confusing, and it is not really sustained throughout the book. Yet the idea is innovative, had Wells only had the patience to carry his conception through. With a writer who wrote as much as Wells did, we must take the word for the deed occasionally. With all its faults, *A Modern Utopia* is one of the very first books to realize — to incarnate — the fact that henceforth the art of storytelling would be shared out between the printed form of the word and the photographed, filmed form of the action.

II

Turning now from H.G. Wells on film, what about H.G. Wells in film: film versions of his most famous and influential novels? What of H.G. Wells and film: Wells's influence on the whole tradition of the science fiction film?

Between 1895 and 1901 Wells published five "scientific romances" that effectively established the boundaries of science fiction: *The Time Machine*; *The Island of Dr. Moreau* (1896); *The Invisible Man*; *The War of the Worlds* (1898); and *The First Men in the Moon*. To be sure, he published much else in those years. Yet those five novels are by general consent his lasting claim to be the "father" of science fiction. It is hard to find a theme in the repertoire of science fiction plots that is not anticipated in them. And each, in turn, has been translated into a major science fiction film.

Méliès's *Voyage to the Moon* is a free adaptation of *The First Men in the Moon*. By 1914, Wells had signed a contract for film versions of his novels, and by 1919 he had to endure another dreary version of *The First Men in the Moon*. By 1932, however, his luck changed. *The Island of Dr. Moreau* became on film *The Island of Lost Souls*, starring Charles Laughton as the crazed genius Moreau, and featuring one of the most brilliantly atmospheric horror-film sets of the decade. Wells's novel was a grim — some thought a disgusting — parable about the implications of Darwinian theory. And though the undercurrents of sadism and atheism abate somewhat in the film, *Island of Lost Souls* remains an unsettling, "Wellsian" encounter with the hard facts of existence.

The next year, 1933, saw the release of *The Invisible Man*, directed by James Whale, who had first brought *Frankenstein* to the screen. In the title role, his first screen appearance, Claude Rains never appeared! The movie is a masterpiece of wit, dialogue and state-of-the-art special effects. Writers are famous or notorious for complaining about the film treatments of their books. But *The Invisible Man* is a nearly perfect translation of the spirit of the tale as written into the spirit of the tale as filmed. In Griffin, the Invisible Man, Wells may have invented the first modern terrorist, the first enthusiast of random and irresponsible violence. Reading the book today, or seeing the film, one can only feel a shiver of recognition.

He had written *The War of the Worlds* in 1898 after the national disgrace of the Boer War and in expectation of the outbreak of the First World War, which was surprising only because it took so long to break out (I.F. Clarke writes splendidly about this in his book, *Voices Prophesying War*). Why do we imagine invaders from another planet? Because we are terrified of invaders from another country. The famous radio broadcast by Orson Welles of *The War of the Worlds* could not have worked as much havoc as it did had it not been aired on Halloween Night, 1938 — the year when all America knew, and tried to forget, that the world was about to spiral into the abyss of the century's second bloodbath. Fear begets fiction, and fiction gives a shape to fear.

Wells's Martians attacked London and rode in war machines that resembled gigantic tripod barbecue grills. The Martians in George Pal's 1953 film version attacked northern California and rode in war machines that looked remarkably like floating Chryslers. Purists may complain. But their complaints both miss the point and, by missing it, make the point. Wells's fable about alien invasion has less to do with extraterrestrial incursion than with our fear of the War That Might Come. Despite the discrepancies between the original and the filmed version of the tale, the central myth remains the same: "Fear not," says Wells at his most heroic. "Man will survive."

Man will survive even the mast arduous of his tasks, the imagination of the end of civilization. It is interesting that, of Wells's five great science fiction novels, the last to be made into a film was *The Time Machine* (1960), the first published. Again produced by George Pal, it is a fairly faithful rendition of the story, although without a representation of the Time Traveller's chilling final vision of the end of all things.

The message of *The Time Machine* is, finally, hopeful. Man may be dammed to cosmic irrelevancy, but until that final damm is pronounced, he is right to hope, to aspire, and to tell stories. In the film version of *The Time Machine* the Time Traveller returns to the future with three books from his library to educate the people of the future out of their all but invincible ignorance. The inevitable question is asked, "Which three books would you choose?" It is the classic, corny desert-island question, but the film — and the enduring power of Wells's conception — makes it real again. Wells, like Shakespeare and other strong writers, reminds us that confusing "corny" with "bad" in art can be merely a sign of unsophisticated naïveté.

These then are the seminal films. Later versions of some of his novels appeared — *The Food of the Gods* (1976), and a remake of *The Island of Dr.*

Moreau (1977), and even a remake of *Things to Come* (1979) — none of them very interesting or, far that matter, very Wellsian.

III

What of Wells as filmmaker? In 1929 he published *The King Who Was a King*, effectively a script for a film he never made. At the time of his death he was contemplating a screenplay on the perils of nuclear war. How remarkable that this man, who was as much as anybody else the first modern mind, should write so few screenplays. In part, one might say, it was almost out of spite. Wells loved writing, and he quite properly hated seeing his writing turned into pabulum. The German writer Thea von Harbou — later a member of the Nazi party — had done so in her book *Metropolis*, a sentimentalized version of *The Time Machine*, where the Eloi and Morlocks become simply upstairs and downstairs dwellers in the same city. Another bad book would not have bothered Wells. But another bad film would, and did. Thea von Harbou's husband, the great Fritz Lang, filmed *Metropolis* in 1927. It became one of the enduring classics of the silent screen. Wells hated it. "The silliest film" he had ever seen, he said, and he had good reasons for saying so.[7] *Metropolis* argues for spontaneous enlightenment (which Wells did not believe in), instant social rapprochement (which Wells did not believe in), and final peace between workers and bosses (which Wells knew could never happen).

Having written *The Shape of Things to Come* in 1933, he wrote the screenplay for *Things to Come* in 1936. There is really very little resemblance between the book and the film. Both predict a massive global war in the near future, leading to the collapse of civilization and its eventual rebirth under a benign dictatorship of engineers and scientists. But in the book, Wells casts this history of the future as if it were a history, with much general observation and very few moments of personal encounter. The film, directed by William Cameron Menzies, becomes enthusiastically melodramatic. It traces the future history of mankind in the fates of the adventurous scientist John Cabal (Raymond Massey) and his timid friend Pippa Passworthy (Edward Chapman), both of whom live through the Great War to Come and into the exciting, scientific future. Their names themselves are significant. Pippa Passworthy represents that part of the Wells soul that wants things to be always pleasant and harmless. The name comes from Browning's "Pippa Passes," the poem famous for its pollyannish "God's in his heaven — /All's right with the world."[8] John Cabal, on the other hand, is a member of a cabal, a secret group or "Open Conspiracy" of intellectuals determined to save the world in spite of itself.

Called "Wings over the World" in the film, the group is another one of those organizations of the best and the brightest in whom Wells invested so much faith, both in his fiction and in his non-fiction writing.

The film created a mild sensation. Wells, after all, was one of the most famous and influential gurus in Europe. Under Menzies's direction, the scenes depicting the global war, its aftermath, and the rebuilding of a rational civilization are still — even after *Star Wars* and *Close Encounters*— among the most impressive science fiction scenes on film. Significantly when global war breaks out, the first shot we see is of a ruined street and a bombed movie theater. Wells not only understood the importance of film for the twentieth century, he also understood the nature of the craft. From the evidence of *Things to Come* alone, we can speculate that he would have been a subtle and creative screenwriter.

But 1936 marked a turning point in the history of Europe and in Wells's career. Both arcs began to go downhill. The war came that Wells had warned of for nearly two decades. There would not be another screenplay from that sick, tired, despairing man. It would be a disservice to his own rigorous honesty with himself to deny that Wells's life ended in unhappiness: in the cosmic unhappiness he had heroically fended off for almost eighty years. And it would be unfair to deny that *Things to Come* is so poignant because it is one of the last flashes of a once dazzling, and now dwindling, imagination.

IV

And, then, what of H.G. Wells and film? Not films of his books, not the screenplay he wrote for *Things to Come*, but the influence and presence of the man in the art of the film. I think it is fair to say that Wells is a presence behind the evolution of the movies. Precisely because he is virtually the last writer in English to believe, and believe strenuously, in the Victorian marriage of artist and audience, he believed fundamentally in the movies. In maintaining that faith — the faith that you could be a teacher, storyteller, and an entertainer all at the same time — he set a model for the filmmakers who, in the first three decades of this century, would create a new art. In the simplest and most sentimental of terms, he kept the faith and passed it on.

Yet there is more. George Orwell once observed that all art is propaganda, though not all propaganda is necessarily art. What a Wellsian thing to say: the artist who tells you that he does not have designs upon you is, prima facie, lying to you. From Sergei Eisenstein through Leni Riefenstahl to Michael Cimino, the film has remained a storytelling device that is also a powerful device for reinterpreting and redirecting history: propaganda. "If the world does not please you *you can change it.*" The famous statement comes from Wells's *History of Mr. Polly*, and it perfectly summarizes his own attitude toward fiction as propaganda.[9] It even might be true that all his novels are the first drafts of screenplays waiting to be made.

Part II
Slouching Toward Bedlam: The Early Eaton Essays

This first five essays in this section show Frank adjusting to the special atmosphere of the Eaton Conference and perfecting the subgenre of the McConnell Eaton paper—learned, eclectic, insightful, and wildly amusing. He brought the same style to the sixth item, an essay written for a projected new journal focused on the study of fantasy, and another Eaton paper first presented in 1990. Still, while some of his characteristic themes reverberate through these essays—the shaky foundations of the concept of genre, the importance of storytelling, the folly of literary theorists—he has not yet hit upon the key relationship between science fiction and Gnosticism that will further enrich his later efforts.

5
Sturgeon's Law
First Corollary

My purpose here is to discuss the distinction between "hard" and "soft" science fiction. Or — to speak in the picturesque if curious terms of the topic as officially announced, we are here to discuss "hard-core science fiction." Now, what can *that* mean, I wonder? My own mind, ineluctably Victorian and therefore unreservedly prurient, conjures up for the idea of "hard-core" science fiction any number of titles that, I am sure, you don't want to hear more about: *Deep Transistor*, say; or *The Capacitor in Miss Jones*; or, worst of all, *Beyond the Green Spacewarp*. Consider, as they used to say on movie marquees, the possibilities.

I hope you see my problem. I am driven to discuss a very seriously conceived topic — the distinction between "hard" or "pure" science fiction and its — what? — *less* hard and pure avatars, and I am driven to discuss it in terms of jokes. Let me be the devil's advocate, and let me suggest that there is *not* such a thing as "hard-core science fiction." Or if there is, let me suggest that we ought to do to it the same thing the present administration has done to the ideal of detente: get rid of it.

Most of us have taught, or talked about, or lectured on, or simply babbled on the subject of science fiction. And that means that we have, most of us, babbled at one time or another about the difference between "hard" and "new wave" science fiction. We have explained, carefully or sloppily, with more or less references to mythology, structuralism, and James Joyce, the difference between Robert A. Heinlein's *Starship Troopers* (1959) and Roger Zelazny's *Nine Princes in Amber* (1970), Isaac Asimov's *Foundation* (1951), and Samuel R. Delany's *Dhalgren* (1975), Larry Niven's "Neutron Star" (1966) and Harlan Ellison's "I Have No Mouth, and I Must Scream" (1967). It is one of the great truisms of popular culture criticism, this distinction between mainstream and new-wave science fiction; like the distinction between the British and the American traditions of detective fiction (Conan Doyle — Christie — Sayers vs. Hammett — Chandler — MacDonald, say).

And like all truisms, this one is at least partly true. And like all truisms, it is mainly, boringly, off the point.

The point is this, and let us admit it once and for all: science fiction is *fiction*, no more and no less. Some of the nice-nellying adjectives that well-meaning editors and writers have applied to it — "extrapolative," "speculative," "experimental" — only help point up the *conventionality* of the mode. What fiction, God help us, is *not* extrapolative or speculative or experimental?

Quite honestly, I can no longer tell the differences among Saul Bellow's *Mr. Sammler's Planet* (1970), Thomas Pynchon's *V.* (1963), Alfred Bester's *The Stars My Destination* (1956), Stephen R. Donaldson's The Chronicles of Thomas Covenant the Unbeliever and — for that matter — Bruce Springsteen's "Born to Run." Or, rather, I no longer think it is important to tell the differences among them. All are fictions — and splendid fictions, at that — involving protagonists who *do not understand* the situation into which they are thrown, and whose heroic struggle is to understand, and through understanding to master, a universe of mechanisms that seem set to destroy them.

Mechanisms: either the machinery of the plot itself or the machinery described by the plot itself. Does it make a difference whether the mechanism is more or less explicitly described *in* the story? Charles Dickens's London is, at this point in time, a no less strange technology for living than Alfred Bester's meticulously imagined future in *The Stars My Destination*. What this suggests to me, at least, is that Oliver Twist and Gully Foyle — or Clarissa Harlowe and Paul Atreides, or Emma Bovary and Thomas Covenant — are equally products of the storytelling imagination and equally to be regarded, and honored, as projections of *ourselves* struggling with the impingements of the fictions of the self life wants and tries to impose upon us.

"Hard-core science fiction": what might that be? In the terms I have just suggested for fiction altogether, I suppose that we could define "hard-core" science fiction as fiction that depends in an especially acute way on a sense of the intransigence of matter and the complexity with which that intransigence tends to manifest itself. A Buddhist, say, for whom such intransigence is mere illusion, or a Taoist, for whom it is sublimely unimportant, could not write hard-core science fiction. Nor, presumably, could a Franciscan mystic, for whom the intransigence would collapse into a kind of cosmic chumminess (consider the concepts of "Brother White Dwarf" or "Sister Entropy").

But the mainstream Western tradition of thought — the *whole* mainstream — is structured on precisely the sense of the impermeability and the hostility of matter. Herbert Schneidau, in his brilliant study of the Bible,

Sacred Discontent (1976), argues persuasively that the Judeo-Christian heritage of mythmaking is in fact a heritage of antimythmaking, a narrative tradition whose inmost form blocks the identification of self and world which is at the heart of the mythological imagination.[1] And even more interestingly, Leszek Kolakowski in his book, *Religion*, suggests that "by appointing man the lord of the earth and by subordinating Nature to his needs the Judaeo-Christian tradition encouraged the great thrust of technological and scientific progress on which Western civilization was to be built."[2]

Now what this suggests is, I think, a revision of our idea of science fiction as a genre, or maybe of the idea of fictional genre altogether. Let me draw an analogy. You will remember that in Arthur C. Clarke's *Childhood's End* (1953), when the mysterious "Overlords" arrive from outer space to reorganize earth's society — and eventually lead it toward its own annihilation and self-transcendence — they keep themselves hidden at first. When they finally make their appearance, they are all in the classic shape of medieval devils — leather wings, pointed tails, horns, and complete satanic *ensemble*. The reason for this remarkable coalescence of myth and reality, Clarke hypothesizes, is that mankind, in a sort of proleptic vision of its ultimate fate — of childhood's end — remembered *forward* to the Overlords and placed their shape at the point of an aboriginal, rather than a terminal, catastrophe.

The analogy is this: I want to suggest that we consider hard-core science fiction, not as a recently evolved form of Western storytelling, but as the form toward which Western storytelling has been tending all along, the perfect antimythological mythology or the perfect technological theology, whose form is implicit in the very roots of our tradition. Hard-core science fiction, in other words, like the Overlords of Clarke, so frequently looks like a recapitulation of our earliest past because our earliest past was dreaming of it before it became possible.

This kind of formulation will, of course, offend academic intellectuals because it seems to give a kind of evolutionary primacy to a form which is still not officially respectable. And it will offend science fiction fans because it seems to assimilate their chosen and revered imaginative escape to the great tradition of so-called "serious" writing. And this gives me solace, since a formulation that offends nearly everybody cannot, I think, be wholly wrong.

And let us admit, too, that we are all ideological prisoners of Hugo Gernsback, who coined the grotesque term, "scientifiction," in 1926. It is not even *science fiction*: it is technological fiction. If science is the nonintrusionist (*pace* Heisenberg) contemplation of nature, then there can be no real science fiction. But once man does intrude on the environment; once he does begin to use his pure contemplation for impure, acquisitive ends; then technology is possible, and then fiction is possible. From Cain to Genghis Khan to James Watt, despoilers of the landscape have always been the stuff of epic and romance: just because fiction, in the Western tradition, *is* the story of technology and technology is the dynamics of our exile from the primal Garden by instruments of our own devising.

Jules Verne, one of the fathers of the form (did ever a child have so many fathers?) was asked in 1903 to comment on the resemblance of his work to that of H.G. Wells. Verne's testy response virtually encapsulates and exhausts the distinction between "hard" and "other" science fiction. Verne sputtered, *il invente!*

"He *invents!*"[3] And so Wells did, and so Verne did not. Or, rather, so Verne *thought* he didn't. The hard science fiction writer, from Verne to Asimov to Niven, has always made it a point of personal pride that his work is strict extrapolation from the known, with no — or as little as possible — adulterating admixture from the purely fantastic. This is the boast that produces, among other things, Niven's very funny series of time travel stories, collected in *The Flight of the Horse* (1973). For since time travel is a manifest absurdity in terms of contemporary physics, what Niven's time travelers do — but don't *know* they do — is travel, not into the past, but into fantasy, into the world of the never-was (e.g., the traveler, sent back to find a horse, brings home a unicorn). The journey, for Niven, is not across barriers of time, but across the barriers between genres.

The counter-example to Niven's stories would be, I think, most baldly Isaac Asimov's robot stories: there the fiction is not simply an extrapolation from known laws, but is, really, simply a redemonstration, again and again, of the "Three Laws of Robotics" that are the entire fictive universe of the tales. Reading the robot stories, wonderful as they are, is in fact rather like playing a classic game from the chess column of the newspaper: your interest is not diminished, but is qualified by your sure knowledge that the rules will *always* be established again, in full primacy, at the end. Outside of the romances of Barbara Cartland, this is probably the closest approach fiction can make to playing pinball without using the levers. You just watch the ball take its predestined, gravity-ridden course down the board.

But however hard a hard-core science fiction writer tries, he cannot help transgressing the artificial generic barriers he may impose upon himself. Not even Asimov can keep his stories from giving delight — and the special kind of delight that belongs to storytelling, not to logical or pseudoscientific demonstration. (Indeed, I would suggest that Asimov's vaunted "hardness" is on a par with the "rationalism" of Arthur Conan Doyle: both men, whether they knew it or not, are really involved with creating a *myth* of rationality, not rationality itself.)

To be sure, there is *some* sort of difference between science fiction and fantasy. But I think that difference is only apparent, or obtrusive, when one form impinges ludicrously on the other. Like identical twins, they are easiest to tell apart when their sibling rivalry erupts into fistfights or name-calling.

There is, for example, what I like to think of as the "Princess Aura" syndrome (after everyone's favorite seductress from the Flash Gordon serials). A set of technological heroes, full-hardware-equipped space travelers, reach a distant and inhospitable world only to find it populated by venal tyrants, deposed princes, and breathtaking court ladies — all speaking flawless English — straight out of Anthony Hope Hawkins's *The Prisoner of Zenda* (1894) or, for that matter, William Shakespeare's *As You Like It*.

But this often-remarked triviality of space opera is, really, not a triviality at all. It is part of the inevitable contamination of technological fiction by romance: because, as I have been saying, technological fiction and romance really are the same imaginative endeavor. And though the discovery of such improbably British aliens is the sort of thing that gives nightmares to the Carl Sagans of the world, a healthy course of reading Rabelais, James Fenimore Cooper, and Edgar Rice Burroughs can work wonders to allay the fright.

To be sure, there are counter-examples, moments when explicit fantasy impinges ludicrously upon the domain of hard SF. In a fantasy I very much admire, Harold Bloom's *The Flight to Lucifer* (1979), a character remarks, early on and offhandedly, "I cross the cosmos through black holes"— prompting one to ask things like, "What time does the next black hole come through?" And when questioned about the nature of his spaceship, this same being laughs. "An illegal borrowing, from your space shuttle perhaps. We will say no more about that."[4] Bloom at least has the wit to see that anything as hardware-rich as the space shuttle *is* an illegal borrowing from one fiction universe into another, and to turn a generic absurdity into a self-conscious joke.

But these, as I said, are instances of the extreme incompatibility of the modes we loosely call "hard" and "soft" science fiction.

I invoke one of the very greatest theorists of narrative modes: Søren Kierkegaard, in *The Sickness Unto Death*, remarks that there are two elementary forms of despair. "The Despair of possibility is due to the lack of necessity," and "The Despair of necessity is due to the lack of possibility."[5] Or, as he also puts it, the despair of the infinite sense is its hunger for the finite, and the despair of the finite sense is its hunger for the infinite. I do no more than follow Kierkegaard in remarking that these complementary despairs produce complementary narrative modes, the one a fantastic quest longing for the specificity of the limited and the material, the other an exploration of the limited and the material longing for the transcendence of the fantastic. "Eternity is in love with the productions of time," wrote William Blake a half-century before Kierkegaard.[6] And the feeling is mutual: the productions of time are in love with eternity. Out of that star-crossed love is generated all our uneasiness with our lives, all our hopes for curing that uneasiness, and, of course, all our storytelling.

Consider the ideas of the quest and the return. They are the prime constituents, the major moments, of any human voyage. And yet how different they are! The quester's journey is always into strangeness, into the unformed or the unformulable, and yet he tends to discover that in that inchoate landscape the forms of the familiar. And the journey home, the return after the quest, is always a journey back to the familiar; but what returnee, from Gulliver to Gully Foyle, has not come home only to find the entire universe altered into the strange? "There are two ways of getting home," wrote G.K. Chesterton, "and one of them is to stay there."[7] But even staying there is a kind of voyaging: you don't know you *have* stayed until things begin to look different, perhaps even frightening. And this, very hard-core phenomenological fact is at the heart of two great modern masters of the everyday nightmarish, Samuel Beckett and Philip K. Dick.

In a brilliant paper presented at the first Eaton Conference, Thomas A. Hanzo examined "The Past of Science Fiction." All Science fiction, argued Hanzo, is a version of *prolepsis*—i.e. the presentation of future events as if they had already occurred.[8] When you place a ten dollar bet on a horse I *know* is going to lose in the fifth at Santa Anita, and I tell you, "You just blew ten bucks," I have performed a rhetorical act of prolepsis: and, according to Hanzo, I have also just created a very short science fiction story. (Whether "hard" or "soft," I suppose, depends upon whether or not your horse actually wins.)

But this obsession with the past tense, Hanzo suggests, really involves an obsession with two *kinds* of past tense, to which we are all thrall, and within which we all make our feeble gestures toward a human life. There is the primal past, the irrevocable past before the trauma of the separation of self and other. And there is the historical past, the past of your individual life and mine, and the past of civilization itself. These pasts are irreconcilable. To have a history is to not retain the aboriginal sense of unity, and to return to the aboriginal sense of unity is to abolish history.

And yet we do both, because we must, because we are compelled to do both. "Hard" science fiction can be taken as the architecture of our banishment into time, into the irreversibility of process. And, in fact, one way of imagining the unimaginable Big Bang is *precisely* in terms of this crypto-cosmo-Freudian birth trauma. Fantasy, on the other hand, can be taken as the fiction of the return — the return to that primal scene before action, even before fiction, is possible or necessary. These two possibilities, in fact, are really Kierkegaard's two kinds of creative despair, but articulated with a little more relevance to the business of storytelling itself.

And you see how they implicate, and demand, rather than impinge upon one another. Robert A. Heinlein's *The Puppet Masters* (1951) and *Starship Troopers* must surely be among the most incontestably non-new-wave of science fiction tales. They are both quest-adventures, inventions of putative future history based on the most cautious extrapolation from present-day technology. In fact, the future culture imagined in *The Puppet Masters*, relying heavily on an extension of contemporary pharmacology and communications-technology, is almost uncomfortably close to the tv-dominated, tranquilized and/or hyped lives many of us lead now, thirty years after the book was written. And *Starship Troopers* may well be the ultimately convincing space-war epic, with weaponry and tactics so precisely imagined that, a generation later, Joe Haldeman could use their details as the basis for his own, anti–Heinlein and antiwar novel, *The Forever War* (1974).

And yet these extrapolations, like so many others, collapse finally into that alternate time, that alternate past which is the myth of our recovery of the primal scene. Sam Nivens and Johnny Rico, the respective heroes of *The Puppet Masters* and *Starship Troopers*, are finally questers for a reunion with their fathers, which is to say questers after the pre–Oedipal paradise that is the landscape of childhood and of pastoral romance. The voyage out — the "hard" science fiction voyage out — turns in on itself and becomes a voyage inward, into fiction and the stuff of fiction rather than into the inhospitable cosmos. The process is especially clear in Heinlein, but we can remark that the questees in Larry Niven's *Protector* (1973) and in his Ringworld novels also find themselves impelled backward to a rediscovery of the elder race, to cosmogenesis, and even that Asimov's Second Foundation proves to be the scene that preceded the establishing of the First Foundation.

The process is nowhere better incarnated, though, than in Arthur C. Clarke's *2010: Odyssey Two* (1982). The novel is by no means a towering achievement. It is, in fact, an attempt to reinvent the structure and nature of the universe in less than 300 pages: rather like a disco version of Olaf Stapledon at his profoundest. But it is also an exceptionally clever book. Careful and sometimes even tedious in its attention to scientific detail, it is also packed with references to J.R.R. Tolkien's *The Lord of the Rings* (1955–1956), to the film *Alien* (1979), and indeed, to the whole tradition of science fantasy. Clarke, in other words, understands — and makes great fun of — the inevitable interchange between science fiction and fantasy science fiction.

I will not divulge the mainsprings of the plot for those of you who have not yet read it, but I will observe that in this sequel to the most famous science fiction story of recent years, voyages out and voyages within are constantly impinging upon one another, and the boundaries between science fiction and fiction itself are constantly on the point — as they should be — of dissipating. Even HAL, that most put-upon of gadgets, finally gets the treatment we all think he really deserves: but only at the expense of becoming *fully* the human being we always knew he was, which is to say only at the cost of crossing the generic border between hard-core science fiction and psychological narrative.

I one saw a T-shirt at a science fiction convention that said "Reality is a crutch for people who can't deal with science fiction." The slogan is truer, I think, than the writer of it knew. For what I have been arguing is that science fiction does not and cannot make real sense to us until we understand that it is misnamed, and that it acts out the ancient, and only, task of fiction altogether. It is more "hard-core," to be sure, as it deals more explicitly with the technological facts of the universe we inhabit at the present moment. But precisely as it becomes more hard core, at its best and most valuable it also becomes more and more an approximation of the forms of those ancient modes of storytelling whose natal ground is the subconscious and whose fruits are the strange and lovely and invariant shapes of the racial mythic consciousness.

And since I have already mentioned that awesome man, Olaf Stapledon, let me conclude with a reference to his work. In *Star Maker* (1937), Stapledon invents a situation that is stunning in its coalescence of the matters we have been discussing. The narrator tells us how, musing one night on the place of consciousness in the universe, he suddenly finds himself transported — a "body-less view-point," he calls himself — into interstellar space, and is there gifted with the power to journey from planet to planet, inhabiting alien mind after alien mind, in his search for the underlying principle of consciousness.[9] Now this is both the most outrageous of fantastic details, and *at the same time* the most satisfying of "scientific" devices: for it allows us to understand that the *real* science fiction deals with is the science of thought itself, and that first human technology, language, which allows us to tell stories about the world and compels us to try and make sense of the world through that language. Stapledon simply does away with, jettisons, the whole clanking paraphernalia of spacecraft, vacuum suits, and life-support systems. And by doing so he reminds us how fanciful, how romantic, those paraphernalia really are: as much so as the shield of Achilles or the lance and sword of Sir Gawain. *Star Maker*, in other words, is the hardest of hard science fiction stories, because its quest is as unrelenting and as unpicturesque, as single-minded and as pure, as the quest of pure science itself.

And at the heart of that purity there is a terrifying and austere poetry. Early in the tale, the narrator explains to us that it is only with great difficulty and great inaccuracy that he can describe the real nature of his galactic experiences: "Of the less human worlds," he writes, "and the many fantastic kinds of beings which we encountered up and down the galaxy and throughout the whole cosmos, and even beyond it, I shall perforce make statements which, literally regarded, must be almost wholly false. I can only hope that they have the kind of truth that we sometimes find in myths."[10]

"The kind of truth that we sometimes find in myths": it is the only kind of truth, really, that we shall probably ever find to make our lives joyful or habitable. It is the only life-support system we can rely on for very long. And it is the honor, not just of Stapledon, but of the great tradition of mainstream science fiction, to continued unabated the activity of incarnating that lying truth, that most precise of false analogies, that waking dream.

6

Boring Dates

Reflections on the Apocalypse Game

To satisfy what I am sure must be keen anticipation at my title, let me give you the complete list of boring dates, in chronological order. They are 1984, 1999, 2001, 2010, 2419, and — the first shall be last, I recall hearing somewhere — 802,701.

Of course you recognize most of them. But, without being condescending, let me remind you that 2419 is the date of Philip Francis Nowlan's original Buck Rogers story, *Armageddon 2419 A.D.* (1928). 802,701 is the date of the central action of H.G. Wells's *The Time Machine* (1895). And "1999" is the title of a song by the outrageous rock and roller, Prince, which contains some brilliantly apocalyptic lyrics. Prince, that other party animal named Petronius, and the man who called himself John of Patmos and wrote the Book of Revelation share not only an initial but a sense of the terminal, the sense — as Frank Kermode calls it in his splendid book — of an ending, the imagination of the end. It is an imagination George Orwell shares, and those are the terms under which I choose to celebrate him.

Mind you, it is the numbers which are boring, and not by any means the texts those numbers inhabit. And, in its way, that is an indication of one of the problems of apocalyptic writing, and one of the more virulent bacteria infesting science fiction criticism, that is, the belief that science fiction is in any way *predictive*.

Many of my distinguished colleagues and friends, I know, disagree fraternally but severely with my opinion — especially that kind and wise man, Frederik Pohl. But, each year at the Eaton Conference, I introduce that divisive theme into the proceedings: a harmlessly academic and diffident version of Edgar Allan Poe's Red Death.

William Blake, the first great theorist of science fiction, put it this way:

a prophet does not tell you what is *going* to happen, he tells you that, if you go on the way you're going, this is what you're going to *look* like. And Eric S. Rabkin, a spiritual heir of Blake, has argued that science fiction matters precisely because it raises in an especially acute fashion the general phenomenological and historical problems of storytelling altogether. I would go farther than Rabkin and suggest that at least the utopian/dystopian variety of science fiction raises serious questions about the nature of writing itself.

Let me put it this way: my boring dates are boring because they *are* inscribed, and because the act of inscription is, *per se*, a fixative that can tend to diminish the radiance or the luster of the very image it preserves.

Now that sounds almost perverse and paradoxical enough to have been translated from the French. But anyone who has ever written will recognize that the proposition is not so complicated. To write it down is to *fix* it; and to fix it is to confront, inevitably, the fissure between expectation and execution, idea and act. Jean Genet, that maestro of unpleasantness, compares his writing, in *Our Lady of the Flowers* (1948), to fecal matter that, once produced, grows progressively cold and alien to the producer.

To be sure, many readers of Genet will want to observe that, in his case, this is a remarkable act of self-assessment. But it *generally* true. Genet writes from prison, and for him to write is simultaneously to be freed from confinement and to realize a new, other kind of confinement: the confinement of having *uttered*.

Genet in prison, Frederick Douglass in slavery, Winston Smith in the bowels of the Party, Jack Abbott in the belly of the beast: for all of them, to write is to realize what it is to be free, and what it is to be enslaved. Remember that *Nineteen Eighty-Four* (1949) is primarily, the record of a record, a book about the production of Winston Smith's journal and its effect upon his consciousness. "He was a lonely ghost uttering a truth that nobody would ever hear. But so long as he uttered it, in some obscure way the continuity was not broken." That is what Winston thinks to himself at the very inception of his journal. "It was not by making yourself heard but by staying sane that you carried on the human heritage." And on the very next page he comes to the central insight of the prison journalist: "Now that he had recognized himself as a dead man it became important to stay alive as long as possible."[1]

There speak, I submit, both the crucial political and prophetic voice of the novel, and also the peculiarly despairing voice of the professional writer who understands both the importance and the folly of his elected vocation. As Peter Stansky and William Abrahams reassert in their splendid biography of Orwell, his initial commitment was not to politics, but to that distinctively modern disease, the idea of being a writer[2]: the political prophecy followed upon the artistic quest, as it did in the case of that other great esthete-turned-polymath, H.G. Wells. Indeed, *Homage to Catalonia* (1938), where Orwell discovers in the same moment his passionate political libertarianism and his full vigor as a writer, may almost be taken as the mirror image of Winston Smith's journal. For the author of *Homage*, writing shows him the way out of his self-constructed cage; for the author *in Nineteen Eighty-Four*, the writing shows him the bars of his cell.

Or rather, not the bars, but the screens. Notice again the brilliance of the scene in which Winston begins to write. He has to hide the blank notebook from the omnipresent telescreen: which is to say he has to conceal his seditious act of inscription from the very technology that, in our age, most threatens the privacy, the loneliness, and the sublime arrogance of the act of writing. And under that indictment I include, of course, not just television but its older brother, film. The second film version of *Nineteen Eighty-Four* (1984), vastly wiser than the first version, concentrates on this aspect of the novel, on screens within screens and the omnipresence of the visual, as opposed to the written, image. And on that level, it cannot help but remind us of a film like George Lucas's *THX 1138* (1971)(another arbitrary number!) where the entire structure of society is video-monitored; which is to say simply that we are reminded of how much Orwell's vision *is* a vision not only of our world but of our nightmares about that world.

Twenty-four hours before I wrote this, I had a long conversation and a rather Daliesque dinner with a hyperintelligent and distinguished science fiction writer who has also written extensively for and about television. He made the compelling point, over the lamb tandoori, that trying to write *good* television is an immoral act, since watching television is itself an immoral act, and good television would only seduce us into more time in front of the tube, more time not writing or reading or thinking for ourselves.

To be sure, the argument can be described as paradoxical. The cure for America's malaise of the spirit is not less but more *Laverne and Shirley*: homeopathic medicine, indeed (as in "emetic"). But it is not necessarily wrong. Here is a distinguished imaginative writer — he despises the term science fiction — Harlan Ellison, in the preface to his collection, *Strange Wine*: "The *act* of watching television for protracted periods (and there's no way to insure the narcotic effects won't take you over) is deleterious to the human animal. The medium itself insists you sit there quietly and cease thinking."[3]

Having expended a number of words, and a larger amount of energy, upon arguing that film and literature are equivalently noble and serious acts of the primal, mythmaking imagination, I find this a distressing utterance. But part of my distress is that I cannot entirely dismiss it. Remember that

Orwell's overriding passion was to be a *writer,* a writer of any sort, but a man whose life was lived with and within words. Indeed, it is difficult to think of Orwell, with his love of the language and his compulsive sense of the work to be done, without thinking of that other magisterial British consumptive, John Keats. Both men were obsessed with, dedicated to, the business of inscription. And both men felt it to be an existential gamble.

What Ellison is saying is really a paraphrase of the myth of *Nineteen Eighty-Four,* and a fine paraphrase at that: I find it significant and moving that one of his best stories, "'Repent, Harlequin!' Said the Ticktockman" (1965), virtually concludes with a reference to Orwell's book. To produce a sound and image track is not to write, but, precisely, to *produce*— to manufacture an object of consumption that bears no more relationship to your inner life than your next pack of cigarettes or your next White Tower hamburger. Maybe, come to think of it, less.

Now I do not really believe this. But I think it is important *not* to believe it, and to understand why we don't have to believe it. Notice that one of the first things Winston remembers in his journal is the propaganda film showing Oceanian helicopters strafing Eurasian soldiers and citizens alike. The audience — except for Winston, who is already an embryonic humanist — is delighted at the carnage. This may have appeared, in 1948, to be a perverse view of film, or a pessimistically unreal view of human nature. But of course we have watched audiences watch *Straw Dogs* (1971), *Dirty Harry* (1971), and any number of even more shocking films (*I Spit on Your Grave* [1978] and *Bring Me the Head of Alfredo Garcia* [1974] come to mind as two of the more elegantly self-descriptive titles in human history). And so we know that Orwell may never have been more of a prophet than in this area.

But that is a secondary point. The main point is that Orwell perceives a tension between the written and the filmed tale — a tension that can be either therapeutic or deleterious. The 1956 film of *Nineteen Eighty-Four* has not been re-released, thanks mainly to the venality of theatrical distributors. This is a pity, because it is a very fine film. But, in fact, in that film of this book about books and film, the important scene of Winston viewing the helicopters is not shown. It is a thematic mistake of the first order. Think, for example, of what a François Truffaut or a Stanley Kubrick could have done with it.

Because, of course, both Truffaut and Kubrick *did* do something with it. *2001: A Space Odyssey* (1968), which may well be the most nonverbal sound film ever made, features printed legends — as in a silent film, reminding us once again that we are hearing what we see — at each major junction of the film. It is a film about language: THE DAWN OF MAN is the first legend we see on the screen, and that writing is not solely writing, but also writing *about* writing. After the development of sound, it is impossible to make a truly silent film (Charlie Chaplin in *Modern Times* [1936] and Mel Brooks in *Silent Movie* [1976] both tried, with failed if wonderful results): but Kubrick comes as close as any director can to that precarious eminence. For *2001* is, ultimately, a film about language and the ways in which language not only reflects, but constitutes human consciousness. We did not need, nor did we want, Arthur C. Clarke's *2010: Odyssey Two* (1982) to explain to us that Hal goes bonkers in *2001* because he has become truly linguistic (i.e., truly human; i.e., has been taught to lie). We *knew* that, if we had watched the film successfully at all. Clarke, like Hal, has failed to learn one important lesson: when to shut up.

Truffaut's *Fahrenheit 451* (1966) plays even more subtly with the tension between writing and filming than does *2001*—and a great deal more subtly than Ray Bradbury's original novel (1953). To begin with, there is one place in the film where the written word is absolutely necessary: the main title sequence, of course. But in *Fahrenheit 451*, this dyslexic dystopia, the credits are only spoken, while the camera shows us a forest — an electromagnetic *selva oscura*— of television antennae. It is a clever trick, but it is also (as is usual with Truffaut's clever tricks) more than that. It is a reminder that the spoken word, even when spoken through the medium of the sound track, is perishable, and that the written word, even when only seen on the screen, somehow *stays*. Jacques Derrida argues seriously that, at least in the metaphysical acceptance of priority, writing is *before* speech. Bradbury's novel argues the same thing, rather faintly, and Truffaut's film establishes it with, for me, unrelenting authority. *Fahrenheit 451* is in its way the ideal reverse-image of the novel *Nineteen Eighty-Four*: for just as in the novel, the written word is continually threatened by the video image, so in the film, the video image continually impinges upon the authority of the written word.

Montag the fireman — his job is to set fire to books — becomes seduced by literature and finally becomes a subversive, which is to say, in this world, a literate man. He is an anti–Winston Smith in that for him freedom is the discovery of reading rather than writing, and in that the television screens in his world are primarily things that you watch rather than things that watch you. Nevertheless, the same fundamental equations apply in both stories.

Except that they apply more bitterly, and perhaps more realistically, in Orwell's tale than in Bradbury/Truffaut's. For *Fahrenheit 451*, after all, depends upon the same thesis that sustains almost every second-rate humanities and literature course taught in American or British universities: the brave but pathetic faith, that is, that in a soulless society literature will save you because it is, God help us all, *good* for you. Depressed? Read Jane Austen. In despair? Check out Charles Dickens. Suicidal? Try William Shakespeare.

Orwell will not allow us that easy option. Not because he knows more about life than Bradbury does, but precisely because he knows more about literature, more about being a writer. If we are the words we live by, then the possibility of cheapening those words is also the possibility of cheapening ourselves. George Steiner, in a brilliant discussion of *Mein Kampf* in his book *Language and Silence*, observes that the cheapening of the national psyche under the Third Reich is anticipated by the cheapening of that marvelous instrument, the German language, in Adolf Hitler's autobiography.[4] Of course it is Orwell's "Politics and the English Language" (1946), and of course it is the grammatology of the Vietnam War and every other officially sanctioned debacle of a sickening century. But it is also an indication of the degree to which Orwell perceived, and preserved for us, the right semantics of our time.

Nineteen Eighty-Four is not a book, it is a mythogem; a metaphor that we can not really escape even if we wanted to, a boring date that will remain forever one of the *words* by which we define ourselves. Orwell succeeded better at his act of inscription than he perhaps intended, but succeed he did. "The philosophers have only *interpreted* the world, in various ways," wrote the young Karl Marx in the most famous of his theses on Ludwig Feuerbach. "The point is to *change* it."[5] It is Orwell's permanent glory that he wrote us a book and forged us a myth that inverts the Marxian formula and convinces us again that, in some range of identity, understanding still matters.

7
Frames in Search of a Genre

A poll conducted in the 1960s found that the most popular daily comic strips in America were, in order, *Blondie, Dick Tracy, Little Orphan Annie, Peanuts,* and *Rex Morgan, M.D.* I offer this fact as proof that evolution, at least in the arts, is not always downward. *Dick Tracy* and *Little Orphan Annie* have long since gone to that great syndicate in the sky, although neither without a final, sadly optimistic spasm of hoped for contemporaneity: Tracy was even drawn, near the last, in three-quarter face instead of the classic and inevitable, full and hawk-face profile, and Annie, though she never got eyeballs, did get involved with drug dealers and social radicals in her penultimate, etiolated days. This is known as profanation. Peace to their ashes, or to their dried ink. As with all truly popular forms of popular art, they were there and they were great when we needed them to be. *Blondie*, boringly, continues. *Peanuts* continues boringly and pretentiously: how many times must we hear Linus quote the Gospel according to St. John before we admit that Mr. Schulz is a well-read man? And Rex Morgan, the Ronald Reagan of comics — you don't trust him, but you can't dislike him — still acts out the interminable soap opera of his life and nonloves to the affectionate yawn of the cosmos. Mary Worth, at least — because of a change in writers — has moved to Santa Barbara. All of which is beside my point. My point is that you don't read these strips. Or if you do, you do because, like me, you are hopelessly nostalgic or because you are so hopelessly old-fashioned that you don't want to hear the rest of what I have to say. I'd like us, after all, to part friends, even if only in the first paragraph.

But if you're still with me, let me suggest this as preface and premise. In a culture increasingly torn between the alternatives of science fiction and fantasy; magic and technology; the possibility of infinite possibility and the risk of unfathomable guilt; in a culture at the break of noon between aspiration and despair; in a culture like that, one of our best guides to who we think we are and where we think we are is the comic strip, which is to say the purest contemporary form of the joke. The joke or the cartoon, where sf and fantasy meet, kiss, and dance — my favorite form of modern fiction.

L'histoire drôle, the French, with their seemingly endless gift for tediously irrefutable analytic brilliance, call it. It is a *histoire*: every joke, every cartoon worth the cost of publication, is in fact a short story ("This guy walks into a bar, see? And he's got this duck on his shoulder, right? And the bartender says to him..."). Rudolf Bultmann distinguished between *Geschichtliche* and *Historische* utterance because the latter not only tells you where you are, it tells you in a way you can't, except if you are a Philistine, forget for the rest of the day. The greatest of Galilean *zaddiks* was also — and I say this with the deepest reverence — a kind of *Historische*, religious stand-up comic. What is the Kingdom of heaven like? Well, maybe a mustard seed. See, a mustard seed when it starts out is, like, real small, you dig? You can almost hear Peter chortling and digging Matthew in the ribs. Damn! There he goes again.

But *l'histoire drôle* is not only a *histoire*, it is also *drôle*. Violette Morin, in a brilliant essay on cartoon jokes, concludes by invoking Todorov's studies on fantasy, and by observing that while "literary" fantasy is naturally enlightening, cartoon fantasy is naturally shocking — not éclairante but *foudroyante*. The joke, in other words, has this difference from the true story: it doesn't teach us, it simply jumps out from around the corner and says "booga-booga!" to the soul. Violette Morin's essay is, as I have said, brilliant. It is also wrong. A better theorist of fiction, Barbara Herrnstein Smith, tells us in *On the Margins of Discourse* (1978) that fiction is indeed, as Aristotle said, a *mimesis* or imitation — not an imitation of *the real*, but rather an imitation of so-called natural forms of discourse. Thus, the epistolary novel is an imitation of letter writing, the drama is an imitation of conversation, the Valentine Day's card is an imitation of saying "I love you," and so forth. So what is the cartoon joke, *l'histoire drôle*, an imitation of? I think, of that most natural and unnatural of human activities, the act of storytelling and mythmaking itself.

Let me begin with an example from *Garfield*. In frame one, Garfield the cat, about to grab a vine hanging from the ceiling, thinks "I'm going to swing down this vine and steal Jon's [his owner's] chicken." In frame two, Garfield swoops down on the vine, grabbing the roast chicken off Jon's plate. In frame three Jon, bemused, stares at the ceiling and asks, "Where did the vine come from?"

Søren Kierkegaard is about as perceptive about the nature of narrative, but not many others. There is, of course, the magic sword Beowulf finds when he is fighting Grendel's mother, that enables him to kill her. Where did the sword come from? There is the white gold wedding ring in Stephen R. Donaldson's Thomas Covenant cycle that makes Covenant the most important character in the magic Land. Where did the ring come from? There is the shield of Achilles, the garter of Sir Gawain, Cinderella's glass slipper.... There is Mark Twain's immortal comment that a character in one of James Fenimore Cooper's Leatherstocking tales is slain by a random bullet fired by the author.

The joke tells us, in one way or the other, that the universe — that very large machine that we know is out to get us — can be, if not conquered, at least circumvented by our very admission of its alienness. The joke, in other words, is man's first inkling and first denial of the irreversibility of the entropy arrow. *Raffiniert ist der Herrgott, aber böshaft ist er niche*, said Albert Einstein in a famous utterance: the Lord God is subtle, but he is not malicious.[1] Niels Bohr was not as sweet a man as Einstein but he would not have committed such a *gaffe*. Every joke, every fantasy, and every science fiction story tells us that the Lord God is *böshaft*. And since it has become my personal ritual to tell you that there is no such distinct entity as science fiction or fantasy, I shall do so once again and insist that all storytelling fits the crucial matrix of the joke.

Where did the vine in the Garfield cartoon come from? From the same place the universe, the scene of all stories, came from: from nowhere. Ilya Prigogine, Hugh Everett, and John Gribbin all entertain the possibility that the universe, from big bang to contemporary whimper, is a vacuum fluctuation, a random permutation of sheer probability that will eventually permute back to absolute, Brahman-like nonbeing. There is a free lunch, in other words, but it turns out to be a wake. I am, to be sure, Huckleberry Finnishy innocent of the mathematics behind this hypothesis. But since Jerry Falwell has denounced it from the pulpit as a hellish, damnable doctrine, I am sufficiently persuaded of its righteousness. The world, like the tales he tell about the world, loves to jump from around the corner and shout "booga-booga!" at us. Why else would the *Herrgott* have given elementary particles a quality called "strangeness"? The only real question is whether or not the joke is on us. If the joke is on us, we are writing what can roughly be called science fiction. If we get to share in the joke, we are writing what can roughly be called fantasy. There is a third alternative, but I haven't yet the courage to address it; bear with me.

There are two elementary forms of the joke: the one-liner and the shaggy dog story. Of course, the one-liner doesn't have to be restrained to only one line any more than the shaggy dog story has to involve an overhirsute canine. The distinction is in the punch line: the one-liner has one and the shaggy dog story doesn't. Henny Youngman's famous gag will illustrate the first model. "Women are funny, you know? Take my wife. Please." That "Please," I submit, is brilliant. It turns what promises to be a rambling set of anecdotes about women into an ironic statement of domestic less than bliss, at the same time effecting an epistemological leap in the interpretation of the word *take*: not "take her as an example" but "take her off my hands." (Arthur Koestler discusses jokes as synaptic leaps of this sort in his splendid and underrated *The Act of Creation* [1964].) The punch line — or, in this case, punch-word — gives meaning, finality, the sense of an ending and even of a kind of epiphany to the joke. In a night club, the drummer would do a roll and a rim-shot to punctuate it. It is the equivalent of the Grand Unified Theory that would explain, once and for all, the interrelationship of the four elemental forces and the reason for, as Douglas Adams puts it, *Life, the Universe, and Everything* (1982).

Tiddley-bum (one man's approximation of a rim-shot).

How different is the shaggy dog story.

A little old man — Murray, say, is his name — is walking through the garment district in New York late at night. A UFO lands and an alien steps out.

"Ach," says Murray, "are you ugly! Where you from?"

"I am from Mars," says the alien.

"Mars, schmars. *Nu*? But you got seven arms. Everybody on Mars got seven arms?"

"Everyone on Mars has seven arms."

"Yeah, but *feh*! On each arm you got six fingers, like tentacles or something. Everybody up there got that?"

"Everyone on Mars," with a patient sigh, "has six fingers on each of their seven arms."

"Yeah, yeah, *sei gesund*. But on each of your fingers you got all kinds rings. Topaz, emerald, diamond, ruby. Everybody on Mars got rings like that?"

"Well — not the *goyim*."

As Murray himself might say: this, already, is a *joke*? "Not the *goyim*" is, maybe a punch line? What, there's Jews on Mars? That is funny? That is to do a rim-shot? What's the point? The point is that there is no point: no answer, no epiphany, no Grand Unified Theory. No rim-shot. If you love shaggy dog stories, you love them because they are celebrations of the fundamental unknowability of the cosmos, and therefore of its infinite capacity to surprise, delight, or murder us. And by cosmos I mean not only the galaxy, but also the neighborhood — yours or mine.

Robert Scholes and Frank Kermode both suggest that the distinctive form of the classical novel may be the idea of absolutely transmissible information (the punch line model, in my reductivist argot), and that the postmodern novel, from James Joyce to Thomas Pynchon, can be best described as a version of the shaggy dog story. What does Molly Bloom's "Yes" mean? Who is V? Where does the meaning come from? In his recent, brilliant fantasy *Jitterbug Perfume* (1984), Tom Robbins narrates a conversation between two women. "Do you ever pray?" asks woman A. "Sure I do, honey. I pray all the time," says woman B. "Well, when you talk to God, does he answer?" "Absolutely." "What does God say?" "God says the check is in the mail."[2] This, I submit, is not only very good theology but also a very good four-frame cartoon: it has been said that if Thomas Pynchon were a muppet, he would write like Tom Robbins. The punch line writer believes that the world owes us an explanation — benevolent or malevolent — of its workings. The despair of infinitude, says Søren Kierkegaard in *Fear and Trembling* (1843), is the lack of finitude. Such people like to listen to Wolfgang Amadeus Mozart or the Beatles, read *Doonesbury*, and play bridge. The shaggy-dog writer believes that the final explanation, if we ever got one, would be incomprehensible anyway. The despair of finitude is the lack of infinitude, says Kierkegaard. Such people like to listen to Stravinsky and Thelonious Monk, read *Garfield*, and play poker.

Job believes fervently in punch lines. He demands one of the Lord God. The Lord God, speaking out of the whirlwind, tells him instead the greatest of shaggy dog stories. Why did all this happen to you? *Why*? Because. As the shortest and best shaggy dog joke in the world puts it: "Are we lost, Daddy?" "Shut up," he explained.

Literature is littered with left-to-dies, founded upon foundlings. Oedipus is abandoned. Moses is abandoned. Arthur is abandoned. Donald Duck never knew his papa drake, Garfield as all the world knows was found in the kitchen of an Italian restaurant — hence his lasagna addiction — and Opus, the saintly penguin of Berke Breathed's *Bloom County*, was abandoned by his mother on an Antarctic ice floe. If the joke is the model for fiction, and if fiction is the model for human consciousness, then the sub-subtext of both articulations is the quest of the son/daughter for the parent who will justify, validate existence itself. Am I lost, Daddy? Odysseus tries to get home. But Telemachus journeys out to find the father he seeks and who is seeking him. Joyce did not misread the aboriginal tale as much as he retaught us to read it aright. We begin and end all quests with Telemachus, Stephen Dedalus, thee and me looking for the punch line — or the lack of same — that will finally tell us whether we are lost.

If most literature and most jokes — by now you know that to me they are the same — express the search of the son for the father, then William

Shakespeare's *King Lear* is the elemental joke turned inside out. For years I wondered why that play, of all plays, is the most truly terrifying. (Doctor Johnson said he could never read the last act again, and he was right.) Now I know. The play is about being a father. And that means it is about organizing, not being organized by, your universe. And *that* means it is about delivering, not waiting for, the punch line or non-punch line the universe ultimately has in store for you. It is a play about the difference between science fiction and fantasy.

The Duke of Gloucester has only sons — one good and one bad. Lear has only daughters — two bad and one good. Male chauvinism aside (John Milton might have given Lear even more bad daughters), it is important that both old men choose the wrong moiety of offspring, and both pay for their wrong choice.

But how differently they pay. Gloucester lives through a tragedy. Having given his love to the wrong son and having been horribly blinded (this, apparently, is a professional hazard of tragic heroes), he can deliver the best tragic punch line in English literature: "As flies to wanton boys are we to the gods;/They kill us for their sport."[3] The universe is meaningful, even if inimical, and to suffer because the Lord God is subtle, even if sadistic, is at least to suffer for a reason.

That is what Gloucester knows. Lear knows worse. When Cordelia is strangled because of an absurd oversight ("great thing of us forgot"[4] is William Shakespeare's immortally silly line), Lear, entering with his dead daughter in his arms, can manage one imperishable line, perhaps the most difficult of all lines to deliver: the single word, "Howl,"[5] repeated three times.

It is an anti-punch line. It is the question, "Where did the vine come from?" It is Lear's, once-uttered indelible affirmation that there is no affirmation; that the world is a zero-sum game; that death is death, and death and death indeed; and that all life from the birth and perishing of star systems to the birth and perishing of those like you and me is accidental, pointless, devoid of even the consolation of a cosmic rim-shot.

That is the way the world ends: not with a tiddley-bum but with a howl.

Or is it? Every morning I buy the *San Francisco Chronicle*. Each day in the *San Francisco Chronicle*, on the comics page, at the top of the page, I read what has become known in my household as "the big three"—*Doonesbury*, by Garry Trudeau; *Garfield*, by Jim Davis; and *Bloom County*, by Berke Breathed. Of course, I read everything else on the comics page—Lynn Johnston's *For Better or Worse*, Phil Frank's *Travels with Farley*, and so on. And, in the *Los Angeles Times* I read Tom K. Ryan's *Tumbleweeds*, William Overgard's very strange and extraordinarily hip *Rudy*, and Gary Larson's *The Far Side*. If I were ordered to deliver a course on the theory of fiction and the theory of narrative, I could not think of a better reading list.

Doonesbury, which thinks it is a fantasy, is actually a novel in spite of itself: *un roman malgre soi*, if you think Gallicisms lend authenticity to the obvious. The ongoing story of Mike Doonesbury — patron saint of the Yuppies — of Uncle Duke, patron saint of the chemically addicted, and of everybody else in Trudeau's imaginative menagerie is, notwithstanding Trudeau's year-and-a-half retirement, a chronicle of the late 1960s sensibility. Remember that back then we all thought there were answers: the war in Vietnam was wrong, civil rights was (were?) right, and we all read Frank Herbert's *Dune* (1965) and *The Autobiography of Malcolm X* (1965). Those are two great books, and that was, even allowing for the fear and the pain and the ugliness, one great decade. It was a Gloucester decade, a punch line decade; a decade in which we believed that, however hostile the universe might be to our chances for survival, there was still a point to the hostility. When *2001: A Space Odyssey* was released in 1968, only John Simon had the good sense, in his initial review, to describe it as a "shaggy God story."[6] The rest of us tried to figure out what the monolith meant, and whether it was Louis Quatorze or Louis Quinze furniture in that galactic motel room at the end, and why HAL was so disturbed in the first place. The rest of us, in other words, not being gifted with John Simon's universal distaste — rather like the absolute solvent, which nothing can hold — believed that there was a reason for what was going on. *Why Are We in Vietnam?* Norman Mailer had asked only a year before. Well, to ask why is to suggest that there ought to be a why?— is that not so?

Of course, there wasn't; any more than there was a why for the carnage Ezra Pound memorialized in "Hugh Selwyn Mauberly" (1920). But we thought there was, and those of us who went through the decade thought and think there was, and so does Garry Trudeau. One of his recent running gags in the reborn *Doonesbury* is the implantation of a liberal heart into the mind and body of a conservative. It makes, perhaps every other day, for great fun; but it is also rather grimly confessional. Trudeau's strip has not been nearly as funny since he has come back — and it hasn't been, I suggest, because the age of the punch line is, at least temporarily, over.

It is now the age of Reagan, and of *Garfield*: the vain, self-satisfied, eternally hungry fat cat. Garfield looks like a punch line strip, and is actually a shaggy dog — or shaggy cat — one. Where did the vine come from? *Garfield*, actually, is ritualized; and ritual, as any liturgist will tell you, is inimical to punch lines.

Garfield is a three-frame strip, and *Doonesbury* is a four-frame strip. This makes a very large difference in the respective psychic realities of the two mythologies. In four frames you can set up a situation, a complication of the situation, a pause, and a summation. In what may be the best and most Swiftian cartoon ever, Mike Doonesbury and the eternal hippie, Zonker Harris, are staring across the field. Frame one: Zonker says, "It's a very nice day today." Frame two: Zonker says, "They say it was a very nice day one year ago today at Kent State." Frame three: silence. Frame four: Zonker says, "Have a nice day, John Mitchell." If this is not the moral use of language — which is to say, a holy thing — then I do not know what is. Frame one: Garfield strolls into the yard, saying, "Hello, flowers, hello trees, hello grass." Frame two: Garfield passing an extinct bird says, "Hello, daisies, hello, Apteryx." Frame three: Garfield does a double take. You see, I hope, the difference. I do not mean to privilege one or the other form of the joke. But Garry Trudeau, I think, could write great science fiction and Jim Davis could write great fantasy. Or put it this way: Zonker thinks there is a point to it all, while the Great Gar knows there isn't.

I suggest to you that all artists are disingenuous. Plato, braver than I, simply observed that all poets are liars. Samuel R. Delany wants us to believe that his novels, from *Nova* (1968) through *Dhalgren* (1975) to *Stars in My Pocket Like Grains of Sand* (1984), are science fiction. And Roger Zelazny wants us to believe that the *Nine Princes in Amber* series is fantasy. Of course, we all know that there is no real distinction between the two forms. A story is a story, and a joke is a joke, and the *Iliad* and the *Odyssey*, the best punch line and the best shaggy dog stories, respectively, ever told, were created by the same committee. But, as good readers of the comics, we also know that the distinction, though false, is useful. Life is like that. Ask any lawyer.

You will recall that I gave you the option of exiting this discussion at the beginning. But I would be disappointed in you if, at this point, you were not mumbling to yourself, "Okay, fine, for sure — but what the heck is he trying to *say?*" Harold Bloom, in *Agon* (1982), defines fantasy as that form of mythmaking in which the pleasure-pain principle predominates over the reality principle but, through overdetermination, collapses back into the very *thanatos*-drive it came into existence to overcome. That is a brilliant, since Bloomian, and baffling, since Bloomian, description of the mechanism of fantasy and the daily life of Garfield. What the heck I am trying to say, in other words, is that from the Homeric poems and the Torah to yesterday's comic page, all storytelling is storytelling, and that the differences matter less than the similarities. And if you tell me the jokes you laugh at, I will tell you how you stand with the universe. Or if you tell me what animals you laugh at, to paraphrase, by their brutes you shall know them.

Subtle is the Lord God, but malicious he is not, said Einstein, that greatest of believers in the punch line theory of reality. But Pan was a trickster, and so was Anansi the Spider who, when he migrated from Africa to America, changed his name to Brer Rabbit. So were a number of deities, all of whom are, in their ways, the tutelary deities of fantasy, and of the comic strip. I am not fond of people who are fond of Snoopy, and I like almost everyone who likes *Fred Bassett* (Garfield, of course, is *hors de combat*). There: you have my personal metaphysics. I believe in the radical unknowability of the universe, in the Second Law of Thermodynamics, in the ineluctability of the darkness that is going to descend upon us all, and in Thelonious Monk and Garfield. And that is what fantasy believes in. I find it significant that there are no animals in *Doonesbury*: in a punch line universe, the trickster figure, the innocent who observes that the Emperor is naked, is not welcome, not any more welcome, indeed, than poets in Plato's *Republic*, the Mule in Isaac Asimov's *Foundation* trilogy, or hobbits in *The Lord of the Rings* (1955–1956) as it might have been written by E.E. "Doc" Smith or Jerry Pournelle. Tricksters, like charm particles, muons, and monopoles, upset as much as they clarify, and teach us that the pleasure-pain principle is really not different from the reality principle. Penguins, cats, and bassett hounds are not supposed to talk; neither, by the way, are subtle serpents in certain gardens. And if they do, what they have to tell us is our own alienness, our own strangeness in an otherwise ordered and healthy cosmos. The serpent, after all, did not lie to Eve. She did eat the fruit, and she discovered exactly what the serpent told her she would discover: that she was not the woods she wandered in. Then — and only then — did she receive her name. Havah, meaning "life" or, specifically, "human life."

The story of the Fall in Genesis is shot through with the gaping absence of a tiddley-bum. Because what Adam and Havah enter, thanks to the ministrations of the serpent, is nothing less than human history — where, one suspects, YHVH meant them to be all along, to where fantasy always returns us (Thomas Covenant will awaken from his dream of the Land, Garfield will rediscover and redemonstrate the law of gravity), and where we live our lives without more than the hope of punch lines, Grand Unified Theories, or reasonable answers out of the whirlwind.

But there is more. I told you that there are two kinds of jokes; and then I told you that there is a third alternative. It is now time to discuss that third alternative. It is what that very bright man, Christian Metz, calls the "witticism." It is also the hope of imaginative salvation.

If we are torn between the alternatives of the punch line and the shaggy dog universe, then we are damned and doomed. "We live in an old chaos of the sun,"[7] writes Wallace Stevens. Indeed we do. But we need not accept it.

The witticism is harder to illustrate than the two classic forms of the joke, just because it is the point at which consciousness intersects with reality, rather than judges reality. I will try to give you an example.

A few years ago, I found myself separated from a wife of twenty years and in the company of a lady of whom I am, to this day, very fond. It was a time for paranoia, guilt feelings of Olympic proportions, anxiety attacks, and whatever other bad things you can imagine. A friend, whose kindness I will never forget, left a note in my office simply telling me that he knew what I must be going through, and that he was there if I needed to talk to him. I had not spoken to anyone — anyone — since my private apocalypse. So, that afternoon, I called my friend. When I said "Hello," he laughed and said, "Frank! What's new?" That is a witticism. It is not a punch line, because it doesn't give any final answer to my plight. It is not a shaggy dog line, because it does not tell me that the point is that there is no point. It arises out of the absurd, unending possibility of friendship and is therefore like a manifestation of grace. A *mitzvah*. It is a moment when the joke — or the fiction, or the imposed structure, call it what you will — no longer impinges upon but guides and heals reality. Most of us who are still sane — and we are all last-ditch soldiers in the wars of consciousness — *are* still sane because we have been lucky enough to encounter our share of witticisms along the way.

The shortest and the best witticism in the world you will only understand if you are Jewish (I consider myself very reform): it is the word, *Nu?* accompanied, of course, by a shrug of the shoulder. John Ashbery has a poem entitled "I Had Thought Things Were Going Along Well" with a brief text indicating that the poet had made an error."[8] Another witticism, perhaps a shrug, like Kurt Vonnegut, Jr.'s "So it goes" in *Slaughterhouse-Five* (1969), or like the Road Runner's invincible faith that, though coyotes do kill and eat road runners, he will not be killed and eaten by Wile E. Coyote. Where does faith like this come from? From the same place that the vine comes from. You will not mind if I discuss the Road Runner as a paradigm of religious belief, since I have already sufficiently indicated to you that I regard all human culture as having approximately the structure of a Caesar salad. I am merely offering you another anchovy.

Early in his book, *Religion* (1982), Leszek Kolakowski observes that "a religious world perception is indeed able to teach us *how to be a failure*."[9] That strikes me as one of the smartest things I have ever read. The Fool in *King Lear* — wiser than Cordelia, holier than Lear, and bitterer than Gloucester — knows the same thing. He doesn't drop punch lines and he doesn't tell shaggy dog jokes, he utters witticisms. He tries to train his king in failure, how to shrug and say *Nu?* to the omnivorous universe, how to find what lies beyond the pleasure-pain principle and the reality principle.

And what might that be? The knowledge, I suppose, that though we are here by accident we also have a right to be here by accident, and that the nostalgia of infinity for finitude and the nostalgia of finitude for infinity are both, properly considered, the longing of being for meaning. And what the best fiction, and the best jokes, and the best science fiction, and the best fantasy tell us is that that is a longing whose very passion is its own fulfillment.

In the late eighteenth century, in London, someone was marauding the city and murdering cats in the most grisly ways. Dr. Samuel Johnson, when he heard of this, expressed disgust and anger at the sadism and then, stroking his own cat, said, "But they won't get Hodge. No, they won't get Hodge." It is a punch line at Johnson's expense: the great man was incapable of separating his own feelings from the feline carnage abroad. It is a shaggy dog story: what does it matter if one cat more or less is disemboweled? But it is also a witticism: a lesson in failure: an observation that the silliest or grossest of violent acts still can touch the heart and still can move the human spirit to pity. As such, I submit, it is a great joke and a very human story.

Do not mind that it is also, like *Garfield*, about a cat.

8

From Astarte to Barbie and Beyond
The Serious History of Dolls

On the distant planet Symbion, a genetic experiment fails. Frightening changes take place that cannot be stopped. The result? A world where insects grow to frightening proportions. A world where the inhabitants have taken on the awesome characteristics of insects. Where the good of the Shining Realm is locked in mortal combat with the evil of the Dark Domain. Telepathically bonded in combat, Sectaur Warriors join with their insect companions in the ultimate battle for survival. A battle that is now in your hands.

Except for the last sentence, this passage might come from the back cover of a fifties or sixties science fiction paperback. Today, however, when science fiction has almost received its academic laying-on of hands — a mixed *mitzvah* if there ever was one — the jacket copy would read more like this: "In *Sectaur Warrior*, the author continues his exploration of the shadowy interrealm where myth, genetic theory, and man's profoundest religious concerns all collide; and all of it cast in a mold of high adventure reminiscent of *The Lord of the Rings* and Anne McCaffrey's *Dragonriders of Pern*. This is speculative fiction at its best and most provocative."

And, to be sure, there would also be the ritual two-sentence blurb from, say, Norman Spinrad and, with luck, Gregory Benford. I leave it to you to decide which version you prefer, although I know which one would make *me* (apologies to Mr. Spinrad and Mr. Benford) buy the book. I always listen to AM rock stations rather than FM rock stations because I have a woefully low tolerance for pretension and would rather hear Little Richard's "Tutti Frutti" three more times than the Grateful Dead's "Dark Star" once.

At any rate, the more persuasive passage is not, of course, from a paperback. It is from a package containing Sectaur Warrior Zak (and his insect sidekick Bitaur), bought for my far-from-wicked stepson Eric, eight years old and my research assistant for this project. Besides Sectaur Warriors, my home is also populated by GoBots, Power Lords, Masters of the Universe, and Transformers (who are either "Heroic Autobots" or "Evil Decepticons"). Now, *that* is what I call an alien invasion: these aliens attack you through your Mastercard or Visa.

Are they toys? Dolls? Mere counters in a fantasy game played mainly in the head? Or the polyurethane grandchildren of those tin soldiers who fueled the martial instincts of boys about to be warriors, boys about to die from the Crimea through the Argonne and the Battle of the Bulge and into Korea and Vietnam?

I am not a deconstructionist. The only *real* deconstructionists I know are French intellectuals and termites. So my answer to that multiple question is "all of the above." And, more importantly, these aliens are the stuff of which fiction is made, the raw material that can be annealed into that most ancient and most indispensable of human artifacts, storytelling. (I will amend this later.) *Homo neanderthalensis* may not have had a writing system or a concept of the pulley; but it is inconceivable that this dear departed cousin did not tell stories and fashion dolls or icons to reify the characters in his stories.

The Babylonians, we know, not only worshipped the graven images of their gods, but on festival days set especially tasty dishes before them and pretended to feed them: there may be a shorter line than one might think from Astarte to Chatty Cathy. The *ka* of the Egyptians, the immortal yet still somehow physical part of the self, is represented in paintings as a doll-like simulacrum of the deceased. And just as the *ka* was the physical self in its immortal mode, it could be fed with real food or with the representation of food. The pharaohs and high priests would have understood, better than the *New York Times Book Review*, Philip K. Dick's brilliant question, *Do Androids Dream of Electric Sheep?* (1968) And, finally, the most popular fantasy game in the world, with elegantly simple and infinitely suggestive rules, involves toys of various powers and capabilities not unlike those of the many GoBots, Sectaur Warriors, or Transformers: its Persian name, *shah-mat*— our "checkmate"— means "the king is dead." Game is story, story is game.

And let us not forget that H.G. Wells loved to play elaborate games with his hundreds of toy soldiers, that Stanislaw Lem is fascinated with mechanical toys, and that Harlan Ellison has collected enough Shogun Warriors, Masters of the Universe, and so on, to satisfy the Christmas rush in a small town in Iowa.

Our subject is aliens and narrative, or aliens *in* narrative, and I want to suggest that all narrative begins as child's play and that the first and most indispensable tool of child's play, the first alien, is the doll/toy/simulacrum.

It is an alien in the true sense. As Wallace Stevens says in "The Man with the Blue Guitar," it is a "tune beyond us, yet ourselves."[1] It is a projection of ourselves that is, strangely enough, not ourselves, a fun-house mirror image that reflects us, not more accurately, but more tellingly, than an undistorted image.

Emile Benveniste, Gallically gnomic or gnomically Gallic, observes that "language ... is accordingly the possibility of subjectivity" and that the proper definition of the first-person pronoun "I" is "the individual who utters the present instance of discourse containing the linguistic instance *I*."[2]

Never mind that this garble sounds like a Sorbonne lecture as written by Woody Allen. Benveniste's formula is still immensely suggestive. I would paraphrase it thus: "I" is both the most existential and most alien of utterances, the very possibility of narrative, of a "tune beyond us, yet ourselves." "Je est un autre" writes Arthur Rimbaud, sublimely mangling his native tongue: "I is somebody else."[3] It is the very principle of storytelling, the distancing of the self from the self, of the story of your life as you tell it to yourself from the story of your life as it happened to you, of causality from experience. And as such its echo, its Siamese twin in play, is the doll that is and is not us.

What does this have to do with Power Lords or Masters of the Universe?

I am not, mind you, interested in or convinced by the arguments of child psychologists about the "educative value" of toys, that is, make it out of wood and don't paint it because it stimulates the kid's imagination. Only in Departments of Education and in remote reaches of Marin County can people believe that, in our culture, wood is a more "natural" substance than plastic. I am with G.K. Chesterton, who observed that there is more natural spontaneity in the man who eats caviar on impulse than in the man who eats grape nuts on principle. I am interested in toys, in other words, not as relics of the childhood world, but as building blocks of the grown-up world.

Let me invoke two very intelligent women for elucidation. Jacquetta Hawkes, in her magisterial book *Prehistory*, remarks that everything we call "art" is intimately connected to the evolution of tool using. The human impulse to make representations of people and animals, according to Hawkes, seems to have developed at about the same time as the emergence of *secondary* tools, that is, stone fragments whose purpose it is to chip other stone fragments into axes, adzes, hammers, or spear points.[4] This subtle refinement of what must have been the original chipping technique may, in its way, be a stage of development as crucial as the Neolithic Revolution itself. For, if you can make a tool that makes a tool, why not build a better axe by making a tool that makes a tool that makes a tool, and so on to infinity? Self-consciousness becomes possible; and so does play in the most serious sense of the word (*play* being, of course, one of the few words that can never be used frivolously).

Art and technology are not combatants but rather mirror siblings, like Helen and Klytemnestra, hatched from the same egg. The Magdalenian cave drawings — are they art or ritual or metaphysical technology? — overtrump John Ruskin and G.W.F. Hegel in their idea of the growth of culture.

There is another intelligent lady: my daughter Kathy. When Kathy was ten, she had a rather shabby alien, a stuffed dog named Murray, and a friend, little Sally, who was a terrible child but who, since she was the daughter of good friends, was to be treated nicely. One day, as Kathy and Murray and I were sitting in my car, I asked Kathy is she really liked Sally. Kathy's answer was predictable: "Oh, yes, Daddy, I *love* Sally." So far, so good. But then, hefting hapless Murray onto her lap and staring seriously into his button eyes, she said, "Murray doesn't like Sally, you know. Murray *hates* Sally. Yes, he does." "Good for old Murray!" I thought. Not yet having read Roland Barthes on the omnipresence of the "I" in all fictive utterance and having stupidly forgotten Rimbaud's "Je est un autre," I did not realize that I was witnessing the birth of fiction and the reason for fiction. Kathy, the human, was expressing through Murray, the alien, that Sally, the other human, was a brat. If we could not invent simulacra to act out our unacted desires, speak our unspeakable wishes, how could we — a species burdened with the killing burden of consciousness — survive?

Sigmund Freud, in *The Interpretation of Dreams* (1900), describes the business of dreaming, the *Traumwerk*, as if he were describing the composition of a nineteenth-century novel. Fiction, in other words, is daydreaming. And I think Freud's epochal insight can be expanded to argue that *all* fantasy activity is not just the raw stuff of story, but is story.

Four years after *The Interpretation of Dreams*, in *The Psychopathology of Everyday Life*— a kind of streamlined version of his earlier book — Freud writes of the unreliability of childhood memories. "Thus the 'childhood memories' of individuals come in general to acquire the significance of 'screen memories' [that is, *edited* memories], and in doing so offer a remarkable analogy with the childhood memories that a nation preserves in its store of legends and myths."[5]

Bridging the gap between the private and the cultural level of storytelling, in one of its early phases of transmutation, we find the doll. We are moving toward the exegesis of the Evil Decepticons and their colleagues. But, since I believe that literary commentary is like cross-country travel and courtship, in that half the fun is getting there, let me approach the world of my table-top aliens by an indirect route.

My wife, who is not a research assistant but in fact a collaborator on this essay, remembers Barbie. So do I, but deep and silly psychic mechanisms best described by Freud and best understood by Gloria Steinem and Vivian Sobchack force me, in my less liberated modes, to repress the memory.

Think about Barbie as an alien, a Philip K. Dick alien, to be sure: that is, something so like us as to be a tune beyond us, yet ourselves. Barbie is a charming, foxy teenager with a boyfriend, Ken, a best friend, Midge, a little sister, a black girlfriend, and the black girlfriend's black boyfriend, and, as the years have rolled on, an endlessly proliferating accumulation of sky clothes, surfing gear, evening gowns, and even cardboard chalets and beach houses. The Babylonians would have understood, and not found laughable, this headlong buildup of *things* to shore up the identity, the radiant "thereness" of the central and at-all-cost-to-be-venerated goddess. And so would Jay Gatsby, able to win the gaze of the golden girl in the high castle only by his vulgar, absurd, and holy accumulation of shirts. "I've never seen such — such beautiful shirts," exclaims Daisy, crying as he tosses them on his bed, showing her what he has done for her.[6] And the person who finds that great scene funny is disenfranchised from reading the novel. Remember that the pharaohs went into eternity with their favorite toys: what else would you take with you on such an awful journey?

How easy it is to attack Barbie as a fallacious role model for women or as a celebration of capitalism at its most poisonous. Both positions are simple-minded enough to have been held by people whose political sophistication is bounded by *Rolling Stone* on the right and *Marx for Beginners* on the left. How easy, and how very tedious.

How interesting it is, on the other hand, to realize that Barbie — poor, plastic, neglected, and now collecting dust in a continent-full of attics or basements — may have been as much a woman warrior in the emerging feminist cause as Maxine Hong Kingston. She was, for the decade of her birth, independent, self-reliant, and able to use, rather than be used by, her feminine identity. Queen of the prom? Certainly. But also efficient mistress of the capitalism system and nobody's fool. And that means something. Like chess or Dungeons and Dragons or the Transformers, the universe called "Barbie" is the algorithm of a war game; it is only that Barbie, Ken, and the rest of the crew are warriors in those social and sexual battles better described by John Updike and John Cheever than by Philip K. Dick and Philip José Farmer.

Nevertheless, remember that one of Philip K. Dick's stories, "The Days of Perky Pat" (1963), imagines a postnuclear, impoverished Earth, where the survivors gamble their meager provisions on fantasy games played with Barbie-style dolls, reenacting the comfortable, middle-class existence detonated irrevocably beyond their reach. It would be fine to read this story simply as a satire on the foolishness of the bourgeoisie, obsessed with the trivialities of middle-class life even on the brink of the abyss. But oversimplifying Dick is about as wise — maybe less so — as oversimplifying Franz Kafka or Jorge Luis Borges. "Perky Pat" may represent capitalism gone rancid. But she also represents the continued possibility of invention, of storytelling, of making something out of nothing, which is after all Dick's generative obsession as a writer.

Stanislaw Lem writes that "the peculiarities of Dick's worlds arise especially from the fact that in them it is waking reality which undergoes profound dissociation and duplication." Or, elsewhere: "The end-effect is always the same: distinguishing between waking reality and visions proves to be impossible."[7] Readers of Lem's stunning novel *Solaris* (1961) or of his collection *The Cyberiad* (1967) will of course recognize that in discussing Dick's purposeful confusion of reality with imitation, Lem is also discussing his own work. Lem reads Dick with his own interpretive swerve, as of course we all do. But I interpret Lem's interpretation of Dick to mean this: from his earliest stories to the genius of *The Man in the High Castle* (1962), to the mad sublimity of *Ubik* (1969) and *Valis* (1981) and *The Divine Invasion* (1981), Dick has been concerned with the relationship between simulacrum and reality, which is to say that a perfect imitation *of* a thing is that thing, be it an 1844 Colt revolver, a 1910 American advertising poster, or a human being. Who writes *The Man in the High Castle*? At one level, the *I Ching*, the most rigorous and most random, most tychistic of oracles. Causality is what we impose upon, or flatter into, our lives. And to say that is to say that Dick, more than Vladimir Nabokov and maybe even more than James Joyce, is brooded over, intimately and terribly, by the core shadow of Story itself. He is, in short, our indispensable theorist of dolls.

And now we have come, at last, to the Transformers, the GoBots, Power Lords, Masters of the Universe, and whatever else may come along over the next few years. They are all toys, or dolls, who are aliens at a double remove. For they are, prima facie, aliens because they are dolls. But they are also dolls of aliens, of honest-to-God extraterrestrials: projections of ourselves, or of our children's selves if we are shy, into figures of wonder and terror who are, nonetheless, demonstrably of our world and of our dreams. I have already used the metaphor of the alien as a fun-house mirror reflection of ourselves; but it is extraordinary to realize that all the aliens we invent or produce are, from H.G. Wells's Martians to Larry Niven's Puppeteers and the Sectaur Warriors, deflections and declensions of us, the tedious Carl Sagan notwithstanding.

Even Ggriptogg, the most brutal and pitiless of the bad Power Lords, even that four-armed monster has a copyright stamped under his left foot: just as Caliban in William Shakespeare's *The Tempest* becomes an efficient monster only after Prospero teaches him how to speak English.

It is always a battle between ultimate good and ultimate evil with these toys and with their accompanying mythologies. That, as far as I can see, differentiates them from maybe 10 percent of the world's stories. Let me take my favorite mytheme, that of the Transformers, to stand for the lot.

Eons ago, alien robots from the planet Cybertron crash-landed on Earth. Awakened from suspended animation after thousands of years of sleep, they are now engaged in a battle that will determine the fate of our planet. The evil Decepticons, led by the powerful Megatron — whose slogan is "Peace through Tyranny" — seek to return to Cybertron after draining all of the Earth's energy. They are resisted, thwarted in their dark quest by the Heroic Autobots, led by the wise Optimus Prime, whose somewhat question-begging motto (he is, after all, a robot) is "Freedom is the right of all sentient beings." They are called "Transformers" because, in order to deceive or in order not to alarm the unsuspecting earthlings, they can transform themselves from their warrior form into automobiles, airplanes, cassette decks, insects, dinosaurs, and dune buggies. As of the last catalog I bought, there were forty-three Heroic Autobots and twenty-nine Evil Decepticons on the market. By now, there may be more. Each box ranks its occupant in terms of strength, intelligence, speed, endurance, rank, courage, firepower, and skill on a scale of one to ten, proof that the mind-set of the Educational Testing Service at Princeton may be a universal principle and that the Homer who described the warriors before Troy could have been the E.T.S.'s first chairman of the board.

But I do not mean to make light of these toys. Quite the contrary. I find it rich and heartening that these highly technological toys are also toys *about* technology. They are alien invaders or alien friends who remind us — or our children, all of whom we hope will grow up to be Larry Nivens or Ursula K. Le Guins — that the truest and most immediately available aliens in our world are the machines with which we surround ourselves and out of which we build our culture. A Corvette Stingray or a transistor radio can, in the right circumstances, be a good guy, just as a laser pistol or a demolition truck can be a bad guy. The alternate universes of these toy worlds, played out on table tops or on that most magical of places, a child's counterpane at night with one, clandestine light on in the room, are alternate universes indeed and deserve to be treated as such.

We have heard, by now, so many versions of the pun between "alien" and "alienation" that one more cannot possibly hurt. Let us note, then, that "alienated labor" is Karl Marx's phrase for the separation of man from the fruits of his technology and that an "alienist," in the nineteenth century, would be called a psychoanalyst in ours. The toys of which I am speaking heal or help to thaw the ice, the schism between those two great imaginations of alienation, as do any storytelling tools, since all stories are about the aliens we carry in our heads and our hearts and since all stories are desperate, playful stabs at healing the wounds that make us human. And my toys help us, too, to understand the games we play later about aliens, with the more cumbersome counters of typewriters, word processors, and — save us — the mature human mind.

9

The Playing Fields of Eden

Our general subject is imaginary landscapes in science fiction and fantasy, and the way we have phrased things suggests that science fiction and fantasy are primordial human activities that somehow imply, or necessitate, the inventions of worlds elsewhere or elsewhen. I have written and taught for years that man is the storytelling animal, and that the act of tale-weaving is the first truly human activity.

I was, of course, wrong. Never fear, it is an old habit of mine. For recently thinking about this essay, watching the Chicago Bears blow their Super Bowl chances, losing at chess to my son, at dominoes to my wife, and worst of all at a high rate to my bookie (Lakers 106, Celtics 103), I came to realize that Mircea Eliade is subtly wrong in *Myth and Reality* (1963) and Johan Huizinga subtly right in *Homo Ludens* (1938). (I also submit to you that a man who, after dropping two hundred dollars on the Celtics, thinks about comparative anthropology, is at the very least deserving of your compassion.)

There is an older urge than the urge to tell stories. It is the urge to play, and to play with strict rules. I now believe that, even before they began telling anecdotes to one another, Og and Skag, the first fully enfranchised human beings, tried to match the number of stones one or the other held in his hand, or raced to the salt lick, or enacted some elaborate and forever lost combination of the two contests. And then they told anecdotes, because the game had given them the possibility of a landscape they could control, rather than vice versa, and had thereby given them the possibility of fiction.

I want, in other words, to reverse the perspective of these proceedings, and to suggest that imagined landscapes invent stories, rather than the other way around. In Stevens's great metaphor for metaphor:

> They said, "You have a blue guitar,
> You do not play things as they are."

9. The Playing Fields of Eden

> The man replied, "Things as they are
> Are changed upon the blue guitar."[1]

Never mind that this resonant wedding of rhythm and simplicity is obviously the strong precursor of that master fantasist, Dr. Seuss. I am more concerned with the fact that here, as everywhere in Stevens, the landscape comes *before* the story, just because it is an artificial landscape, the landscape of story or of dreams or of game. Why is the man with the blue guitar a shearsman of sorts? Because he cuts into patterns: because he partitions the world of experience as it is given to us — or attacks us — into a habitable place for the imagination. Things as they are, as we all know, are intolerable. So we invent games to organize the chaos, and if we have the spirit to take the games seriously enough, later in our psychic evolution we invent stories that carry the grace of the games into a more expansive sphere. From chessboard to basketball court to Dungeons and Dragons playsheet, the playing field is the primal scene, the Eden, in which grows the Tree of the Knowledge of Good and Evil.

George C. Scott, in *Patton*, always raises a smile when he snarls, "I wouldn't give a hoot in hell for a man who lost — and laughed!"[2] But that is actually very good theology. If you play a game with anything but absolute seriousness, you are not really playing the game. You are only watching, and the difference between watching and playing is like the difference between wanting and desiring. All sentient species do the first, but only a few are lucky and unfortunate enough to be capable of the latter. The game *must* be serious, just because it is cosmically trivial, triviality being, like Jean-Paul Sartre's "Nothingness," the gift consciousness alone brings into the world. "We are a bit of stellar matter gone wrong," writes Sir Arthur Eddington of you and me[3]; it is not that far from Lord Byron's description of you and me, a century earlier, as "faery dust,"[4] or Hamlet's description of you and me as "this quintessence of dust,"[5] or the observation of Lucretius, in *De Rerum Natura*, that human life is merely an epiphenomenon of a closed, uncaring universe.

We are a cosmic triviality, and we did not have to wait for radio telescopy to find out how tiny we really are. But, as far as we know, we are the only creatures who *have* heard the bad news. Blessed though they might be, presumably no dolphin has ever stared at the moon and felt longing.

But we have, and have realized that the dimensions of our world are not fitted to the dimensions of our hope. So we have, traditionally, done one of two things. We have invented a god who ultimately reconciles the world outside the head and the world inside the head, or we have invented playing boards or playing fields or rules of procedure that limit reality to bits we can deal with. Nick Adams's fishing trip in Ernest Hemingway's "Big Two-Hearted

River" (1925) and the Pauli Exclusion Principle are both attempts to say that, if the cosmos is radically unknowable, we may at least define the things we do know, and deal with them as if they were the all. One fishes with a sense of ethics: you do not drop a percussion grenade into the middle of the lake and wait for your dead victims to float to the surface. For to do so would be to violate the rules, and that is an unholy thing. The playing board is a shield against disorder whose vulnerability is its own best defense.

I am supposed to be talking about landscapes, and, remarkably enough, I am. For a landscape is not a world. It is a world as perceived, which is to say a prospect with rules of perception, which is to say a playing board.

I have grown prematurely metaphysical. Let me attempt to retreat from portentousness by asking you why you do *not* move your bishop vertically as opposed to diagonally, why you do *not* pass to an ineligible receiver, or why you do *not* cheat at cards. You do not because to do so would be to violate, not just the rules of the game, but the fragile, endangered structure of consciousness itself. Ludwig Wittgenstein, that unhappy and godlike man, dated the second phase of his philosophical career from the moment when he realized that language could most accurately be perceived as a game. And to cheat at the game, to lie, is to utter a deep and maybe irrevocable challenge to the authenticity of consciousness altogether. But what is a lie? "How can you charge me with heresy?" shouted a priest friend of mine to his cardinal a few years ago. "You don't even know what orthodoxy is, you toad!"

A lie is a violation of the conventions of speech, or truth, of the rules of the game as they have been promulgated. And nothing else. It is easy, and therein lies its terror. You cannot lie until you have a convention about "the truth": you cannot cheat until you know the rules to violate. "Civilization," said another friend of mine to me, "is an agreement to leave the abyss alone." But then civilization is the invention of the abyss it chooses, regally, to ignore. The first act of the Holy One in Genesis is to divide the light from the darkness: a shearsman of sorts. Some busy years later, Alexander Pope would re-create the creation in "The Rape of the Lock," in terms of a card game: "The skillful nymph reviews her force with care: '*Let spades be trumps!*' she said, and trumps they were."[6]

Tom Robbins, in *Even Cowgirls Get the Blues* (1976), observes quite correctly that earthquakes only happen in cities. That is, if one continental plate decides to get on closer terms with another, rabbits, deer, and nomads will notice the ensuing perturbation as no more "unnatural" or "extraordinary" than a thunderstorm or a snowfall. But we have built cities, and cities are as vulnerable to fault lines as language is to lies or games to rule violations. We know that Jericho is the earliest city of the Neolithic Revolution; and we know, from the song we all sang as children, that its walls came tumbling down. Joshua, in other words, not only fought the battle of Jericho, he also, in a world-historical sense, invented the Richter scale.

King Lear knew this, too. That most inexhaustible of plays may be read as, among much else, a parable about human as opposed to inhuman space and a paradigm of the landscapes of fantasy.

In *The Poetics of Space*, Gaston Bachelard makes the crucial observation that "space" has two meanings. Our first association, when we are being self-consciously intellectual — always a bad move, by the way — our first association is usually with the Cartesian abstraction of emptiness incarnate or with the infinite and cold vistas of John Milton's *Paradise Lost* (1667), Goethe's *Faust* (1808, 1832), and *Star Wars* (1977). But, says Bachelard, there is another kind of space, and one much closer to us. Call it human space: the warm encirclement of mother's arms, of your blanket on a frosty morning, of the living room at night after the children are in bed, of your lover's arms. It is the space of the cave, and perhaps we do not write about it as much as we do about the space of the galaxies because it is so much more dear to us. Sacred things are not to be lightly spoken of.[7]

Bachelard, at least, has the great good sense to admit the importance of this perception. Among his phenomenological, deconstructionist, or otherwise distracted countrymen, he is the prose poet of the cozy, and of the home truth — and that is high praise — rather as if Beatrix Potter had married G.W.F. Hegel and begotten a critic.

Think about Lear in the storm. He has already learned about the difference between inside and outside, inside his clothes, inside the castle walls, inside the security of his kingship, and outside, terribly outside, all these things. And now it is raining on him. And he does not even care about coming in from the rain, for, as he says to Kent, "This tempest in my mind/Doth from my senses take all feeling else,/Save what beats there."[8]

George Orwell says that when Lear is in his right mind he hardly ever says anything sensible. Leaving aside the question whether Lear ever *is* in his right mind, here at least he is at the height of his rage, and therefore also at his wisest. Inside is civilized space, the space of the playing board of the story, the space we have humanized. Outside is the abyss. And *King Lear*, more unrelentingly than any fantasy I know, reminds us again and again that once you cross that boundary, you may never —*ever*— return. The tempest in the mind is the breaking of the rules of the game, the admission of the barbarians within the gates. It is the end of the civilization that invents, and then defends itself against, the void.

This is why, of Cuchulain, it is recorded that "the poets were encouraged to record his points of excellence, as follows: excellence of body, shape, and build. His grades in the following skills were also excellent: swimming, horsemanship, checkers, chess, and competitions of various sorts. In combat he was, as we have seen, unmatched in all Ireland."[9]

It should strike us as curious that a mighty warrior is praised for, among other things, his prowess at checkers and chess. Not even Howard Cosell, one imagines, would ask Sugar Ray Leonard about his bridge game. Indeed, it should strike us as Homeric. William Empson, in *Some Versions of Pastoral* (1935), remarks upon the scene in Homer's *Iliad* where Ajax cooks his own dinner. Only in the primal perception of the epic or pastoral world, says Empson, could we see the connection between martial heroism and the most elementary of human technologies; because only that perception shows us how intimately related are primitive *and* sophisticated technologies. Think about the famous shock cut from tossed bone to orbiting nuclear warhead in *2001: A Space Odyssey* (1968); the landscape defined by both tools is human, antinatural, and therefore essentially the same.

Or think about my own favorite example of "heroic" ethics, from *Beowulf*. There the bard tells us that when Beowulf became king he was a mighty warrior, a fair dispenser of treasure to his people, and when "Drunk, he slew no hearth-companions."[10]

It is a funny line, and a profound one. The rules of the game are revealed in all their simplicity and all their resonance. "You will *not* kill," says the Mosaic Decalogue. "Even when you're drunk, *don't* kill your friends," says *Beowulf*. Perhaps we could interpret most serious fiction as subtly encoded rules of conduct, as models for social and psychic games we might like to play.

Let me quote from a brilliant novel published in 1986, John Hough's *The Conduct of the Game*. It is about baseball umpires, about storytelling, and about theology. In one scene a young man, Roy Van Arsdale, is asked to serve as umpire in an informal softball game between the teams of lawyers — a harmless, even a trivial event. Roy calls a batter out on strikes, the batter swears at him, Roy ejects him from the game, and the lawyers tell Roy he is dismissed as their umpire.

Then comes a moment worth waiting to have been written. "*Wait just a goddamn minute!*" shouts Roy:

"If you want me to leave.... I'll leave. I'll go. But if you do this — if you dismiss me in the middle of a game — you make the game meaningless, do you understand? Whoever wins, it'll mean nothing. Your man here took a good pitch and struck out. He swore at the umpire; he's out of the game. That's baseball. *Those* are the rules. Do you want to play the game right, or do you want to play a made-up game that'll suit your tantrums and your mistakes?"

"That's baseball. Those are the rules." In this extraordinary book, that is an extraordinary passage. The lawyers, overcome by logic (this is, after all, a work of fiction), ask Roy if he will at least leave Clark, the erring player, in the game. "No," replies Roy. "I cannot *leave* Clark in the game, because Clark is no longer *in* the game. What did I just finish saying?"[11]

There is a direct line, I suggest, from this passage back to "*Let spades be trumps!* she said, and trumps they were" and back to Lear's discovery that the tempest in the mind overwhelms the tempest outside the mind, and finally back to the only fiction I know that has the courage, or the audacity, to begin "In the beginning." You will notice that I have presumed upon your attention without really, so far, addressing the topic. I will be brief, and do not remind me that Polonius said the same thing. The imagination of landscape produces the possibility of fiction, and the activity of the game produces the imagination of landscape. Storytelling, no less than checkers or chess or football, is a kind of game, and the opponents are the storyteller and the listener.

But are we not already guilty of an insulting limitation in calling storytelling a game? Isn't it also a science, an art, hovering between these two categories as Muhammad's coffin hovered between heaven and earth? Isn't it a unique bond between every pair of opponents, ancient and yet eternally new; mechanical in its framework and yet only functioning through use of the imagination; confined in geometrically fixed space and at the same time released from confinement by its permutations; continuously evolving yet sterile; thought that leads nowhere, mathematics that add up to nothing, art without an end product, architecture without substance, and nevertheless demonstrably more durable in its true nature and existence than any books or creative works? Isn't it the only game that belongs to all peoples and all times? And who knows whether God put it on earth to kill boredom, to sharpen the wits, or to lift the spirits? Where is its beginning and where its end?

That is the best definition of storytelling I have ever written, and I did not write it first. From "But are we not already guilty" to "Where is its beginning and where its end" the passage is a direct quotation from Stefan Zweig's great story, "The Royal Game." I only cheated once in my hygienic plagiarism, and that was in using the word *storytelling*. For Zweig is not writing about storytelling. He is writing about chess.[12]

There is a Zen of archery, and of the tea service. If there were a Zen of criticism, and if I were one of its masters, I would propose this *koan* to my apprentices: you may wager your life against the matador or a chess grand master. Choose.

(Since there is no Zen of criticism, and since this essay is *my* game, there is an answer, a right answer, to the *koan*. But you have to wait for it. Isn't Deep Thought *fun?*)

Not really, I say answering my preceding parenthetical paragraph. The game is not fun, and is not meant to be. Or, rather, the game as game redefines what fun is and what it can be. The chess grand master and the matador both know that the game is deadly serious.

So do the theologian and the storyteller. "I am convinced," writes Karl Rahner in *The Practice of Faith*, "that a human being's historical life moves in freedom toward a point of decision, that it contains this decision in itself, that life as a whole must be answered for and does not simply run away into a void in these details. Of course, this outlook on which my life is based, which is almost inescapable and yet required of me, is nothing but breathtaking optimism, so terrifying that everything trembles with the sheer audacity of it."[13]

Game, narrative, and theology are a kind of spectrum of human attempts to impose *direction*, or *sense*, on the random series of absolutely unrepeatable moments that are experience. "Personality," writes F. Scott Fitzgerald in *Gatsby*, "is an unbroken series of successful gestures."[14] But this series can only have sense in retrospect, from the point of view of the goal that has been arrived at: that is what turns the random series into the unbroken series. If you had not spilled punch on her dress at the senior prom, would you be happily married to her today? As a detective writer of distinctly limited talent, I can tell you that beginning a novel without knowing how it will end is very bad for the blood pressure. Millennia before television, Homer invented the instant replay when Odysseus recounts his misadventures in the *Odyssey*— because, in being recounted, they are transformed into adventures. Pouring over maps of the campaigns he fought in, Ernest Hemingway's veteran in "Soldier's Home" thinks, "Now he was really learning about the war. He had been a good soldier. That made a difference."[15]

What distinguishes game from storytelling from theology is, probably, the degree of the involvement in the randomness of the playing field itself. It is a game if the field — the landscape — predominates over the control of the field. It is theology if the knowledge of the field renders the reality of the field all but irrelevant. *Prakriti* and *purusha*, the field and the knower of the field, are the central concepts of the branch of Hinduism called Samkhya. Between these extremes lies the area in which the random and the planned share an uncomfortable, if exciting bed, in which "what could be" flirts with "what had to happen." It is the field I call storytelling.

The four suits in a deck of cards represent the sociological landscape of a classic Neolithic culture (like the one we live in): priestly nobility, knights, merchants, and day laborers. Brahmins, Kshatryas, Vaisyas, and Sudras, if you are an Indologist. The Mayans played a form of basketball, pok-a-tok, in which the players attempted to bounce a rubber ball with their hips through a ring fixed vertically, not horizontally to the ground. We may guess that high scoring in pok-a-tok meant something different than it does in the NBA; but we know that court astrologers followed the movement of the ball carefully in order to forecast the fate of the empire. And the Aztecs regularly conducted "Wars of the Flowers," stylized mock combats among their captured slaves, the losers in which game would have their hearts ceremonially carved out on one of the following mornings so that the sun could rise.

You wonder where I am tending. I will tell you where I am tending. Games want to be stories, and theology wants to explain stories, and stories, the poor dears — if they are good stories — just want to be told.

My mathematician friends who also design computer game programs are fond of distinguishing between "games of partial information" and "games of perfect information." Most games fall into the first batch, but that does not diminish the importance of the games of perfect information.

Look at your chessboard and think about the opening sentence of Jane Austen's *Pride and Prejudice* (1813). Fan out your poker hand (three-card draw, nothing wild) and think about the opening sentence of Kafka's "The Metamorphosis" (1915). Now you know the difference between games of perfect information and games of partial information. When I open P-K4, nothing — absolutely nothing — that I can do is unavailable to you, and if I lose to you it is because I lost, because the game has, in George Steiner's accurate and chilling phrase, tracked the ego to its final lair. If, on the other hand, I meet the opening bet in a jacks-or-better-to-open poker game, you have no idea whether I am fueled by self-assurance or by hope. Never draw to an inside straight, the grown-ups tell you; just you try not to draw to an inside straight, says your life. If I lose, I can blame the cards, the luck of the draw, the air conditioning, or the bourbon. The poker table strokes losers; we are only human. The chessboard damn them; we are *only* human.

Baseball is like chess and like fantasy. Football is like poker and like science fiction. The diamond is a perfect square poised on one of the corners. The time of the game is the time defined by the game — three strikes to get out, three outs per side per inning, three times three innings per game with each half inning posing one enemy against three times three opponents. The point of the game, as its central metaphysician Bill Veeck once said, is disarmingly simple — to find out if a running man can travel faster than a thrown or hit ball. Not David Lindsay's *A Voyage to Arcturus* (1920), not J.R.R. Tolkien's *The Lord of the Rings* (1955–1956), not Stephen R. Donaldson's

Chronicles of Thomas Covenant the Unbeliever — not Shakespeare's *The Tempest* give us a more overwhelming sense of an other, a clarified world. A baseball game can be annotated as surely as a chess game, can be transfigured into the pure abstraction of statistics — as Robert Coover understood in his stunning novel, *The Universal Baseball Association, Inc., J. Henry Waugh, Prop.* (1968).

The space of baseball is fantasy space, pastoral space — Tolkien's Middle-earth, Donaldson's The Land, C.S. Lewis's Narnia. Football is played, not on a diamond, but on a gridiron. It does not measure the speed of a running man against the speed of a thrown ball, it measures the momentum of a running man against the momentum of other men running against him. "Dancing as a contact sport," snarled — I think — Frank Leahy of Notre Dame. "Football is a collision sport." The space of football is not the space that contains, but the space that is *contained*, the Cartesian vista from which we cannot escape. Like science fiction, football is a matter of cold equations, of space to be traversed rather than filled. In baseball you can commit an error; in football you fumble.

But I pity anyone who cannot, like me, lose at chess as much as at poker; or who cannot be as awed by Reggie Jackson as by Walter Payton; or who cannot read Stephen King *and* Poul Anderson. I pity psychic amputees, in other words. The playing fields of Eden are the landscapes that make storytelling possible. And they are either the peaceful pastoral of *A Midsummer Night's Dream* or the blasted heath of *King Lear*. And they are the same place, just as nirvana, the state of rest, and samsara, the state of frantic to-and-fro, are the same state in classic Buddhism — the same state, but perceived differently.

And I told you there was an answer to my critical *koan*. Would you rather battle for your life against a chess grand master or a matador? Once you have accepted the question, once you have begun to read and write for the only sane reasons that should impel anyone to read or write, you have entered the game and you are lost and won. You are wagering against grand master and matador at once — they are both inside you — and you have no choice of opponents. Your only choice is the choice of the terms upon which you will win. It is distressing, it is inconvenient, and it is ineluctable. It is called consciousness.

10

It's Only a Paper Moon
Fantasy and the Professors

Let's start with four animals:

In *The Wind in the Willows* (1908), four animals hold our particular interest: the Mole, a sensitive, gentle beast who initiates the action of the whole book by venturing forth from his underground home one fine day to explore the big world above; the Water Rat (familiarly, "Ratty"), a knowledgeable and kindly river-farer who befriends Mole and guides him through the mazes of life in the open; Mr. Toad, a hopeless victim of his enthusiasms for machinery whose adventures inevitably collapse into escapades; and Badger, wisest and most inaccessible of the denizens of the wood, who seems to know the answer to everything and gives the answer to nothing.

This quaternity seems perfectly suited to the structure of the fairy tales most widely known and most widely loved among children, the fantasy novels most widely marketed among adults, and the spiritual algorithms most widely employed by psychoanalysts — who may, depending on your point of view, represent the melding of childhood with adulthood or the terminal sclerosis of both. At any rate, C.G. Jung, even if he did not read *The Wind in the Willows*, gave names to the members of the quaternity, which are also the names of the "consolidated personality" in the Jungian myth of the self. The Animus — the male, questing, discovery-borne part of the self — is, of course, Mole, the initiand. The Anima — the kind, caring, and forgiving part — is the wonderful Ratty, the initiator. The Shadow — that part of yourself which is you-at-your-worst, silliest, or most excessive — could be none other than Mr. Toad. And the Syzygy, the very principle of consolidation, the part of the soul that says "I" and means by that most curious of words *all* the aspects of the self in tension and unity, is incarnated in the mysterious, ineluctable Badger. Nor is Jung alone the elected exegete of fairy tales in this fashion. Mircea Eliade, Vladimir Propp, Joseph Campbell, and Stephen Larsen in his vastly underrecognized book *The Shaman's Doorway* (1976), along with a host of others, all recognize that the elementary nature of fairy tales/fantasy/creative daydreaming is the repetitive, infinitely recursive, and never boring iteration of the fact of Individual Being. *De nobis fibula.*

I begin with this relatively unremarkable bit of exegesis because it sets the tone for my differentiation of fantasy from science fiction — at least in terms of their reception and treatment by academics and so-called "mainstream" critics. George Slusser in "Who's Afraid of Science Fiction?" shows eloquently and tellingly why and how science fiction, after all these years, is still ghettoized in that intellectual demi-monde also inhabited by Western novels, vintage radio shows of the forties, and the music of Carl Orff.[1] It will be my task to examine why fantasy, as a genre, is *not* thus treated; and why the treatment it does receive may be, in the long run, just as deleterious to a real understanding of the form.

And I use the word "task" deliberately. Let me complicate the job, at the outset, by saying that I do not believe there *is* a difference between science fiction and fantasy; not really. "Real" is, to be sure, as Vladimir Nabokov says, the one word in English that can only be used between inverted commas. Nevertheless, there we are: I believe that the massively sought and overtalked "difference" between science fiction and fantasy is about as helpful as Jacques Derrida's idea of "*difference,*" which is to say precisely as substantial as Lewis Carroll's Snark. It is simply a product of critical-mainstream prejudice and misconception. The girl you are going to take home to meet the folks may be charming beyond hope. But depending on whether her name is "Celeste" or "Sadie," they are going to expect rather different things. If it is Celeste, buy some sherry, but if it is Sadie, hide the gin. This is unjust, certainly, but nobody ever said that semantics was a pretty game.

Mind you, you are not about to find David Lindsay's *A Voyage to Arcturus* (1920) or Stephen R. Donaldson's The Chronicles of Thomas Covenant the Unbeliever on a required reading list for the English Major; there are ghettos and there are ghettos. But what we choose to call "fantasy" has, at least, moved a little farther uptown than has what we choose to call "science fiction." Why? Ask the marketing department.

When Ursula K. Le Guin was merely a splendid writer of science fiction, she was reviewed in *Analog* and *Galaxy*. But then came the Earthsea Trilogy, and she was suddenly transfigured into a brilliant fantasy writer. Now she's reviewed in the Sunday *New York Times*— and Camelot at last?— the *TLS*. In a ships-in-the-night crossover, Doris Lessing used to write "serious" fiction, and has lately been writing what *she* calls "science fiction." But, since we know that she is a "serious" writer, *we* know that it is really "fantasy," and so she continues to be reviewed by the Olympian journals of the publishing world. Roger Zelazny's Amber novels are, by any humanly knowable criteria, fantasy. But since we know that Zelazny is a science fiction writer, that is where he is shelved. And, though I do not have the computer print-outs, assume that the act of shelving means that Zelazny significantly undersells Marion Zimmer Bradley or Anne McCaffrey or Jean M. Auel's *Clan of the Cave Bear* series. As Harlan Ellison is bitterly fond of saying, literary success depends largely on where your book is placed on the display counter in the drugstore, and *that* has a good deal to do with your resolution to continue writing: your shelf-respect, as one might say.

Let me interject a personal anecdote that has nothing to do with fantasy and science fiction, and everything to do with the kind of marketing/academic snobbism I am discussing. I write, or try to write, mystery novels. And when I mentioned this activity to a colleague of mine in the English Department at Northwestern, his immediately, arched-eyebrow response was, "Oh. Interesting. Do you plan to publish them under your own name?" That the same man could write a book on Saul Bellow, edit a collection of essays on Biblical exegesis, and do a hard-boiled mystery novel was, apparently, beyond my colleague's grasp. But I want to argue that Sadie *could* be Celeste, and Celeste, Sadie. I want to make the world — at least the world of Fantasy Studies — safe for antinomianism.

I am not trying to make easy, ivory-tower fun of the economics of the literary business. Quite the contrary. Northrop Frye once wrote that money is the best reason anybody ever had for writing, and we know that William Shakespeare was not only good at his craft but a terrific accountant as well, and that Homer and the bard of *Beowulf* sang for free drinks. The point I am trying to bring round is that marketing in the bookstore and criticism in the academy or the mainstream journals are really the same thing. Ever since Aristotle, a logician on holiday, wrote the *Poetics*, the central task of criticism (whether in *PMLA* or *Newsweek*) has been to: (a) classify works according to genre and (b) evaluate works according to how well they fulfill the requirements and expectations of those genres. To be sure, this activity has caused any amount of silliness, from Polonius to the Chicago School of criticism. Aristotle would, most likely, be as appalled by his disciples John Dryden and Pierre Corneille as would Moses by the greatest of rabbis and strongest of his interpreters, Akiba and the Baal Shem Tob. But this activity of classifying and judging according to classification is, God help us, what we do. Aristotle, in other words, not only founds the enterprise of literary criticism — a profession still looking for its legitimization — but also founds the profession of bookselling. Walk through your local bookstore, and notice that Norman Mailer's *The Executioner's Song* (1979), which won the Pulitzer Prize for fiction, is sometimes placed in the "Biography" rack; or that Philip K. Dick's *Valis* (1981) may be either in the "Science Fiction" or the "Fantasy" rack; or that Laurence Sanders's *The Seduction of Peter S.* (1983) may be shelved in "Mystery" or in that most serious, hence daunting, of sections, "Fictions" (look out! Jane Austen and Henry James lurk there, too). Aristotle, in other words, could have opened and successfully managed the first B. Dalton's franchise in Athens.

The central assumption of advertising, as any advertising executive will tell you, is that people will like what they are *told* to like. This applies to soap, music, clothing, and literature pretty equally, and Frederik Pohl and C.M. Kornbluth articulated it in *The Space Merchants* (1953) almost before such concepts as "sample market," "target population," and "cognitive dissonance" were invented by the people who use those concepts to sell us things. Jerry Della Femina, the Leonardo of sixties advertising, coined the immortal slogan: "I can sell you anything — once." And he was right. Think about the godfather term for all the books we are discussing: the term, "novel."

Literary historians like Q.D. Leavis, Arnold Kettle, and Ian Watt have long ago told us that the "rise of the novel" is actually a marketing phenomenon tied in with the rise of a literate middle class. George Lukacs (and before him, Max Weber) argued much the same thing and even more persuasively. John Bunyan and Daniel Defoe did not know that they were writing "novels." Samuel Richardson had only an inchoate idea of what he was doing (*Pamela* [1740], he thought, would be a useful — and saleable — manual for young girls interested in the arts of letter-writing and moral choice); but Henry Fielding, Laurence Sterne, and Tobias Smollett, with increasing canniness, realized that they were trafficking in a truly "novel" and highly profitable commodity. One proof of the value of a currency is its tendency toward debasement (i.e., there are probably more counterfeit dollars than there are counterfeit *lire*). Likewise, a strong proof of the economic viability of a literary form is its likeliness to attract second- or third-rate practitioners: its hack quotient. And in that category, no form of the last two hundred years can compete with prose fiction. (No, not even the film, because it is much more expensive to produce a truly bad movie than a truly bad novel; Gresham's Law being one of the corollaries of Aristotle's *Poetics*.) Thus, books that a decade or so ago would have been sold as "science fiction" are now sold as "Fantasy," for the simple, simpleminded, and simply overwhelming reason that fantasy *outsells* science fiction.

Anne McCaffrey's Dragonriders of Pern series is wonderfully written, sometimes brilliant, fantasy: or is it? Among its salient details are telepathy (between humans and dragons), killing spoors or "threads" from outer space, and, above all, the crucial fact that Pern is not an enchanted place or a land of faerie, but a *planet*, a planet located, presumably, in the same space-time continuum as Earth, Mars, or Larry Niven's Ringworld. Or, is not Ringworld — or Philip José Farmer's Riverworld or Frank Herbert's Dune — far the more "fantastic" place? Telepathic dragons, well, maybe: but a pie plate the size of the solar system? infinite death and rebirth? mystical, godseeing sandworms? One thinks not.

The point is that Pern has most of the characteristics of what we normally call science fiction, and yet it is "fantasy." Why? For the same reason that a football in England is a soccer-ball in America, or a basketball in Indianapolis is a round ball in Boston.

By now I have, I hope, reduced the serious discussion of generic norms to a sufficiently crass level of who is selling what to whom, how much of it, and how come? Because from there we can proceed, one hopes without deconstructionist obfuscation, to seeing what fantasy studies are really like today, and how they got that way.

Let me return to the example from *The Wind in the Willows* with which I began. Analogizing Kenneth Grahame to C.G. Jung is not hard to do, and would hardly raise an eyebrow among most of my university colleagues. Jung, after all, is to be taken *very* seriously. And Kenneth Grahame, though not perhaps *really* serious, nevertheless was British and did write a kind of elegant, post–Edwardian prose: A.A. Milne with more vinegar, if you please. He is, as we would say in the academy, legitimately interesting; or, as they would say on Broadway, legit. It comes down to the same thing, canon-formation. Lately, the idea of canon-formation has played a major role in literary theory, mainly in analogy to the history of canon-formation in sacred scripture. But an important difference has not been sufficiently remarked, and which does not redound to the credit or credulity of the academic establishment. In the formation of the canon of the Hebrew Bible and the Christian Scriptures, the central point of debate seems to have been, what can be let in? In the formation of the academic, secular canon, however, the operative question seems to be, what can we throw out? Or, put most crudely, what do we not have to read? It is a curious literary culture we have created for ourselves, where we congratulate ourselves on what we do not like more strenuously than we prize what we appreciate.

The same Jungian quaternity I identified in Kenneth Grahame is also to be found in the work of E.E. "Doc" Smith, Isaac Asimov, and even — letting *everybody* into the party — the adventures of Flash Gordon. But to find these analogies in these latter works would be to raise eyebrows, to seem either to be overrationalizing mere trifles (i.e., rhapsodizing over the preparation of a Big Mac) or tainting the majesty of a sublime system of thought (e.g., taking John Gielgud to a working-class bar in Pittsburgh).

The simple fact is that fantasy is more popular than science fiction because a larger and larger number of the reading public is university-trained, and because American academics, spiritually Anglophiliac and intellectually Gallo-idolatrous, think that "fantasy" means "Tolkien — or something like it."

There: I said it and I am glad. In the canon — the "safe" canon of books you can read for fun and still not be embarrassed about — who is more distinguishedly *déclassé* than J.R.R. Tolkien? Learned, genteel, gentle, and highly articulate, Tolkien and *The Lord of the Rings* (1955–1956) brood, somehow, behind any discussion of the contemporary reception of fantasy — as does C.S. Lewis's Space Trilogy, much of which is written as a charmingly, if second-rank, vitriolic parody of the science fiction of that wretched working-class materialist, H.G. Wells.

Fantasy, in other words, is safe — or perceived as such. A fantasy writer, as opposed to a science fiction writer, is literate, cultured, and aware of the parameters of his art, and very probably Anglo-Catholic to boot. And is this not the code of a literary Boy Scout? And is not Alfred Bester's Gully Foyle (a Gulliver, a gullible foil), in *The Stars My Destination* (1956), engaged on a rather more serious quest for identity?

I am not trying to depreciate *The Lord of the Rings*: it is a great book. I am, however, trying to depreciate the terms in which it has been mainly celebrated. I do not believe that the Hobbits, Elves, Dwarfs, and Men of Tolkien inhabit a universe less severe than David Lindsay's or less charged with irony than that in Peter Beagle's *The Last Unicorn* (1968) or less wittily self-conscious than the one in William Goldman's *The Princess Bride* (1973). But I do think they tend to be presented, and defended, in exactly those negative virtues.

Tolkien himself, in his indispensable essay "On Fairy Stories," does not really help matters, just because he writes so plangently. Fairy stories, he says, are "tales in which the fairies are not themselves illusions; behind the fantasy real wills and powers exist, independent of the minds and purposes of men." Later, reminiscing about his boyhood encounter with fantasy tales, he writes "I desired dragons with a profound desire." And finally, in the epilogue to the essay, he suggests — diffidently, yet still embarrassingly — that fairy stories or fantasy may be so important because they are our closest sublunary approach to the myth of the incarnation. "All tales may come true," he writes. "And yet, at the last, redeemed, they may be as like as yet as unlike the forms that we give them as Man, finally redeemed, will be like and unlike the fallen that we know."[2]

It is the kind of essay that sends deconstructionists running for their Todorov, if not their Maalox. It is also the kind of essay of which a non- or anti-deconstructionist will say, "How graceful! and, for all its possible encumbrance of piety, how very just and reasonable!"

It should be fairly obvious by now which group of respondents my sympathies are with. The "structuralist" approach to fantasy has, as far as I can tell, simply stretched an important and perennial narrative form upon the rack of half-understood and badly applied linguistic theory. Ferdinand de Saussure is not accountable for the sins committed in his name. But that does not erase the fact that the sins have been committed. Henri Lefebvre, one of the most outspoken critics of the reigning Gallic (now Gallo-American) approach, points out in *Le Langage et la Société* (1966) that there are two basic types of "structuralist" criticism. One takes the rigor and method of Saussurean (or Chomskyan) criticism so seriously as to be virtually incapable of applying it to literary or anthropological texts, while the other is so anxious to say new and dazzling things about the text that it transforms the rhythm and rigor of scientific linguistics into a mere metaphor, a "speculative instrument," as I.A. Richards used to say, whose main function is to allow the critic to shine, even to outshine the text, even to *shine on* the text (in the language spoken by Californians, to "shine on" someone means to tell him or her to "buzz off").

Nevertheless, my affection for Tolkien and my incurable prejudice against structuralism do not absolve Tolkien from a certain share of blame for the misdirection of fantasy studies. He does, through the exquisite grace of his style and imagination, what the ponderous academic technologues do through the elephantine complexity of their systems: he makes fantasy seem acceptable, and that is a drastic mistake. For as soon as a form — literary or biological — becomes acceptable or comfortable, it ceases to have interest for those of us (critics, writers, or God) who *like* to watch change, uncertainty, imbalance, and risk: a.k.a. "life."

Tolkien has that good grace — which his friend C.S. Lewis does not — to acknowledge that H.G. Wells might, despite doctrinal differences, be a pretty good writer. He is especially taken with Wells's invention, in *The Time Machine* (1895), of the complementary and adversary races of the Eloi and the Morlocks. I want to take Tolkien's grudging admiration a little further, and suggest that, at least for the critical mainstream, the gentle, vulnerable Eloi are something like the mainstream's idea of fantasy, while the bestial Morlocks, machine-tenders who feed upon the sweet Eloi, are something like the mainstream's idea of science fiction. And with whom would *you* rather have a picnic?

Notice how many prominent fantasy writers, as opposed to science fiction writers, are women. I have mentioned a few, but only a few. And, the last time I looked, Jean Auel's *The Mammoth Hunters* (1985) was on the best-seller list along with eight *Garfield* volumes. Now *that* is what I call fame. It's only a paper moon, this fantasy. It's only an Eloi art. But it sells: Lordy, it sells.

Or *is* it only an Eloi art? Let us face the fact that sexism is implicit in the field we are examining, and that it is quite as stupid and quite as inescapable in this field as in any other. More women do write fantasy than science fiction, and more women probably read fantasy. Not by accident was Judith Merril a contributor to *The Magazine of Fantasy and Science Fiction* while John W. Campbell, Jr. was editing *Analog*. Nor is it an accident that Alice Sheldon, one of the best science fiction writers of the seventies and eighties, published her work until recently under the elaborate pseudonym "James Tiptree, Jr." One is reminded of those nervous ladies, Charlotte, Anne, and Emily Bronte, publishing their novels under the diffident masks of Currer, Acton, and Ellis Bell; or of the greatest ghost in English literature, the "George Eliot" who took all the fame and all the royalties for the novels written by Mary Ann Evans.

"Science" is a male province, "fantasy" a female one. That is a very crude formulation of a very vulgar and quite universally accepted assumption. Since we are all speakers of Indo-European, we have only three tenses for our verbs: past, present and future (the Navajos, Aztecs, and Trobriand Islanders had others but they were not much more interesting). And the present tense is both tantalizingly unapproachable and boring. It is the tense of jokes ("This guy walks into a bar, see...") and of the novels of Saul Bellow. The past tense is the tense of fantasy: "A long time ago, in a galaxy far, far away," begins the most popular fantasy ever filmed. But the past tense is also the tense of bedtime stories and tales around the fire: a comforting, motherly space in time. Science fiction occupies the future tense, the tense of unease and anxiety. Tolkien, in his great essay "*Beowulf*: The Monsters and the Critics," identifies the peculiar tang of fantasy with the sense of irrecoverable vistas of *time* underlying the action as it is played out. In this sense, *Macbeth* and The Chronicles of Thomas Covenant the Unbeliever are both fantasy tales, in that they are concerned with the intersection, or collision, of ordinary with "magic" time. The word "time" occurs, I think, more often in *Macbeth* than in any of Shakespeare's other plays; and of course *Macbeth* is the shortest and most precipitate of his plays. In the same — or the reverse-image, which is to say the same — fashion, Stephen R. Donaldson's Covenant series plays with the fact that Thomas Covenant, failed writer and leper in the "real" world, is a divinely ordained hero in "The Land," which he only enters in his dreams. But — and this is Donaldson's special brilliance — Covenant *knows* that he is dreaming, and cannot decide whether the "Land" or the "real world" is the right one. As with *Macbeth*, we are here faced with a character who knows himself to be in *Faerie*, the land of unlikeness, of timeslips, and yet cannot find his way out.

And does this make fantasy a "woman's art"? Well, perhaps it does, if you want to accept the established differentiation between male and female personalities. What is marketed as fantasy tends to be more sensitive, lyrical and generally smarmy than what is marketed as science fiction. No one would shelve *Dragonsong* (1976) and *The Ringworld Engineers* (1980) in the same bin; though perhaps one should.

Thomas Hanzo, in a remarkable essay on science fiction, describes the whole craft as an extended version of the ancient rhetorical figure of *prolepsis*, i.e., describing future events as if they had already happened.[3] If you bet on horse number six in the second race at Santa Anita, and I tell you "You've just lost two dollars," then I am practicing prolepsis; I have also written a brief science fiction story. Perhaps the difference between fantasy and science fiction — which, we know, does not really exist in the first place — is in its time sense. Fantasy is set in the irrecoverable past (hence dragons, dungeons, swords, and sorcery) while science fiction is set in the unattainable future (hence ray guns, rocket ships, anomalies, and aliens).

This may be a distinction, though I do not for a minute believe it valid. I do not believe it valid any more than I believe that women are "naturally" afraid of science or that men are "naturally" averse to fantasizing. The real distinction between science fiction and fantasy is *what will be accepted by the marketplace*: and *what will be accepted by the marketplace* determines *who will enter the marketplace*. The conventional, unspoken assumption of literary criticism is here literally inverted: the best of the genre does not rise to the top because it is chosen by the informed masses, but rather the "best" of the genre is determined by what can be imposed upon those sheep, the masses, who *think* they are informed.

The extraordinary Stanislaw Lem, in *Microworlds* (1984), heroically refuses to differentiate between science fiction and fantasy. So does his strong precursor (whom he surpasses), Jorge Luis Borges. Horsemen in the sky or ICBMs penetrating the atmosphere, it is all the same. Lem has high good fun with Tzvetan Todorov's influential study, *The Fantastic* (1973), which he — writer *and* critic — finds an uninformative exercise in overclassification based upon an insufficiently rich number of primary texts. And Lem also argues that studies like Todorov's eviscerate fantasy precisely by making it respectable.

Fantasy heroes from Aladdin to David Copperfield to Jay Gatsby have found out that respectability is not always the best thing that can happen to you. Harold Bloom, a great critic and the author of a fine fantasy novel, *The Flight to Lucifer* (1979), describes fantasy in Freudian terms: i.e., an overplus of the pleasure principle that, through sheer accumulated weight, collapses back into the reality principle from which it was striving to escape. "Why was all this necessary?" asks a character surveying the carnage at the end of *A Voyage to Arcturus*, and that question may be the subtlest anybody ever asked about the form.[4] There is something perennially in excess about the genre, just as the pleasure principle is always in excess, absurdly in excess, of the reality principle. The more you win, in other words, the more you stand to lose. Sir Gawain, Frodo Baggins, or any croupier in Las Vegas can tell you as much. Marie-Louise von Franz, in her little-regarded *The Interpretation of Fairy Tales* (1970), articulates much the same attitude when she writes:

> I have come to the conclusion that all fairy tales endeavour to describe one and the same psychic fact, but a fact so complex and far-reaching and so difficult for us to realize in all its different aspects that hundreds of tales and thousands of repetitions with a musician's variations are needed until this unknown fact is delivered into consciousness.... This unknown fact is what Jung calls the Self....[5]

And, earlier, than Bloom or von Franz, Kierkegaard in *Fear and Trembling* (1843) describes fantasy, quite simply, as the nostalgia of the infinite for the finite.

These definitions are all more serious than deconstructionist tinkerings or coy witticisms. And they all suggest that fantasy is not just "Eloi writing" any more than science fiction is just "Morlock prose."

And yet something is still missing. What is missing is a straight confrontation with the real problem of fantasy studies. And the real problem is this: people—even students, who are almost people—are reading more and more science fiction and fantasy; and the academic/critical establishment, enfranchised and paid well to explain literature to those people, is at a loss to explicate these texts because it has lagged so far behind the taste or curiosity of the very masses it was created to educate. We were all rereading Ernest Hemingway's *The Sun Also Rises* (1926) while they were well into the second of Marion Zimmer Bradley's Darkover series, or could name all of the characters from *Return of the Jedi* (1983). And our response, in general, was to say that science fiction could not matter because it was written by hacks, and fantasy was all right—as a diversion—because it displayed some watered-down mythic elements. This is a version of what sociologists used to call the "Black Bourgeoisie" syndrome: you can move into my neighborhood, but only if you dress and talk the way I do, and trade in that outrageous red Cadillac for a nice, sensible station wagon. Assimilate, *then* integrate: it is, of course, a losing proposition.

A very valued friend of mine, a medievalist, reads contemporary fantasy voraciously, but reads it only to reassure himself that it is all hopelessly second-rate, and cannot rival *Pearl*, or *Sir Gawain and the Green Knight*. I find his attitude puzzling but symptomatic. It is not so much fear of the new as it is insistence upon the order of things. But the order of things, as we should know after a century of relativity theory and quantum physics, is nothing if not fluid. Sir Arthur Eddington once paraphrased the whole of quantum theory by saying, "Something unknown is doing we don't know what": that is also, I admit, a fine premise for fantasy at its most interesting and dangerous, and a good slogan for the only literary criticism that could be really useful.

In *What Was Literature?* (1982) the professionally scandalous Leslie Fiedler discusses this phenomenon, and has the temerity to suggest that perhaps the popular taste may be more ultimately *right* than the ivory-tower taste. I do not know that I would go that far: I *do* value Hemingway, F. Scott Fitzgerald, William Faulkner, etc. But I am also not prepared to say that they are better than Stephen King, Stephen R. Donaldson, Marion Zimmer Bradley, or Peter S. Beagle. And I *know* none of them is better than Philip K. Dick.

But "better" is itself a poisonous concept. Is *Paradise Lost* "better" than *King Lear*? Is Saul Bellow "better" than Norman Mailer? The only answers to questions like that is: "You should not have asked." As Kenneth Burke long ago observed about bogus differentiations of "high" and "low" culture, a ladder without its lower rungs is not a ladder you can really use.

And that is my final point. Science fiction, as George Slusser says, still has to break out of the ghetto. But fantasy has to move out of the suburbs, and that may be even a harder move. Serious study of the form has to reforge its connections with the elemental mythic qualities from which it sprung, and to re-realize that reading any literary text worth the bother is engaging in a high adventure of psychic risk. Who knows? Learning to read Grahame's *The Wind in the Willows* dangerously might even reteach us to read Leo Tolstoy's *Anna Karenina* well.

In that enterprise this volume will at least try. Or, to put it another way, it will attempt to make the world — and the university — safe for red Cadillacs and for Mole.

11

"Turn That Shit Down!" Or, How to Market an Underground

A funny thing happened as I started writing this. I wanted to begin — as much out of love as for any real or fancied reasons of discourse — by quoting the first lines of Allen Ginsberg's *Howl*, the poem that changed the way I read poems and taught me you could do things *with* words as scary and dazzling and holy as the things the greatest American artist of this century, Charlie Parker, did *without* words. And I could not find the book. *The* book: the black-and-white cover, stapler-bound, eighteenth printing of the original City Lights Books Pocket Poets Series Number Four, seventy-five cents in 1967, that I have carried through four changes of venue, one divorce (I kept all the Charlie Parker records, too), and as much good and bad karma as normally fills up a quarter-century.

Everyone knows the special panic and guilt of losing a treasured book: it is how we understand Desdemona's handkerchief, Frodo's ring, or Holden Caulfield's red hunting cap. But I assured myself that the book must be in my office at the university (it was — this is not a melodrama), and I remembered the complete text of *Howl* was also staring at me from my bookshelf in *British and American Poets, Chaucer to the Present*, edited by — talk about your Olympus — W. Jackson Bate and David Perkins, published by Harcourt Brace Jovanovich, 1986. Here are the opening lines of *Howl*:

> I saw the best minds of my generation destroyed by madness,
>   starving hysterical naked,
> dragging themselves through the negro streets at dawn
>   looking for an angry fix,
> angelheaded hipsters burning for the ancient heavenly
>   connection to the starry dynamo in the machinery of
>   night....[1]

11. "Turn That Shit Down!"

And that is the funny thing that happened. I expected that, reading those to-me indelible lines now enshrined in a sanctified, official, annotated, and academically kosher textbook would bring on an attack of the midlife bends, reminding me that in twenty-five years even Ginsberg — Ginsberg! — had been assimilated into the Lit-Crit establishment and what, for God's sake, did that say about Prufrockian *me*? Or alternatively I expected that, even ensconced in the masonry of the ivy edifice Ginsberg had tried to explode, his lines would still flare and sear, a time bomb under the cathedral of "official" art — like Charlie Parker with strings, or Blake's "Jerusalem," now in the Anglican hymnal. The *funny* thing, you see, is that there was no question of "alternatively": both of the expected, and mutually contradictory, responses were my response, and they were a single response.

I trust that you see how crucially relevant all this is to the idea of science fiction and the marketplace.

Frank Kafka's parable "Leopards in the Temple" is an indispensable text here, as it is for any attempt at reading. Leopards periodically break into the Temple during the sacrifice and eat the consecrated bread; eventually this becomes predictable and accepted as part of the ritual. Also indispensable is Walter Benjamin's idea of the "aura" surrounding or inhabiting or illuminating the artwork in late-capitalist culture, that special radiance — based, to be sure, partly on the concept of private ownership — that the *original* always has vis à vis its copy. And this is not very far from Philip K. Dick's articulation, in *The Man in the High Castle* (1962), of the Chinese concept of *wu*, the indefinable but undeniable spiritual charge — something like permanent static electricity — that resides in a work of art not necessarily well, but passionately, made.

In Dick's novel, Frank Frink, one of the multiple nonheroes, is an artisan making near-perfect counterfeits of pre–World War II U.S. artifacts that are highly prized by the Japanese who, in the novel, actually won the war and colonized the western United States (the date of the novel is 1962, so it qualifies as science fiction). He and his partner decide to produce their own original jewelry to market through an antique-dealer, the relatively feckless Robert Childan. In a crucial scene, Childan takes a piece of Frink's jewelry to Paul Kasoura, a Japanese patron he holds in special awe. A man of impeccable taste, Kasoura tells Childan that, as "art," the pin is nugatory; yet it has *wu*. As he says: "By contemplating it, we gain more *wu* ourselves. We experience the tranquility associated not with art but with holy things.... In other words, an entire new world is pointed to, by this. The name for it is neither art, for it has no form, nor religion.... It is an authentically new thing on the face of the world."[2]

Then, despite his stunning analysis of what truly disruptive art really *is*, Kasoura offers Childan a deal. For all its *wu*, he says, the pin is not saleable as a work of art. Maybe it could be mass-produced as cheap trinkets, souvenirs, etc. It is Childan's moment of testing, or *kairos*, the critical time of moral choice theologians distinguish from *chronos*, the neutral, quotidian time of mere habit and duration. After some agonized to-and-fro-ing, he decides he cannot cheapen the work of his countrymen and even — in an act of real heroism for a marginalized colonialized person — demands of Kasoura an apology for the insult to his people and, implicitly, himself.

We hear little of Childan for the rest of *The Man in the High Castle*, although, at the beginning of the book, he appears to be a central, if not the central, character. That, too, is what chess players call a "brilliancy." For in a book that is nothing if not a meditation on the parameters of "artifice" and "reality" and the chances for artifice to validate itself *as* reality, the little art dealer, in choosing to honor the *wu* of his countrymen's art, has in fact achieved his own *wu* and thereby passes from the limbo that is the world of the novel into the authenticity, the radiance of the authentic — what the Kabbala calls the *Shekinah*—to which the book points and for which it longs. To compare Dick to one of the few writers on his level of subtlety and strength: Childan's choice is like a positive rewriting of Kafka's chilling parable from *The Trial*, "Before the Law." It is as if, this time, the seeker after the Law, the Shekinah, mustered the will to walk past the terrible guardian at the door into the holy presence, discovering — this is Kafka's point as much as Dick's — that the one thing needful to approach the Law is the courage to approach the Law.

Dick's parable, whatever *he* may have meant by it, is also about underground art — be it science fiction or beat poetry, bop, free jazz, or rock and roll — and the marketplace, especially that most venal and petty booth in the marketplace, more venal and petty than Hollywood agents or publishers or nightclub owners, the critical establishment which, from the inanities of *Critical Inquiry* to the shibboleths of *Newsweek*, has one clear purpose: to locate and identify *wu* and render it replicable.

Kasoura says "to have no historicity ... and yet to partake of some ethereal value — that is a marvel."[3] His aesthetics is that of classical Japanese culture — or rather, of Dick's understanding of classical Japanese culture — but it is really no more or less inadequate as a way of comprehending than established European modes. Theodor W. Adorno, in a moment of breathtaking though not uncharacteristic ignorance, says of jazz that "art is permitted to survive only if it renounces the right to be different, and integrates itself into the omnipotent realm of the profane.... Jazz is the false liquidation of art."[4]

Adorno, in fact, would have been an interesting character in *The Man in the High Castle*, a Germanic counterpoint and double to Kasoura's Oriental disdain. One recognizes the presence of *wu* in chaotic, aboriginal artwork and wants to mass-market it; whereas the other, just *because* the work is quotidian, is blind to its *wu*—or its aura—altogether.

Trust me, this will not be an exercise in critic-bashing. Diverting as that activity is, it is also—particularly since the recent and, one hopes, ephemeral triumph of deconstruction—about as sterile as miniature golf. Nevertheless, let me remind you that I said Childan's heroic choice is that he refuses to "cheapen" the jewelry he offers for inspection by letting it be mass-produced. And let me remind you also that "cheap" comes from a word—old English *ceap*—which does not mean "inexpensive" or "devalued" but simply "market" or "object of exchanges." When you visit London's Cheapside, you are visiting not the tacky part of the town, but the place the market used to be. If you go to one of the lovely small towns in English with the name "Chipping"—East Chipping, Chipping Wombat, etc.—you are going to a place where, in less stressful days, the weekly farmer's market was held. A generation ago the last gasp of this semantic peculiarity would have still been audible. If I called a woman in 1940 a "chippie," I implied that she was a prostitute *not* because she was "cheap" but because she marketed, bargained for, her favors. And since we have mentioned prostitution, let's talk again about artists and critics.

"Turn That Shit Down!" is my title, and I take some pride in it, especially because it is not really mine, but the title of a paper a student wrote for me in a class in American literature and American popular music. The point of the essay—she was writing about Heavy Metal—was that *that* phrase, uttered or shouted from any parent to any child, is the ultimate validation, benediction, or accolade: the guarantee that you have found an art that is your own, something that cannot be co-opted, marketed, commercialized, academicized, or other nice-nellied to death just because it is, when you father says it, the least valuable commodity on the planet. It's shit: and you can't cheapen that.

But of course you can. Norman Mailer—who, I think, knows as much or more about our language as anybody now writing—said somewhere in *The Armies of the Night* (1968) that the great thing about the word *shit* is that it lets you use the word *noble*. Except for Ludwig Wittgenstein, I do not know anyone who has noticed anything smarter about language, especially the language that is our daily bread (what Wittgenstein called *das Wesentlich unserer Sprache*).

My student heard "turn that shit down!" from her father when she listened to Twisted Sister. I heard it, thirty years ago, from my dad when I listened to Dave Brubeck and Paul Desmond thread their way—Dave clumping, Paul sailing—through Rodgers and Hart's "Little Girl Blue." You have heard it: somewhere, sometime, and with some tune or painting or movie, you were told what you liked was shit and, implicitly, that if you wanted to be accepted as a grown-up, you would have to turn that shit down, leave it behind—what else do you do with shit?—and join the march of civilization, or, as the Clash put it, start working for the clampdown.

At that moment in your life I suggest you were Robert Childan. *They* were telling you—and don't you know by now who *they* are, who they have *always* been?—that this stuff was bad stuff, but that you could still qualify as a member of the club if you treated it like bad stuff—or at least like stuff that only made sense when you compared it with officially *good* stuff. This is how you publish an essay on Philip K. Dick in *PMLA, JEGP, ELH,* or any of the other acronymic and unread journals that constellate, like cenotaphs, the potter's field of literary discourse. Think of an essay: "*Howl* and Its Debt to Blake." You could write it: but why would you?

How do you market an underground? It is the simplest thing in the world. *Tell them* it is an underground, and they will knock down your front door. *Tell* the parents it is bad for the kids, you will get the kids—have I ever lied to you?—you will get the kids in the palm of your hand. Then, of course, you can begin thinking about making some real money—about singing "Hope I die before I get old" at the age of forty-seven, hearing-impaired, before cheering millions on a tour underwritten by Annheuser-Busch; or, if you are a "noted futurist," doing TV commercials hawking imported cars while you allegedly work on the last volume of *Dangerous Visions*.

Let me be clear: Peter Townshend and Harlan Ellison both have tenure in my private pantheon. I am not talking about, or accusing them of, "selling out": quite the contrary, I see their careers as self-conscious dramatizations—"inscription" is the currently fashionable term—of the undergrounder's complex, capitalist fate. For as Marcuse said in *One-Dimensional Man* (1964) and as Townshend, Ellison, and many other good people have brilliantly articulated and *live,* the "underground" is not, and never really was, *there* in our culture. When everything can be marketed, everything can be—in all senses of the world—"cheapened," and thus may be diminished in its aura. On how many bourgeois walls do perfect reproductions of Picasso's "The Lovers" have to hang before the half-life of its *wu* has emitted all but its next-to-last scintilla of power? Or—conversely and the same thing—do the pushing, gawking crowds who gather every day around the Mona Lisa in the Louvre testify to the sempiternity of art or powerfully remind you of the fate of the Elephant Man? Is Fredric Jameson — the highest-paid Marxist in the free world — an absurdity, a walking contradiction, or both?

Perhaps we should define *underground*. *Underground* I take to mean any performance that brings outsiders together and empowers them as outsiders: E.E. "Doc" Smith's *The Skylark of Space* (1947) for the young and insecure Frederik Pohl and Isaac Asimov, Judy Garland for gays in the 1960s, Desmond and Ginsberg for me and some friends you do not know. Pohl remarks in *The Way the Future Was* (1978) that most science fiction writers are a rather homely lot. That is why they are science fiction writers, he goes on: outsiders in grammar school, largely dateless and chosen last for basketball, they sought in Edgar Rice Burroughs's Mars and Alex Raymond's Mongo the validation denied them on the playgrounds of PS 80 or Holy Cross Grade School. Pohl is, of course, as usual making a job at his own expense. But it is not altogether a joke. It explains a lot about how two dreamy, scrawny Cleveland kids — Joe Siegel and Jerry Shuster — could create what is, after all, the one indelibly original U.S. contribution to world mythology. It also explains how another dreamy Brooklyn mama's boy, a century earlier, could reinvent himself as an androgynous democratic Leviathan, the poet of the body and of the soul, containing multitudes, sounding his barbaric yawp over the world, singing the body electric.

And, between them, Superman — Siegel and Shuster's creation — and "Walt" — Walt Whitman's creation — fairly divide the possibilities for art — in our culture — when it scores big in the marketplace. The market can either spit you out or swallow you whole. But the market — Adam Smith is still the only really useful theorist here — will thrive, whatever it does, and only *in* the market will the art, which began as an escape from the market. Be allowed to thrive.

Siegel and Shuster — everyone knows the ugly tale — quickly sold their creation to DC Comics for a pittance, and grew old poor while their omnipotent, extraterrestrial goyische double garnered millions. Maybe they had — the term is curiously addictive — somehow "inscribed" themselves as losers in the very formation of the *ur*-myth: why else Clark Kent? From the Scarlet Pimpernel through Zorro to Batman, the heroes' alter egos have never had to be so definitively wimpish: Bruce Wayne could outclass Clark Kent six ways from Tuesday before breakfast. So, is the invention of the hapless, bungling reporter for a great metropolitan newspaper something besides a mere convention? Reading the early *Superman* strips, one cannot really tell whether the gravamen of the stories is the exaltation of the god or the humiliation of the nebbish — both are, of course, the same character. Or put it this way: the Clark Kents of the world are drawn together by a subversive hope — or is it faith? —

that somewhere inside them there is a Kal-El waiting to emerge. Jacob, whose greatest talents seem to be for lying and running away, has an uncanny encounter at the ford of Peniel and emerges as Yisra-El, whose heroic name means either "fighter for" or "struggler with" God — depending, I suppose, upon whether you read Genesis with Martin Buber or Friedrich Nietzsche.

I want to argue that Superman is the marketed, "cheapened," and successful version of his underground double, Clark Kent: the quality-paperback edition, if you will, of the once-contraband *Howl*. In the same way, "Walt" is the we-made-it, writ large version of the Walter Whitman — doesn't the name, Walter, sound odd, Clark-Kentish here? — who had to discover and *announce* "Walt." The difference is that Siegel and Shuster and Clark Kent were absorbed against their will into the mechanism of success, while Walter Whitman — and Ernest Hemingway and Isaac Asimov and Saul Bellow and Ray Bradbury — found the process of absorption quite congenial.

Here, we are not discussing literary "quality" — if indeed such a fugitive concept still survives, hiding out and living off the land in the underbrush of the academy — but something there is still no very good name for, though Dick's *wu* is a strong contender. We talk about the special quality a book, tune, or movie has as a *shared secret* and what happens to that quality when it is shared by too many. Oscar Wilde perfectly defined the quality of a *coterie* work in the preface to *The Picture of Dorian Gray* when he noted that the nineteenth-century dislike of symbolism was the rage of Caliban at not seeing his face in the mirror, and its dislike of realism was the rage of Caliban at seeing his face in the mirror. It is almost as clever as the remark variously attributed to Louis Armstrong or Fats Waller when asked what it meant "to swing": "Lady, if you gotta ask, you'll never know."

But what about the boredom of Caliban at living in a hall of mirrors? Or what about a world where everyone knows what it means "to swing," and if you don't, you can take a course in it?

That particular sensibility — which Wilde himself in some important ways anticipates — is what has lately become marketable under the name "postmodern." If that much-overused phrase means anything, it means simply that for us, our culture and *sensibility* about culture, there are no more shared secrets, all genre simply is a marketing label, and the claims of any art to a speciality, to *wu* — to whatever is on the other side of "market realities" — are just that: *claims*, like the claims to satisfy your daily vitamin requirement on the package of pseudo-cereal you had for breakfast this morning. It is not just the emperor whose new clothes are an illusion, in other words. It is also the little boy shouting in the crowd — archetype of the underground poet — and the crowd itself — archetypes of all of us as readers — who are hopelessly naked.

11. "Turn That Shit Down!"

To restate and paraphrase Marcuse: when everything can and *will* be sold, no discourse can possibly articulate the sublime, since the sublime has already been co-opted into the discourse of exchange, and exchange is one relationship where the sublime cannot exist. Or — let me attempt a midrash here — we always assume, don't we, that Jesus drives the moneylenders from the temple because he is angry at them. But what if he *fears* them? What if he sees that they, pitted against the Holy of Holies, could *win*? This is a fairly grim scenario if you want to believe in the idea of art as a holy thing. But it is a scenario established by entrepreneurs like Andy Warhol — and one must say, Robert Mapplethorpe — justified by critics like Stanley Fish, even incarnated by writers like John Ashbery at his most boring and Barry N. Malzberg at his most interesting.

Malzberg's splendid and infuriating novel *Galaxies* (1975) is, among many other things — including virtually unteachable — a meditative jeremiad on precisely the topic of this volume. How, he asks, can a writer possessed of genius yet trapped in the market realities of science fiction — indeed of the whole venal literary establishment — hope to do anything except gnash his teeth at the debasing and debased conventions of the forms he is forced to write in? How can one create a holy thing when all holy things have been typed and cataloged? This is what, on the level of the creative imagination, Harold Bloom has christened "the anxiety of influence." It is also what, on the socioeconomic level, the papers in this volume and Malzberg help us see as "the anxiety of affluence." And is *that* the promised end? Do the pure products of America not only go crazy but also become simply pure product?

At the risk of sounding optimistic, I think not. I suggest that what lies on the other side of the postmodern — inelegant phrase! — is and can only be a reemergence of the spare and strange, the stuff, the *wu* that makes discourse a humanizing shared secret in the first place. Can you *tell*, without cheating and looking at the footnote, whether I quoted from the original or the officially sanctioned edition of *Howl*? And if you were hearing those lines for the first — or the fiftieth — time, can you fail to have been shocked and moved by the lines? Ginsberg himself repudiated the poem as an early excrescence, but it makes no different: flash-frozen history outlasts all its exegetes, even its author.

And I suggest the same for science fiction, now a securely established and immensely remunerative mode of production. Take two relatively recent books, William Gibson's *Neuromancer* (1984) and Orson Scott Card's *Ender's Game* (1985): both are mass-marketed, mass-marketable successes, and both are well within the parameters of the kind of book Malzberg loathes — slick, dramatic, full of easy action and easy moralizing. And both also, at heart, contain secrets and hidden imaginative scandals that, I think, eminently qualify them as human utterance. In *Neuromancer*, Gibson literally finds the divine at the heart of the digital machine in a plot modeled, as far as I can see, point for point on the plot of Dante's *Divine Comedy*. And in *Ender's Game*, Card rewrites the problematic Gospel of Mark in terms of a universe — our universe — where reality partakes of the quality of a video game.

Despite all we say and do, in other words, the act of creation goes on: I am enough of a Kabbalist (or Anabaptist) to insist that the age of the prophets is not closed and can never be. And perhaps that is where all meditations about "science fiction and market realities" will or should lead us: simply back to recognizing that the market realities are finally no more "real" than the "fictions" — scientific or otherwise — that we spin.

I began by misplacing Allen Ginsberg, so I end by misreading — I hope usefully — Robert Lowell and the last line of "The Quaker Graveyard at Nantucket." If we see the *business* of writing as the business of writing and the craft of fiction as an ongoing struggle between the desire to say something important and the desire to say something that will be heard; if we realize that, as storytellers, we are all at once entertainers, stand-up comics, and, with luck, conduits for whatever voice makes and keeps us human; then we can say of our nostalgia for the sublime in the midst of the sublime's detritus: "The Lord survives the rainbow of his will."[5]

Part III
Gnostic Lunch:
The Later Eaton Essays

It was very difficult to persuade Frank to present a paper at the 1991 Eaton Conference because he could not abide its topic, "food in science fiction and fantasy." Yet wrestling with that unpalatable subject led Frank to recognize the link between science fiction and gnosticism, an idea which helped to make his final five Eaton papers, in my opinion, his very best work. As if sensing his own imminent demise, Frank transformed his final effort, ostensibly focused on the topic of "science fiction and the two cultures," into a brilliant summary of all the themes that had formed the basis of his Eaton papers.

12

Alimentary, My Dear Watson
Food and Eating and Scientific and Mystery Fiction

Food in science fiction? Let's face it: at first blush the topic sounds like one of those term-paper-from-hell assignments we all, at one time or another, got from one of our (we prayed) anti–role model undergraduate teachers, swore we would never inflict upon *our* students when *we* assumed the captain's chair, and — since the worm dieth not — sometimes still do, just because — cards on the table — we've got to assign *something*, and we're, for crying out loud, *tired*.

So, sure: food in science fiction. And the role of money in pastoral romance. And visual imagery in the songs of Stevie Wonder. And the image of the Negro in the novels of Henry James. And urban planning in romantic poetry. The list could go on forever, and is fun to play with. Ever think about playing *Wheel of Fortune* in Tel Aviv? "Uh — can I buy a vowel?" "NO!"

You get, I guess, my drift. There's precious little food — food, that is, as an object of desire — *in* science fiction, at least as opposed to the "mainstream novel" — whatever the hell *that* is — or to — something you're going to hear a lot about — the detective novel. What interests me about the subject is *why* that should be the case: why food, the celebration of food, the *pleasure* of eating — a pleasure of which I am quite literally an incarnation — should be so all-but-absent from the genre.

To be sure, this sort of exercise carries with it the cheap frisson of deconstruction, which at its most perverse delights in reading the "text" — that's lit-speak for "book" — for what is peripheral to it, sort of like going to a ballgame and watching the umpires.

Okay, okay, I know the game couldn't be played without the umpires, who, precisely by being "under erasure" (see? I can do it, too), validate and "empower" the illusion of unique, free, and absolutely unrepeatable action that *is* the game. So food, too, let's say for the moment, is under erasure in most, or a lot of, science fiction. In fact, since genre criticism is largely an infinite restatement from an infinite number of vantages of the *nature* of the genre — doing chess problems as opposed to playing chess — I'd go so far as to suggest that the absence, erasure, or *etiolation* of food is one of the defining characters of science fiction in contradistinction to other genres; a true sememe since, like the classic definition of *morpheme* or *phoneme*, it is a palpable absence — a semiotic Maxwell's Demon — marking the distinction between two things that otherwise might be confused (put/pot, run/ran, as/ass, and all that). Or, as that *really* smart deconstructionist, G.K. Chesterton, once observed, in a riddle to which the answer is "pudding," there is only one word whose use is absolutely disallowed, that word being, of course, "pudding."

Segue to some — for me — significant appearances of food in sf. They turn out to be, in funny ways, *dis*appearances.

Item. In Samuel R. Delany's wonderful — and predictably out of print — *Babel-17* (1966), Captain Rydra Wong and the crew of her starship, the *Rimbaud*, become involved in a web of piracy, interstellar war, and Byzantine politics. The story, in other words, is pretty close to the classic simplicities of space opera. (This is, of course, Delany, so never fear: the "classic simplicities" are put through some pretty stunning changes, Delany being the Amadeus of pulp.) Among the book's brilliancies is what seems at first just an elegant running gag. The ship's cook, whose name — heh heh — is Diavalo is always serving the crew the most elaborate, gourmet, straight-from-Escoffier meals. And then, near the book's climax, Rydra takes some of her crew to a fancy-schmantzy, planetside restaurant. The meal, over which the spacemen go into ecstasy, is hamburgers and French fries. As one crew member exclaims:

> "Diavalo should be here now.... He's an artist with a carbo-synth, and he's got a feel for a protein-dispenser that's fine for good solid meals like nut stuffed pheasant, fillet of snapper-creyonnaise, and good stick-to-your-ribs food for a hungry spaceship crew. But this fancy stuff"— he spread mustard carefully across his bun — "give him a pound of real chopped meat, and I bet he'd run out of the galley 'cause it might bite him."[1]

I have to observe that part of the great wit of this passage is that phrases like "carbo-synth" and "protein-dispenser" are such obviously creaky props from the space opera warehouse that their very cliché quality adds weight to the quite serious point being made about the abstraction of food in the messily quotidian. It is like Mozart building the last movement of the "Jupiter" symphony on the same four-note theme as the "Twinkle, twinkle, little star" theme of Haydn's "Surprise" symphony; or, for that matter, Springsteen singing "Santa Claus Is Coming to Town."

Item. In Delany's *Nova* (1968), at one point two members of a spaceship crew are standing on the observation bridge, talking. One is sucking on a piece of sugar candy; as they talk, he takes it out of his mouth and offers it to his friend, who declines. He then remarks, casually, that such a gesture would have shocked people who lived before the evolution of space travel brought about the elimination of all harmful bacteria in the human body. It's a subtle moment. Like his strong precursor, H.G. Wells, Delany seems to me at once celebratory and cautious about the inevitable self-refashioning of humankind under technology, creatively embarrassed by the tension between his expectations of liberation and his nostalgia for the erotic — that's the *erotic*, which, unlike its idiot twin the pornographic, always welcomes and makes holy the sweat and funk of the body as body. (Think about his great story, "Aye, and Gomorrah" [1967].) Do we really *want* a world in which we span the stars like a walk around the block but, in doing so, lose the quintessential, authentic pleasure of being able to say *my* meal, *my* glass of beer, and, yes, *my* good time in bed? Chip ain't saying.

Item. In Norman Spinrad's *The Void Captain's Tale* (1983), which is actually Spinrad's astonishingly successful retelling of chapters 2 and 3 of Genesis, Genro Kane Gupta, captain of the sybaritic starline *Dragon Zephyr* (the ship *is* the serpent, dig) falls in love with his navigator, Dominique Alia Wu, and finally yields to her urgings to let the ship, on one of its hyperspace jumps, fly out of control, destinationless, into the interstellar abyss. In Spinrad's novel, you see, starship navigators are all women. They have to be, since spacewarp navigation in this story consists in the navigator interfacing *completely* with the ship's computer and *feeling* her way to the destination, and in the process experiencing a kind of Olympic-class orgasm. Dominique wants Genro to let her put the ship on blind-spin because she wants, quite literally — Spinrad doesn't make this obvious pun, so I will — to go all the way.

The point, for our present purposes, of this rather brilliant invention is a moment that comes early in the story. The *Dragon Zephyr*—a kind of Vegas with hyperdrive — has a gourmet chef who caters to his rich passengers' every caprice. After the first hyperspace jump, when Genro accidentally sees Dominique being wheeled out of the navigator's room with a seraphic, blissed-out (yes, there *are* other words for it) smile on her face, he is summoned to the dining room by an hysterical chef — named, naturally, Bocuse — complaining about the meal Dominique has ordered. It is — depending of course upon how much time you've done in highway franchise restaurants — pretty bizarre: a pitcher of milk and, on one plate, a slab of seared beef with boiled beans topped with melted cheese and three fried eggs, peppercorns, and a sprig of greens. (I especially like the sprig of greens — is Spinrad a Californian?) Genro expostulates with Dominique that this mess is unseemly and potentially offensive to the passengers, and she explains that she eats not for pleasure but to keep her body together for the next great orgasmic hyperspace jump. As she says to the puzzled, *moyen sensuel* captain — I can't help but see this as a scene between Tracy and Hepburn in their prime:

> "So you see, liebe Genro, the purpose of nutritive ingestion is to preserve the corpus material as long as possible, and the purpose of corporeal preservation is to experience as many jumps as possible until some day...."
>
> She stared silently into my eyes [the void captain tells us], and for a moment I saw not the black circles under them, the pinkening of her whites, the wasted physiognomy. What I saw was ... two empty opaque orbs in an archetypal mask, empty yet bottomless like the void itself.[2]

It is an irregular full circle — which is to say, back to the same place — from *Babel-17*, and it is shattering. Space travel, which is to say science fiction, which is to say whatever is behind or beneath or articulating itself through science fiction, tends to dissociate the body from its appetites, and finally — you're surprised, already? — from itself. As Wallace Stevens, the central theologian of the machine age, asks in "Sunday Morning":

> Is there no change of death in paradise?
> Does ripe fruit never fall?[3]

I know the name, by the way, of what is beneath and articulating itself through science fiction: I'll tell you in a while. For the moment, just hold in mind the picture of Dominique, anorexic, ravenous, and obsessed with a transcendence that will both ratify and annihilate her "corporeal preservation": she is the necessary angel, the Sophia, of this discussion.

Item: the last but one, and that one will be a while coming. In William Gibson's second published story and one of the best things he's ever done, "The Gernsback Continuum," the narrator finds himself either hallucinating or time-warped, anyhow transported into the future the America of the sf 1930s dreamed for the America of the 1980s, the *Amazing, Astounding, Things to Come, Popular Mechanics*, all chrome and tile and immense flying wings future of bright and brave young people preparing fearlessly to finalize mankind's empire over matter. And it is a nightmare.

"Here," says the narrator, "we'd gone on and on, in a dream logic that knew nothing of pollution, the finite bounds of fossil fuel, or foreign wars it was possible to lose. They were smug, happy, and utterly content with themselves and their world."

The narrator's nightmare reaches its climax with, parked on the road out of Tucson, he awakes to see a man and woman — splendid, tunic-clad, fair *Hitler-jugend* from the Dream-future — emerge from a futuristic car parked in front of his — they can't see him, of course — and strike a few noble poses and engage in some vapid conversation. And then: "'John,' I heard the woman say, 'we've forgotten to take our food pills.' She clicked two bright wafers from a thing on her belt and passed one to him. I backed onto the highway and headed for Los Angeles, wincing and shaking my head."[4]

We wince in unison with Gibson's hapless narrator. And we wince, at least in part, because we know — Gibson knows this, too — that the grotesque future of magnificent blond beasts swallowing food pills has, to an alarming degree, come to pass. Julia Child — who, given our topic, is *at least* as authoritative a voice as Todorov or, God save us, Derrida — writes eloquently in her latest cookbook about "fear of food," our national obsession with cholesterol-counts, calories, and roughage, as if the purpose of eating at all was to stay out of danger. Justin Wilson, the simply wonderful Cajun raconteur and, when he thinks about it, chef, says, even more to the point, that if your doctor tells you salt is bad for you, stop using the stuff or get another doctor.

Look around — unless you think literary texts are *only* literary texts, and in that case you can leave the room now. They want to sell you margarine instead of butter, Miracle Whip instead of mayonnaise, fish instead of beef, and light beer instead of anything remotely potable because, they tell you, *that* way you won't have a heart attack, a stroke, or the screaming fantods and die. And if you're pregnant and order a glass of wine in a public place, or dare to smoke anywhere where there may be virginal lungs, then you are of course beyond the pale of civilized behavior.

Has any culture ever lived in such — the phrase is carefully chosen — blind-shit fear of its own mortality? Have any people ever hated their bodies so much? Or — to put it the way it must be put, unless we are just playing at thinking — feared death so completely, so abjectly?

You *will* die, you know. Or, to nail things down maybe a little more existentially, *I* will, too. The older I get, in fact, the more I think that reading, listening to music, watching movies, etc. — all the things that make life worth the bother — are a way of prepping for the supreme, last-bet-of-the-evening roll, and if that's morbid then so are Byron, Camus, and Mailer, and I'll play on their team, thanks.

Anyhow, Thomas Pynchon, whom I regard brooking no dispute as the best writer America has produced, says something in the Introduction to *Slow Learner*, the 1984 collection of his early stories, that I found troubling when I first read it — for I do love science fiction — and that now I think encapsulates, as Pynchon almost always does, a bitter wisdom:

When we speak of "seriousness" in fiction ultimately we are talking about an attitude toward death — how characters may act in its presence, for example, or how they handle it when it isn't so immediate. Everybody knows this, but the subject is hardly ever brought up with younger writers, possibly because given to anyone at the apprentice age, such advice is widely felt to be effort wasted. (I suspect one of the reasons that fantasy and science fiction appeal so much to younger readers is that, when the space and time have been altered to allow characters to travel easily anywhere through the continuum and thus escape physical dangers and timepiece inevitabilities, mortality is so seldom an issue.)[5]

Mortality is "so seldom an issue" in science fiction: like food. And like food, of course, by being under erasure, by being present as naggingly as the missing word, "pudding," in Chesterton's "pudding" riddle, it exerts a constant, sometimes all-but-intolerable pressure on the form. Which may explain why Pynchon himself, of all our most valued so-called serious writers, is the one most deeply and obviously influenced by and imbued with the mythology of science fiction (Norman Mailer and William S. Burroughs in a photo-finish for second place, here — and they are both indispensable influences upon young Tom).

But I told you I was going to tell you about food and science fiction and the detective story.

The great Jean Anthelme Brillat-Savarin, in one of the introductory aphorisms to his 1825 *Physiologie du goût*, writers, "*Les animaux se repaissent; l'homme mange; l'homme d'esprit seul sait manger.*" [Animals feed; man eats; but only civilized man knows *how* to eat.][6] This is not far from — indeed, may be a source of— Douglas Adams's observation at the end of *The Hitchhiker's Guide to the Galaxy*, that all great civilizations go through three phases — "Survival," "Inquiry," and "Sophistication" — which may be summarized by the questions, "How can we eat?," "Why do we eat?," and "Where shall we have lunch?"[7]

But *l'homme d'esprit*: where in the world is the right English translation for that? "Civilized man" doesn't even begin to cut it; way too general and pretentious, and all other attempts fail equally, either on the side of the too-trivial or the too-thuddingly earnest. Maybe — and I say this with jaw-grinding chauvinism — there's no right translation because the Anglo-Norman-Saxon-whitebread culture has not, after all this time, produced an individual worthy of calling forth the appropriate name. I mean, what's the Eskimo for "surf"? And why can't Pat Boone sing the blues?

Or maybe — just maybe — *l'homme d'esprit* exists in the Anglo-American language after all, but not as a name as much as a character and a situation, one that the French themselves are obsessed with and have never gotten quite right: the private eye.

III. Gnostic Lunch

I trust that by now you're sufficiently tired of quotations, allusions, evasions, and deferrals — the gossamer out of which conference papers are woven — to wonder what the hell I *really* have to tell you. So, okay: here it is:

THE GENRE OF SCIENCE FICTION — IF THERE ARE SUCH THINGS AS GENRES — IS ONE THAT LOATHES AND FEARS THE BODY AND LONGS — AS DO WE ALL — TO MAKE FOOD EITHER A SACRAMENT OR AN EXCRESCENCE, A PASSAGE TO A HIGHER WORLD OR A CASTOFF RELIC OF THE MORTALITY WE HAVE.

Now, that definition makes the form sound pretty austere. It does fit the bill, though: with only a few exceptions, and the great thing about doing d-con style criticism is that facts and counterexamples don't matter, anyway: *le discours, c'est tout.*

And for the corollary:

THE GENRE OF DETECTIVE FICTION IS ONE THAT IS OBSESSED WITH THE BODY EVEN TO THE POINT OF THE DARK EROTICISM OF THE BODY'S DECAY, AND IN WHICH, THEREFORE, FOOD AND SEX ARE VIRTUALLY INVISIBLE JUST *BECAUSE* OF THEIR OMNIPRESENCE.

(You may have noticed, by the way, that I have gone from my initial scoffing at our topic to believing that it is, in fact, a rich — nay, a most excellent topic: such is the danger of actually *thinking* about things.)

Very simply, we almost always see the detective, in whatever novel, *eating* at one point or another. Holmes and Watson often have dinner brought up by Mrs. Hudson; Philip Marlowe and Lew Archer usually stop and grab a bite somewhere as they careen through southern California; Hercule Poirot is a finicky gourmand (Poirot is a finicky *everything*); Mike Hammer's favorite meals, we know, include fried chicken and beer and fried egg sandwiches (*he's not afraid!*); and then there's Nero Wolfe, magnificently and complacently fat, whose adventures one reads almost as much for what Wolfe eats as for the crimes he solves (Rex Stout even put together a Nero Wolfe cookbook and I even bought the thing). And, to compare the great to the very tiny, when I'm writing a Harry Garnish novel and hit one of those sudden deserts where you don't know *where* to go next, I buy Harry a meal.

Why do I do that? Beats me, except I really, really, *really* want to be a detective writer. The point of all these appearances of food in detective fiction, though, is precisely that they are *not* diegetic (if I have managed for once to use that lumpy term correctly): they don't contribute anything to the unfolding of the plot as a significant utterance.

That doesn't mean, though, that they are not important, maybe crucially so. They establish a ground base, a "world," if I may use such a mundane term, in which the detective story can function as a mythology. I know of no better way of getting at what I mean than by citing some of Roland Barthes's observations in his characteristically brilliant introduction to the 150th anniversary edition of Brillat-Savarins' *Physiologie*. (The translations are my own, so they bear the same relation to Barthes's preternaturally limpid prose as, say, a snort of Bartles & Jaymes to a glass of Chateauneuf-du-Pape.)

Barthes, following Brillat-Savarin or B.S., as he writes, insists that eating — no, *dining*—like love (as opposed to rutting) is an indispensable articulation of the truly human:

> The species, needs procreation to survive, as the individual needs to eat to subsist. But the satisfaction of these needs is not enough for man. He must put into play, so to speak, the luxuriousness of desire, either amorous or gastronomic. An enigmatic and useless superfluity, the desired food [B.S.'s subject] is an unconditional waste, a kind of ethnographic ceremony through which man celebrates his power, his freedom to burn his energy "for no reason."[8]

This is to say — Barthes is too subtle to say it, but I'm surely not — that food, or cookery, for Lévi-Strauss of course permeates this discussion, is not only centrally human but irremediably entropic, an irrecoverable heat-loss, *une perte*, a waste, a loss, maybe even a fall, *pour rien*: because it tastes good. The presence or ambiance of food *as* food, that is, what I take to be the domain of detective, as opposed to science fiction, inevitably recalls us to the things of this world or what John Berryman calls, quite wonderfully, "the sweet switch of the body."[9] And I cannot help summoning Chesterton again, who observes that there is more of the "natural" — the human natural — in the man who eats caviar on impulse than in the man who eats Grape-Nuts on principle. Dominique Alia Wu, I submit, would have not the slightest idea what Barthes, B.S., or G.K.C. are talking about: the stuff on *her* plate is sacramental, literally a *viaticum*, to use another name for the Eucharist, that is a *way* to a higher state of being, bread and wine as precisely *not*— or trying their best not to be — bread and wine.

Even more tellingly for our purposes, Barthes discusses Baudelaire's criticism that B.S. doesn't speak adequately about wine. This because, writes Barthes,

> for Baudelaire wine is memory and forgetfulness, joy and melancholy; what permits the subject to be transported out of itself, to abandon the consistency of the ego for the sake of alien, foreign, strange states; a deviant path; in short, a drug.
>
> But, for B.S. wine is not at all an agent of ecstacy. The reason is clear. Wine is a part of food, and food, for B.S., is essentially convivial. Wine cannot involve a

solitary protocol: we drink at the same time as we eat, and we eat, always, in company; a strict sociality determines the pleasures of dining.... Wine, for B.S., has no special privilege: like food, and along with food, it subtly amplifies the body — renders it "*brilliant*" — but does not mute it. It is an anti-drug.[10]

And again, Barthes explains the profundities underlying B.S.'s discussion of the best way to make coffee. The beans can be either ground with a pestle or put through a coffee-mill, and B.S. prefers grinding:

> Now it is not hard to grasp the poetic of their difference. The mill is mechanical: the hand is applied to it as a force, not as an art (the proof is that the hand-mill quite naturally evolves into the electric mill). So what the mill produces — rather abstractly — is a dust of coffee, a dry and depersonalized substance. The pestle, on the contrary, involves an ensemble of physical gestures (pressing and turning in various directions), and these gestures are directly transmitted by the noblest, most human of substances: wood ... the excellence of the tool (as opposed to the machine), the superiority of the artisanal over the industrial, [is] in a word: nostalgia for the Natural.[11]

Never mind that Barthes — and B.S. — constitute a brilliant critique of such silly and aptly, creepily named devices as the "food processor." (I mean, doesn't anyone remember that chopping and paring the veggies is part of the fun of cooking and *eating* the veggies?) What is really important is that these two great connoisseurs — B.S. of food, Barthes of virtually everything he ever looked at — help us define, through the lens of gastronomy, science fiction and detective fiction: not as different genres, since of course I do not believe "genre" is a very useful term at any serious level of literary discussion, but as complementary articulations of a single mythogem, a central mythogem of which they are the two indispensable articulations in industrial and postindustrial culture. I want to talk about the two types of storytelling as two approaches to the idea of the sacramental.

The "sacramental," of course, is by no means a specifically Judeo-Christian concept. As we learn from *The Raw and the Cooked*, or for that matter from the *Iliad* and the *Mahabharata*, eating has always been one of the human activities most readily assimilable — or attractive — to the realm of the sacred. An interesting thing about the history of Christianity, though, is that so many of its most severe controversies have centered around the nature of the sacred food or, to be precise, the validity of the idea of *transubstantiation*.

We know that the Lord's Supper was the *very first* and *sole* manifestation of Christianity, before Paul's Epistles and well before the composition of the Gospels. And as early as the second century CE, arguments about the nature of the sanctified bread and wine: is it *really* a meal, or food, or what? I have to observe here, by the way, that the choice of bread and wine is very Lévi-

Straussian (or Brillat-Savarinish?), in that these two foods are definitely *post*-Neolithic, not just *preparations* of food but technological transformations of the "natural," that is, grain and grapes. As the prayer in the Roman Mass has it, "Father, accept these gifts, the fruits of the earth *and the work of human hands*."

The real bloodshed in the name of the Kingdom, of course, gets going with the Protestant reformation — or Protestant Revolt, as we were taught to refer to it at Holy Cross Grade School in the 1950s. And there, in the counterrevolutionary Council of Trent (1545–1563), the Catholic doctrine on transubstantiation becomes fully articulated — some would say fully sclerotic. It is, quite simply, that at the moment of consecration the bread and wine become *really* the body and blood of Jesus, while retaining "the *appearance* of bread and wine." The Protestant counterpositions, naturally, are much more varied, but — in those churches that retain the communion service at all — they generally fall under the Lutheran term, "transsignification": the bread and wine, that is, remain "only" bread and wine, while taking on the symbolic weight of the Lord's body and blood.

The fascinating thing about this quarrel is that the Catholic, orthodox position, which certainly *seems* the more mystical, in fact affirms the innate dignity of "the fruits of the earth and the work of human hands," their suitability as vehicles of the divine. The Protestant position, on the other hand, which seems commonsensical — and may, indeed, be so — is based upon the assumption that "mere" bread and wine could not possibly be anything more than symbols of the holy, whose radiance annihilates the mundane. Transubstantiation affirms immanence; transsignification desires transcendence.

I told you I know the name of what is below or behind science fiction that compels it to treat food as "under erasure": it is gnosticism. Like gnosticism — cancel that, *as* gnosticism — science fiction asserts the human as the vector-sum of cosmic forces far transcending the human, and among whom the human can hope only for annihilation or assimilation into the Holy Other. Detective fiction, in contrast, is a fiction of immanence, affirming the innate value of the quotidian, and asserting that God, as Graham Greene once said in an interview, "isn't 'up there'; he's down around here somewhere, don't you think?"[12]

I adduce an example from one of the most brilliant contemporary texts I know: one that I use to explain to my students the point of Sartre's *Being and Nothingness* (1956) and Camus's *The Myth of Sisyphus* (1955). In one installment of Bill Watterson's *Calvin and Hobbes* comic strip, Calvin, the fourth-grade Berserker, and Hobbes, his tiger (if you haven't read the strip, don't ask, and I'm sorry for you), are sitting thinking underneath a tree — very Blakean, that. Frame one, Calvin speaks: "I don't get this death business." Frame two, Calvin continues: "I mean, if we're all going to die anyway, what's the point of anything?" Frame three, they meditate silently. Frame four, Hobbes speaks: "Well, there's seafood...."

If this is not great art, then we should trash the concept. Watterson — a political philosophy major — has said that Calvin is named for John Calvin, the most ferociously antisacramental of the early reformers, and Hobbes is named for Thomas Hobbes, whose *Leviathan* may still be the most resolutely realist, creaturely view of life our culture has produced. Calvin — the kid *and* the Reformer — is a Great Gnostic: the world is not enough, can never *be* enough for our unbounded hunger for life, and life more abundantly. Hobbes — the tiger *and* the philosopher — voices an absolute orthodoxy: the world, *tout court*, is *what you've got*, or, as Wittgenstein would write nearly three centuries later, in the *Tractatus Logico-Philosophicus*, "the world is all that is the case."[13]

I hasten to add, as a Reform Kabbalist Roman Catholic atheist — and proud of it — that I believe we humans, poor things, have no real choice but to be both gnostic *and* orthodox, serving the Lord, whoever he or she might be, cannily in the paradoxes and contradictions of our state. Cosmic amphibians all, makers of star charts *and* street maps, kaballahs *and* cookbooks, we survive only by living in — and writing — both mythologies at once. Immanence and transcendence, as Paul Tillich spent a lifetime showing, are not alternate choices, but, in their rich mutual tension, our lot.

And that's why the "genres" are not really "genres," anymore than Gnosticism and orthodoxy, if you take them both seriously enough, are a simple binary exclusion. In Frederik Pohl and C.M. Kornbluth's *The Space Merchants* (1953), Alfred Bester's *The Demolished Man* (1953), Gibson's *Neuromancer* (1984), Burroughs's *Naked Lunch* (1959), Pynchon's *Gravity's Rainbow* (1973), James Crumley's *Dancing Bear* (1983), Lawrence Sanders's *The First Deadly Sin* (1973), and more books than it is worth naming, the alternatives meet, join hands, and dance together, telling us — what all literature has to tell us, if it's worth the eyestrain — that we are the children of light *and* the sons and daughters of darkness, that our daily bread is the gross matter of our mortality *and* the impossible, wished for viaticum, that the stories we love to hear and tell are only — *only?* — possibilities of being or, as that great, good, and mourned man, Northrop Frye, called them, "Fables of Identity."

Which leads me to my last Item. At the end of "The Man with the Blue Guitar," Wallace Stevens summarizes the tension between the two dreams of articulate humankind: the dream of going beyond the human, and the dream of *staying* there and finding it comfortable. His conclusion about that high warfare is also mine, in some of the most heartbreaking, shattering poetry I know:

>...we shall sleep by night.
>We shall forget by day, except
>The moments when we choose to play
>The imagined pine, the imagined jay.[14]

Let the church say, "Amen!" There's seafood.

13

You Bet Your Life
Death and the Storyteller

Let us begin, as all human things begin, with a story.

It is universal, ancient, and simple enough that you might not think it *is* a story, but it is. Here is one of my favorite versions: Wile E. Coyote, as is his wont, is in fervid pursuit of the Road Runner. The Road Runner runs — that's all he *does*, dig — off a cliff and his momentum carries him to the opposite side. Not so Wile E. Midway across, in midair, he looks down, realizes he *is* in midair, stares bug-eyed for an instant at the audience, and then plummets, like a stretched and snapped rubber band, to earth: the way characters plummet only in Warner Brothers cartoons or real life.

Here is another version: an old man who foolishly squandered the love he had earned finds himself alone, in the open, in a storm that is partially a storm of his own despair. And staring at the camera, as it were, not unlike Wile E. Coyote, he tells us, "When the rain came to wet me once and the wind to make me chatter, when the thunder would not peace at my bidding, there I found 'em, there I smelt 'em out. Go to, they are not men o' their words: they told me I was everything; 'tis a lie, I am not ague-proof."[1]

The Road Runner runs, and that's all he does. "Just runnin' down the road's his idea of havin' fun," as his theme song has it. The thunder will not peace at King Lear's bidding, not because it *dislikes* Lear — any more than the Road Runner dislikes or even notices Wile E. — but because the thunder *doesn't even know Lear is there*, and wouldn't give a damn if it did know.

No, grimmer than that: there *is* no thunder, as a conscious force that can cease or continue at Lear's or anyone's bidding, until somebody *imagines* meteorology as personality. Shakespeare knows as well as we do, maybe even beter, since he articulates it with the proper metaphysical shudder rather than with our currently hip, disengaged shrug. Here it is, the pith, the germ, the immense and fecund shaggy-dog joke at the heart of the story I have just told and, I think, at the heart of all the stories there are to tell. We have invented death, and in inventing that have invented ourselves, and in inventing ourselves invent, by necessity, the gods whose service will be a balm for our mortality, but whose very existence — we have always known — is *predicated* not on their resplendent presence but on our own aboriginal and gnawing lack.

This is basically nothing more than an echo of Karl Rahner's haunting observation that to "be religious" — which for him and me means simply to "be human" — is "to believe it is meaningful for a miserable creature to talk into the endless desert of God's silence."[2] It is also an argument that the only really convincing proof of the existence of God is also the most profoundly uncomfortable one. I mean, of course, the Anselmic or ontological proof, which in one form of another insists that life must have some final meaning just because we ourselves thirst so for it. It is what in the old seminarian's joke was called "the proof from wishful thinking." The problem is, you see, is that it is the only proof we can trust, and that, like the anxiety-ridden uncertainties of quantum theory or chaos theory, or for that matter the truly scary act of saying "I love you," we can trust it only on the firm basis of our distrust. What human speech, from the Upanishads to the Mandelbrot set, is *not*, finally, wishful thinking?

I realize I am getting rather thuddingly paradoxical here, sort of like G.K. Chesterton on a *really* bad day. It is just that I do not know any way to talk about death that is not, ultimately, paradoxical or even, when you break it all the way down, *funny*.

My second favorite deathbed speech — familiar in theater lore — is David Garrick's: "Dying is easy. Comedy is hard." It is a wink at the camera, of course, and therefore a triumph. And it is a joke; better yet, a joke *about* joking: almost what a fashionably francophone contemporary theoroid might call "postmodernist" — to use one of the goofiest phrases ever developed by our culture. Apocryphal or not, this last utterance *is* directed into the "endless desert of God's silence," just because it demands either to *impose* order on the radical, quintessential moment of all disorder or to have that human order validated by — what? By whatever or whoever the hell it is that implants in us the expectation and longing for a Sense To It All and, at the same time, curses us with the wit to see through even our most splendid fabrications of that Sense. I *hope* Garrick really said that, because if he did, he joins Job and Samuel Beckett, and the mad King Lear and vertigo-stricken Wile E. Coyote, as chief anatomists of our cosmic discontent. The Anselmic proof is not our solace. It is our cage.

But you want to know what all this has to do with science fiction, fantasy, and the possibility of technologically achieved immortality. Okay.

Henri Bergson in his crucial essay *Laughter* reduces all comedy to variously performed versions of slapstick, and I think that is just right. The impulse to laugh, Bergson says, is our spontaneous aversion response to "something mechanical encrusted on the living."[3] We laugh, in other words, because in any truly comic situation we recognize — and forfend — the killing joke that for all our intimations of immortality we are, God help us, mortal machines wearing ourselves out in the very exercise of our magnificence. The well-dressed gentleman with cane and bowler who trips on a banana peel is the *ur*-mytheme of all comedy because his fall is *the* Fall, showing us again that all our fondest hopes are built on clouds and subject to vapors: that we not, as we have heard, ague-proof.

Now this may remind you of Frank Herbert's *Dune* (1965), or Stanley Kubrick's *2001: A Space Odyssey* (1968), or even Ridley Scott's *Blade Runner* (1982), because in each of those stories the central character comes to a kind of confrontation with the core of human longing — to live forever — and comes to a different kind of realization about what really achieving that wish might be. In each case, though, we are dealing with a manifest version of Bergson's formula or, to nail it down, of Coyote's and Lear's plight.

Paul Atreides in *Dune*—let us discount the unfortunate sequels to that brilliant book—achieves godhead, or at least messiahhood, but at the expense of any faith or hope in the very messianic message he comes to announce, and for which he becomes universally venerated. This crackling irony — Herbert, after all, was raised Catholic — is lost in David Lynch's otherwise splendid film redaction (1984). Immortality for Paul is finally the immortality of becoming the story of his life, knowing the story he becomes can never, never approach the reality he was. I think *Dune*, despite its immense popularity, gets discussed so seldom at science fiction conferences just because it is so close to the cosmic slapstick that is, finally, all discourse on death. You *will* die. *We* will die. *I* will *die*. All storytelling tries to avoid that fact — as, every hour of the day, do we — and all storytelling, in avoiding that fact, only makes it the more inescapable. We want to become stories because stories go on forever and we do not. We are mortal engines, and mortal engines give out, wear down, or break up, and all that is left of them — God is not mean but She sure is strict — is their, every pun intended, plots.

And if we could devise a physical immortality, could invent a way to keep the engine running forever and ever, we would still not be free of the burden of mortality: precisely because mortality is, by honest appraisal, a "burden" not in the sense of a heavy load we must carry and would dearly love to shrug off, but a "burden" in the sense of the bass-note to the song we make for the Lord or ourselves or others, it really does not matter. An immortal man, if he were to remain a man, would still have to be able to tell himself the story of his own life, and that would require a sense of closure — that is, a reinvention of death. Because death is not the enemy to be feared, but rather the origin and goal of any meaning we may choose to call human. With mutants I have no truck.

Mutants like, say, Dave Bowman at the end of *2001*, the most gnostic of the fables we are discussing, and by my definition the most purely "science fiction." Bowman, avatar of our species and last descendant of the cosmically befuddled ape moonwatcher who began the story, breaks on through to the other side, becomes the Star Child — a godlet at the very least — and returns to contemplate Earth from the light-year playing fields that are now his home. And what does his enigmatic expression in that indelible last scene signify? For all the Sturm and Drang sublimity of Strauss's music, I am not sure it does not signify a kind of melancholy. Because the godlet, poor little fella, has passed beyond the possibility of all stories and therefore past the possibility of selfhood: all dressed up and nowhere to go. Or as Wallace Stevens — who I sometimes suspect explains *everything* says — in "Esthétique du Mal":

> The greatest poverty is not to live
> In a physical world, to feel that one's desire
> Is too difficult to tell from despair.[4]

You will notice, by the way, that I am conflating technological and theological ideas of immortality: and you will also notice that I am none too subtly dismissing both of them. It may indeed be possible to extend life indefinitely by transmitting brain waves to silicon chips or through freezing and resuscitation — Swanson's TV Dinners? Or it may be that, Patrick Swayzes all, we will float toward the big Klieg light at the heart of all Being, there to spend eternity — uh — shining on. To reveal the full extent of my recidivism, let me admit that I find neither prospect especially attractive, or indeed interesting. I said at the beginning, paraphrasing William Years, that we have invented death. It is now time to put the formula properly: death has invented us.

Which brings me to the end of *Blade Runner*. The movie — sorry, purists — is better than the novel it is based on, paradoxically because it is closer to what Philip K. Dick at his best is really *about* than is *Do Androids Dream of Electric Sheep?* (1968). Dick is our poet of the simulacrum in his strongest work, exploring that concept before Jean Baudrillard even knew how to spell it. If you can make a perfect replicant of a human — so runs the essential Dick plot — how can you say that your replicant is not, *tout court*, human? It is a serious problem. It bothered the hell out of René Descartes and John Locke but gave Mary Shelley and E.T.A. Hoffmann some terrific ideas for stories. And it is obviously based on the progressive definition of the body *as* an engine that began in 1616 — not long after *King Lear* — with William Harvey's discovery of the circulation of the blood and the human heart as a simple pump.

It is no more than a classic black box problem, really. If I can make a machine that does what *your* machine does, then I will have replicated your machine, although I can never open the impenetrable black box to see what your machine really is. Right?

Wrong. Dick knew and *Blade Runner* knows that the human engine becomes the *human* engine — becomes conscious — only by predicating its mortality. So when Deckard (Harrison Ford) and the replicant Rachel (Sean Young) escape to that improbable pastoral outside hellish Los Angeles at the end of the film, they both know that Rachel is programmed to die at an unspecified date. As Deckard says, "I didn't know how long we'd have together — but who does?"

And *this*, I think, again quoting Stevens, is "The reverberating psalm, the right chorale."[5] The liberating joke that makes *Blade Runner* the most satisfactory of our stories is that Deckard, the "natural" human, learns from Rachel, the "artificial" human, not just about loving somebody but about accepting limits, mortality — that is the precondition to love or, indeed, any truly human act. To live at all, you have to bet your life. Deckard finds neither the ironically messianic immortality of *Dune* nor the dubious transcendence of Bowman in *2001*. He finds, and embraces, the human condition. *Blade Runner*, in fact, is in this respect hardly a science fiction story at all, but rather a story about escaping from science fiction's gnostic shudder at the fact — and the necessity — of death.

Thomas Pynchon, in his disarming autobiographical introduction to *Slow Learner*, says something that angered me when I first read it and continues to anger me because I think it must be true:

> When we speak of "seriousness" in fiction ultimately we are talking about an attitude toward death — how characters may act in its presence, for example, or how they handle it when it isn't so immediate. Everybody knows this, but the subject is hardly ever brought up with younger writers, possibly because given to anyone at the apprentice age, such advice is widely felt to be effort wasted. (I suspect one of the reasons that fantasy and science fiction appeal so much to younger readers is that, when the space and time have been altered to allow characters to travel easily anywhere through the continuum and thus escape physical dangers and timepiece inevitabilities, mortality is so seldom an issue.)[6]

Of course, no so-called mainstream writer has used the motifs of science fiction, and of its parent mode the Gothic, more extensively or more stunningly than has Pynchon. And this, I think, only adds weight to his observation — just as *Blade Runner* strikes me as a supremely "serious" science fiction story exactly in its deconstruction of the genre to which it manifestly belongs.

Science fiction longs for immortality and shuns death just as, by and large, it shuns palatable food and good sex: because these things speak of the body and bodily limitations, and the inevitability of closure. I called it "gnostic" and it certainly is that, but there is an even better, because formal, name for it.

The one time I was lucky enough to have a drink with the great classicist and lovely man Moses Hadas, we were talking about Longus's *Daphnis and Chloe*. And Hadas, sipping his sherry, said, "You know, that's really what science fiction is: pastoral."

And "Bingo!" I said to myself. That was in 1967, and in a funny way I have spent the last twenty-five years trying to figure out *why* I said "Bingo!" (Actually, since it was 1967, what I probably said was "Right on!") And it was not until the topic of immortality and science fiction was proposed that I had my *satori*.

Science fiction is pastoral (and, by the way, pastoral is gnostic) because it posits a place and/or a time where you can play at life rather than bet your life. A place — Arcadia, the Forest of Arden, the Galactic Imperium, cyberspace, same-o same-o — where we can believe for a while that we are ague-proof and that we are not all vectors on and victims of gravity's rainbow.

And of course it is escapist, granting — just for the moment — that that rather stupid word has any meaning. It is as deeply escapist as *Daphnis and Chloe* or *A Midsummer Night's Dream* or *The Winter's Tale* because it tells us that we do not die, while all the time we know that we do. Like all good pastoral, it is the first phase of the Anselmic proof. And like all good pastoral, if it is really good, it brings us through to the second, more difficult phase of that proof. Look. You do not go *to* a pastoral place, you go *through* a pastoral place. You go into the magic forest and dance with the masquers there precisely so you can come back, healed and refreshed and wisely innocent, to the world where agues and gravity — the closure that makes us real — claim their due. To do otherwise is to become other than human and to invite, or invent, another, more meaningless kind of death: what theologians call the "second death," the annihilation of meaningfulness. Edgar Allan Poe knew this. It has to be why the narcissist, death-defying, and therefore life-denying prince in "The Masque of the Red Death" is named Prospero. That act of naming, maybe the crucial act of the whole tale, is what my mentor, rabbi, and *sen-*

sei, Harold Bloom, might call an "antithetical trope." By naming the misguided prince after the most unavoidable and self-limiting of pastoral characters, the presiding genius of *The Tempest,* Poe surely means to suggest that his story is a dark version of the pastoral myth, an assertion that "escapism" is dangerous only when it forgets how grimly serious it really is. (I am assuming, of course, that you are at least old-fashioned enough to believe that sometimes people write stories because there are certain things they want to say, and they know what they are doing, as opposed to being mere ectoplasmic inscriptions of power for the dominant establishment.)

Does that mean that science fiction manifests a fundamental evasion? Yes. As I argued in another essay for this series, the genre privileges the transcendent over the immanent, the gnostic liberation from the body — and that includes the myth of the body as immortal engine — over what Alfred Whitehead called the "witness" of the body. And in this evasion is both its resilience and its weakness. Just as the complementary resilience or weakness of its mirror twin, the mystery, is privileging the *thanatos* principle over the pleasure-pain principle. Put it this way. All mystery stories begin, in one way or another, with a death; all science fiction stories, in one way or another, try not to end with one.

I had intended to talk about *Gilgamesh* here, a story that I take, even more than *King Lear,* to be an unremitting and absolutely essential prelude to any sane discourse on death and storytelling. But since John S. Dunne has addressed that subject, and since no one has written more brilliantly or valuably about that poem, I defer on the same grounds I would defer to sit in with Sonny Rollins. So let us talk about Homer's *Odyssey* instead.

The gnosis, the knowledge that once gained will take us beyond the realms of the corporeal and mortal — beyond the human realm of story — has an opposite. I am glad to give it the punning name *nostos.* It means "homecoming," and classical critics use it to refer to the moment when Odysseus returns to Ithaca. In fact, I realized as I was working through the poem again, it describes the whole movement of the *Odyssey.* Everybody in the poem — Telemachus, Menelaus, Nausicaa, Circe, Calypso — knows the sublime story of the Trojan War and that its heroes will always be the definitive transcendent heroes of the culture. Odysseus has another problem, though. He wants to go home. He wants to go back to his aged wife, his aging life, and — Athena makes this clear — his human death. In other words, his whole fabulous voyage back home is a voyage out of the fabulous and into the quotidian. The *Odyssey* is an antignostic gospel invented centuries before the gnostic itself was named. And its central moment — at least in my current reading — is maybe its most famous and certainly its least understood episode.

What do the Sirens sing? Not the promise of sexual delight; this man, after all, has just left Circe. Not knowledge or power; Odysseus is always already *polutropos*, skilled in all the tricks. What they promise, explicitly, is to tell Odysseus and his men, over and over again, the story of their immortal exploits before Troy; they promise him that he can live forever in the *Iliad*. And the seduction is so strong that one screams to be untied so as to follow its allure, the allure of infinitely deferred closure, the pornography of the spirit. But Odysseus — Stevens's "Central Man," perhaps — both leaves his ears unstopped against the song and binds his will against following it, and the ship sails on, back from gnosis to nostos and into the blessedly flawed paradise that William Wordsworth calls "a simple produce of the common day."[7]

And that, too, is the reverbating psalm, the right chorale. Between the technological and the theological — our less picturesque version of the Sirens and the Wandering Rocks — I will choose neither, wishing them both lots of luck, and cleave to the bitter charity of Story itself, Story that always gives us back a fragmented image of our own fragmentation but also whispers that our proper immortality is the embrace of our proper mortality, and that the world as we tell it to ourselves is never enough and thus is quite enough. This is no more paradoxical than the Anselmic proof. In fact, it is the Anselmic proof, as are you and I in our splendid disorganization and noble, funny quest for a love that will stay.

But I have not yet told you my favorite deathbed speech. It is not really a deathbed speech, although it takes us back to our original story of Wile E. Coyote. It is just the old joke about the guy who falls out of a fiftieth-floor window and is heard to say, as he passes the thirteenth floor, "Well — so far, so good." That guy, along with Wile E., Lear, Deckard, Odysseus, and Stevens, is a hero of the consciousness. And his line, uttered out of the certainty of doom and the gallant refusal to face it with anything but full awareness, is as good a story as you can tell. So may we all.

14

Seven Types of Chopped Liver
My Adventures in the Genre Wars

It's an often-told tale, but it bears — or demands — repeating. When Woodrow Wilson was President of Princeton, one of his political cronies asked him why *academic* politics was so byzantine, vicious, and brutal. "Ah," replied Wilson. "You must realize: there's so little at stake." I have long thought that that should be engraved upon a plaque to be displayed prominently in every department of literature throughout the western world. (And, by the way, just wait and see if some politically correct dwortz with a complete set of Baudrillard *in translation* doesn't, sooner or later, observe that my reference to the "western world" disqualifies me as hopelessly Eurocentric. We are living, brothers and sisters, in the Season of the Silly.)

Emmis: there is so little at stake. But, my God, how much it costs us to admit that. The underside of Wilson's joke is not ironic but gigantically sad. As a former Chicagoan who now lives in, of all places, Lompoc, California, I can attest to the painful truth: the smaller the prize, the more bitter the contest. (Ask the awards jury of the National Book Critics' Circle — or Tonya Harding, whoever's sitting nearer at the bar.) If, as the axiom runs, work expands to fill the time allotted for it, then, contrariwise, anxiety grows in inverse proportion to the real importance of its object. Years ago, at Northwestern, a senior colleague of mine told me, "Look, just publish your book, attend department meetings, and then, when you get tenure, you can do whatever you want. Look at me: I grew a beard." Jesus.

And that's, I guess, where I want to begin: with the simple, ineluctable, and crushing truth that most of what we academics, we teachers, we critics do is in any realistic taking of accounts trivial. We quarrel about the curriculum; we worry about the "canon" of our subject, be it science fiction or lesbian–Chicano postmodernism, and shouldn't that be lesbian–Chican*a* postmodernism? And we gather, as often as we can, at scholarly conferences to draw from one another warmth, and the reassurance that we are *not* as alone as we, most of the time, feel. It's an AA kind of thing: hands trembling around my coffee cup, cigarette precarious in the corner of my mouth, I say, "Hi, my name is Frank and I'm a recovering New Critic," and you all wave, "Hi, Frank!"

Not that there is anything wrong with that. Psychoanalysts, dentists, plumbers, and microbiologists do the same thing — even lawyers, though it must be hell getting the scales off the hotel carpet afterwards. It's the nature of a profession to be esoteric, shamanic: we know something, can do something, says the shaman, that the rest of you don't and can't. But we will do it to, and for, you, and it might hurt a little but that's just because you can't — heh heh — see the big picture the way we do, but it will in the end be good for you. Pay on the way out.

And every once in a while the shamans need to get together, trade a few new tricks, tell a few jokes about the biz, feel like *insiders*. They used to call them "mysteries" or "guilds"; now they're acronyms, like AHA, MLA, or — my personal favorite — the American Society for Eighteenth Century Studies, which parses as ASECS. The only real difference between then and now, as far as I can guess, is that the parties are probably less fun these days.

But I'm doing exactly what I want to accuse *our* profession — the profession of literature — of doing. I'm evading.

"Science Fiction, Canonization, Marginalization, and the Academy" is the jaw-breaking topic that draws us together, and with luck the topic that will pull us apart. Because any belief in our authority to "canonize" or "marginalize" literature is the one delusion beyond all other delusions that is absolutely poisonous to whatever dignity may accrue to the profession we profess.

I remember, in the 1960s, reading one of John W. Campbell, Jr.'s interminable editorials in *Analog Science Fiction/Science Fact*. He was rejoicing over the fact that the English professors had just discovered detective fiction, and were beginning to write intricate, *soigné* essays and books about Ellery Queen and Raymond Chandler, full of references to *Oedipus Rex* and Dostoyevsky, establishing — actually, "vetting" is the right word — the form as a legitimate, though of course diminished, version of the great tradition of humanistic discourse. I no longer have that copy of *Analog*, so cannot quote accurately, but as I remember it, the source of Campbell's joy at this development was, quite simply, that the academics, having discovered detective fiction as a rich and preyable-upon food source, would probably leave science fiction alone, to be pursued only by those who wrote it and loved it.

Peace to his honorable ashes. If he had only known.

For here we are, in the aftermath of the French Invasion of the Anglo-American university, producing forest-annihilating numbers of essays and books, and distillery-supporting numbers of scholarly conferences, on "science fiction"—a term, let us remember, that was invented only in 1927 by that splendid mediocrity, Hugo Gernsback. We are now an established subroutine of the Big Program that is American education, and a lucrative one. When I taught my first course in sf, in 1971 at Northwestern—I was dragooned into it—it seemed fairly *demimondaine* to most of my senior colleagues. (How melancholy to remember that there was a time when the majority of my colleagues were "senior"!) Now, at the University of California at Santa Barbara, the course regularly enrolls six to eight hundred students, supports a large number of graduate student teaching assistants, and is a strong bargaining-chip with the Dean, come budget time. I should feel justified by all that, *nicht wahr*? Well, shouldn't I?

By now it should be clear that I am using the idea of "Science Fiction, Canonization, Marginalization, and the Academy" as a pretext for circling around, and nipping at, the deeper theme that underlies it, namely: what do we really think we're doing?

Let me repeat what I have been saying for more than a decade now: I teach sf, I write about sf, but in my heart of hearts I do not believe that there is any such thing as sf; and if that sounds perversely paradoxical, remember that you are dealing with a reader who was trained mainly by near–Jesuits and near–Rabbis.

My Jewish father and beloved *sensei* Harold Bloom writes, in his stunning introduction to *The Book of J*, about the author of the Yahwist tales in Genesis, that "Genre is an inoperative category when the strongest of authors are involved."[1] As a good—that is, loyally heretical—son, I want to extend that self-evident truth, and insist that genre is an inoperative category when all but the weakest of authors are involved. And to the weakest of authors we owe, in decency, not critique but simply charity. I recently received a book for review called—the title *is* the story—*Outworld Cats*; the kindly man passes by in silence.

Even before Harold Bloomed into my life, though, there was Brother John Vianney, C.F.X.—that's Xavieran Brother to you—my proctor for reading period in my sophomore year at St. Francis Xavier High School, Louisville, 1957. When I asked him for something good to read from the school library, he suggested *The Picture of Dorian Gray* (he thought it a highly moral tale, but that's another story). Besides the *filé-gumbo* sensuality that wafted up as soon as you lifted the cover, and which I surely did dig, what struck me most was one of the aphorisms with which Wilde, a decaffeinated Nietzsche, sprinkles the "Preface" to the novel: "Books are well written, or badly written. That is all."[2]

Imagine, as they used to say in Republic serials, if this information fell into the wrong hands. If we take Wilde's flippancy seriously — and I think because it is absolutely flippant, it is absolutely serious — then it is an assertion even more outrageous than my revision of Father Bloom's thesis: genre is an inoperative category. As they also used to say in Republic serials — the ones where people rode horses instead of rocket sleds — Bad Medicine; bad for Chief, bad for Tribe. (This, by the way, is at least my third violation of our constipational rules of "correct discourse" with which we have inhibited our power to speak rationally about things that really matter.)

I repeat: if Wilde is right, then genre is an inoperative category. I think that Wilde *is* right. I also think — no, I *know*—that this is the innermost mystery of our craft, not to be revealed to those outside the inner circle, lest the circle itself be revealed to be, nakedly, centerless. Course numberings would disappear — why *not* talk about seventeenth-century masques and Astaire-Rogers films at the same time? Departments would tremble; does it really make sense to teach Shakespeare and ignore the fact that, at precisely the same time, Cervantes also was touched by God? Deans would fall; something of a silver lining, that, I grant, but still a perturbation of the order of things-as-they-are-supposed-to-be. (Remember how poignantly the Israelites, in the time of their deliverance, missed the stupidities of their Egyptian taskmasters — and grow wise.)

Could we, as professionals, professors, professing our proficiency in the profession of literature, live at all comfortably with Wilde's axiom? I think not. The burden it lays upon us is too intolerable, too quintessentially human, too truly scary. "Books are well written, or badly written: That is all." What that means, when you break it all down, is that *you* have to decide about the book you're reading. It means — to paraphrase that good man George Steiner — that when you open a book you take your life into your hands. We all know the truth of that, of course. But how much of our time do we spend suppressing that truth? I can answer only for myself, and I am not happy with the answer: a lot.

As usually, uncannily, happens with the topics proposed for the volumes I am asked to contribute to, I find myself wading in deeper and more turbulent waters than I would have chosen to enter. But since I am already half in, like Macbeth, I see no point in turning back, since it would be as exhausting as to go forward. Let's, then, drop the last disguise.

Why are we here? Why do we become students and professors of literature? "Inquire of every thing," says Marcus Aurelius, made famous again by Hannibal Lecter, "what it is in itself." What—*really*—brings us to this place? It can only be that, for each of us in our various ways, the written word— no, strike that, the act of storytelling—is somehow central to our idea of ourselves. It is, to quote John Berryman, our toy, our dream, our rest. It is— how seldom we say these things out loud—our bread and wine. And that makes this—and I have never said anything more seriously here or elsewhere—a kind of communion service. But we are humankind, so we are much more interesting for our flaws and scars than for our hoped-for perfections. And as humans we are also cosmic amphibians, living in the everyday and the visionary, the quotidian and the *alcheringa*, the dream-time, and never quite sure which is which. (That, as a matter of fact, is the point of a great many of our most important stories, from *Gilgamesh* to Alfred Bester's *The Stars My Destination* [1956] to Orson Scott Card's *Ender's Game* [1985].)

Now what I have to say here is difficult: bear with me if the syntax and the logic seem to be turning involuted, counter-intuitive, or even French. We are here because we love, and live, stories. Not "Science Fiction," "Fantasy," or "Horror"; those are marketing labels, like "Mystery," "Western," and "Romance," that make perfect sense on the shelves in B. Dalton's or Borders but none whatsoever in the present context. Just stories. That would be a beautiful fate, to talk forever with trusted friends about the stories you loved most. In fact, with a little wine and a lot of sex, it would be—well, you know. (Loaf of bread optional.)

But this is not paradise, it is the university. And the university, not despite but just *because* of its deeply engrained absurdities, is a nice little model of consciousness itself, at least consciousness in a fallen world (G.K. Chesterton says beautifully that Original Sin is the one theological proposition for which there is empirical evidence). We are brought together by love: I am convinced that the most desiccated, embittered, and alienating teacher of literature you can find preserves, somewhere in the Gothic dungeons of what's left of his heart, the gnostic, aboriginal flame of the first time he fell in love with a story. But how to preserve that flame in this world, where there are, in sequence, exams to be taken, careers to be built, tenure to be sought, and, finally, power over literature to be coveted? The world as idea is diminished to the world as will.

I have become increasingly convinced that "science fiction," Brother Gernsback's label, is scandalously inaccurate. If we must call it anything, I suggest we call it "technological gnosticism." From Mary Shelley to H.G. Wells to William Gibson and Octavia E. Butler, its archetypal plot seems to be the attempt of a hero, a consciousness trapped in a mechanistic universe, to discover whatever there is of transcendence within or beyond the quotidian. Sometimes the quest succeeds (Wells's *In the Days of the Comet* [1906], *2001: A Space Odyssey* [1968]); sometimes it fails (Mary Shelley's *Frankenstein* [1818], Aldous Huxley's *Brave New World* [1932]); sometimes it is ambiguous (Thomas Pynchon's *Gravity's Rainbow* [1973], Gibson's *Neuromancer* [1984], *Blade Runner* [1982]). But always it is the same quest.

Now I want to suggest that the gnostic paradigm applies not just to the fiction, but to the lives of those who write it, write about it, and teach it. In the gnostic *ur*-myth, Sophia, "Wisdom," falls from or departs from the original unity or plenum, the "Father," into the world of the Contingent — our world — from which, eventually, she is redeemed to re-ascend to the Whole. I remark in passing that the power of this myth is evident in its reappearance in venues as disparate as the sublimities of William Blake and the K-Mart soporifics of Scientology.

A graduate student of mine recently told me that one of my colleagues had told her, and the other people in his seminar, that what they should do is read the journals, find out what critical approaches seemed most *au courant*, and plan their dissertations to catch that wave. Sound advice, I told her, if you want to regard this business as a nine-to-five profession. But if that *is* what you want to do, then why not be completely honest and get a gig playing piano in a whorehouse? The pay would be commensurate, and you'd meet a more varied set of people.

Because that kind of thinking, in the context of our lives, is the fall of Sophia into Contingency. It's the moment when we allow theory to usurp reading, when we allow the concept of genre to intrude upon the naked power of the story at hand, when we turn the Book (a holy word) into the Text (a shabby one). It is not even *trahison*, but *révolution des clercs*, the school of resentment's rage to efface what they themselves cannot create, the diffident arrogance of a De Man, a Derrida, a Jameson, a Fish, all of whose productions Pope anticipated well before the fact:

> Beauty that shocks you, parts that none will trust,
> Wit that can creep, and pride to lick the dust.[3]

W.H. Auden, Pope's smarter reincarnation, cut even closer to the bone in his 1946 poem, "Under Which Lyre." Contrasting the antinomian sons of Hermes with the sons of the academically correct, department-forming Apollo, he writes of the god of tenure:

> Unable to invent the lyre,
> [He] Creates with artificial fire
> Official art.[4]

And there it is. Arguments about canonization and marginalization, whether they are about science fiction or the need to hire an "eighteenth-century man" or about the place of Middle English studies in the curriculum, are really about—a phrase as bitter as Campari straight, no rocks—"official art." The power to say that, e.g., *Stranger in A Strange Land* (1961) is science fiction and, e.g., *The Handmaid's Tale* (1985) is not has, finally, nothing whatsoever to do with the nature of either book, nor with the always-already-null category "science fiction," but only with power. I find it grimly amusing that contemporary critics, so acute to note and catalogue inscriptions of hegemony in virtually every stream and tributary of human endeavor, either forget about it or become uneasily complicit in the game when it's a matter of their own profession. When Michel Foucault told us that power always inscribes only itself, I think he *meant* that "*only.*" And I think he was right. Authority in the academy is simply territorial behavior, and territorial behavior in the fashion of the great cats: baring fangs we never intend to use, and spraying the trees we want for our private scratching-posts.

Hence my title, "Seven Types of Chopped Liver." It's chopped liver at a Sabbath meal on the wrong side of Delancey Street, but it's *paté* at a cocktail party in the suburbs. It's "the movies" on Saturday night with your—how to say this in the age of semantic fascism?—with your personfriend whom you desperately want to canoodle, but it's "cinema" when you're writing for *Camera Obscura* on, say, "Homosociality, Anality, and *Gigi.*" In both cases the thing named is the same, but the name is an inscription of power or relative powerlessness—a spraying. And there's so little at stake: only the radiance of the thing in itself.

But let me be autobiographical for a short while: given my age and lifestyle, it's probably high time.

I fell in love with stories—gnostically, entered the plenum—when, on Valentine's Day in the sixth grade, the object of my passion, named, no kidding, Martha Sue Fritz, gave me a Groff Conklin paperback anthology of "science fiction," when I didn't even know what it was. Grumpy and disappointed back home (never mind what I'd hoped for), I flipped at random to a story with at least a catchy title: "Blood's a Rover," by Chad Oliver. Three or four hours later—I had even missed *Dragnet, Big Town, Martin Kane, Private Investigator,* and *Inner Sanctum* on the radio—I had concluded, finishing the book, that there could be nothing neater than being a writer. Not a spaceman, not an interdimensional swashbuckler, not the hero of the stories, but the guy who *made up* the stories. (The scientific term for this condition is, or should be, *Nerditas Incipiens.*) Oliver was the finest of men, as were Poul

Anderson and Frederik Pohl and, even if she *was* a girl, Judith Merril. I'm still not sure I was mistaken.

Martha Sue Fritz sank below the horizon of my desire, or at least of my initiative, not long after. But she had initiated me, though not as expected. Science fiction — especially my beloved *Planet Stories*— comics, my dad's Mickey Spillane mysteries, which he bought for the covers and I read for the stories and then *I* noticed the covers, Ellery Queen, our old Gustave Doré-illustrated Bible, A.L. Rouse's brave and (I was to find) hopelessly inadequate translations of the *Iliad* and the *Odyssey*, and then in high school, Wilde and the forbidden, preached-against-at-Mass *Lolita* (1955) and *Les Fleurs du Mal* (1857) for which I was slammed on the head by Brother Benedict, C.F.X., when he saw it on my desk, as he shouted, "Don't you know this man was a *sinner?*" and tore up the *—my—*book (I guess this was my first argument with literary authority): when I imagine the plenum I remember that time. Because there was not *a* time in *all* that time when stories, when what John Barth calls plangently "the ocean of story,"[5] were not my toy: my dream: my rest.

The point of this perhaps stupefying narrative is that concepts of genre, or of hierarchy, of more and less great, never meant very much to me. Of course I heard about them, and of course I behaved as if I knew what they meant, but to be perfectly honest I never did. I discovered Johann Sebastian Bach, Charlie Parker, and Jerry Lee Lewis at about the same time. Though I still think Bird is better than the other two, it does not seem anarchic to me to put all three on the CD carousel and punch "Random Play"— and while we're talking about carousels, I'll throw Rodgers and Hammerstein and, what the hell, John Phillip Souza into the hopper too. When I arrived at Cornell for my first teaching assignment, I had finished a dissertation on William Wordsworth's *Prelude* and published an essay on William Burroughs's *Naked Lunch* (1959). A very senior colleague, and distinguished scholar of romanticism, asked me how I could reconcile writing about those two authors. I felt like Stevie Wonder in the Louvre: say *what?*

As I did six years later, when I began teaching science fiction at Northwestern. As I said, I was dragooned: the course was already established, but the fellow who taught it was on leave; and I'd written a few things about horror films and such, so the chairman asked me if I'd like to take it over for a quarter. Of course I would, I said. The quarter, it turned out, would extend to over twenty years, doing sf at least once every one of those years.

But here's an interesting detail, the one that brought on that Stevie Wonder feeling again. By my third year of doing the course, I discovered — through the infallible grapevine that, serpentine and anonymous, both undermines and reinforces all workplaces — that I had jeopardized my position in the department by teaching science fiction. Enrollments were large; I had published a book on Wordsworth and a book on film; and that was precisely the problem. It was becoming increasingly unclear what my specialty was — or if I had a specialty at all. In an unforgettable interview with my chairman — the same one who had given me sf in the beginning and a dear and valued friend to this day — I was told, "Frank, you should think very seriously whether you want people to regard you as a generalist."

I had never heard the word before, and I fear I heard it now in a different key — major as opposed to minor — than my friend had intended. "I'm a *generalist*!" I thought to myself, with the excitement of the *bourgeois gentilhomme* discovering that he'd been speaking *prose* all his life. "A *generalist*: Wow." Soon I found myself teaching, besides sf, a year-long course in World Literature and courses in the Film Division, and writing a book on Saul Bellow, Norman Mailer, John Barth, and Thomas Pynchon. My critical heroes, psychopomps in the absolute sense of the word, had been, besides Bloom, R.P. Blackmur, Kenneth Burke, and Northrop Frye; and it is a source of the 3:00 A.M. blues for me that I know I will never approach the splendor of even their minor work. And "generalist," applied to those national treasures, is not only an honorific but a first articulation of their strength; and it may be significant that, of the four, only Bloom holds a Ph.D. in English. Ever get the feeling God is winking at you?

But *basta*! There is one genre in which I *do* believe — autobiography — and only St. Augustine, Benjamin Franklin, Malcolm X, and Graham Greene should be allowed to practice it. I have heard more than my share of public reminiscences by mid-life and mid-talent intellectuals, and they are uniformly underwhelming. ("God," as the actor Jack Cassidy used to proclaim when in his cups, "it's lonely at the middle!") And I do not want to appear *soi-disant* ("And then I wrote..."), *faux-naïf* (Tom Sawyer among the cannibals) or — the ninth circle — old fart ("Listen, youngster, in my day we didn't even *have* Xeroxing and e-mail!"). The point of my tangled tango down memory lane is just to indicate what, and why, I have to feel the way I do about the idea of "canonization and marginalization" as it applies to our racket. I think it is the fallen world of the Contingent and the blind angel Samael, gnosticism's bungling and blind god of the Contingent.

Which brings me to the second half of my title: "My Adventures in the Genre Wars." Truth to tell, there were none. A psychic Switzerland, I made my separate peace with the literary Mods and Rockers, went on teaching and writing about what I cared about — my chocolates and cuckoo clocks, if you must — and largely ignored the battles of the theorists. Because the theorists reminded me of the warring angels in *Paradise Lost* (1667), impossible abstractions crunching about in clunky armor that only got in their way: an NFL of wraiths, or the new clothes with no Emperor inside.

My one brief sortie was when I did an essay for *The Wilson Quarterly*, in 1990, on Deconstruction, observing that D-con brought up some interesting points but was by no means the apocalyptic transvaluation of all values it claimed to be.[6] J. Hillis Miller responded with a charmingly vituperative letter in a later issue, accusing me of intellectual dishonesty tantamount to proposing a threesome in a crack house. And my real problem, he wrote, was that "McConnell is no longer where the action is."[7] As Jack Benny used to say so eloquently: *Well*! I didn't *want* to be where the action was. I didn't want to play piano in a whorehouse, or dance before Samael the blind. I was — wow! again — a generalist, and the plenum and I were getting along just fine, thank you. Kenneth Burke wrote a letter, too. He thought I had a flair for pointed anecdote, but had some suggestions about how to extend my argument. I bought a fifth of brandy, a jar of oysters, and a jar of caviar.

All of this should strike you as excessively smarmy. Authority may be the blind god, but if he did not exist, we would have to invent him, even to our cost. It is only the Contingent that can lead us *to* the plenum, and even Auden admits that, if the sons of Hermes were allowed to run things, things would quite soon go to hell in a handbasket. Apollo, Samael, the Dean, the curriculum, the canon, official art, the profession, the racket: they are not *altogether* the enemy, because without their constrictions — *our* constrictions, *our* mind-forged manacles — we could never really taste the pang, the sudden glory, of our freedom. To paraphrase Gerard Manly Hopkins, it is the mess man was born for, embedded in the *substantifique mo'élle* of consciousness itself, which is language. Ever since Saussure — actually, ever since Augustine — we have known that the paradox of language is that it is *both* authoritarian and anarchic. You can say anything you want (at least before the invasion of the academic brain police); you cannot say anything that is not allowed by the rules of grammar. If a photon is both wave and particle, a word is both a liberation and a binding — quite literally, in the usage of magic, a *spell*. *En chaque signe dort ce monstre: un stéréotype*, writes Roland Barthes: "Within every sign sleeps the monster, the stereotype."[8] (Actually he is reprising here the much stronger observation of E.M. Cioran, *Sous chaque formula gît un cadavre*, "Beneath every formulation lies a corpse."[9]) But, as Wittgenstein says, *Ein Ausdruck hat nur im Ströme des Lebens Bedeutung*: "An expression has meaning only in the stream of life."[10]

I apologize for the near–Talmudic citing of opinions. (Well, in fact, I don't.) But the emergent point is that the arguments against authority are hardwired into our very nature. Given that eternal, internal struggle reaching from our forebrains to our institutions and even to our crucial yearning to give to the Void a human life, are there any sensible things to say?

I think there are, and here are a few. First, we can rethink the idea I have heard, that science fiction is engaged in *contests* for authority. The Greek word for "contest" is *agon*, and it is under this term that we have, in the academy, largely configured our behavior. *Agon* implies "struggle," "competition," even — and obviously — "ant*agon*ism." It suggests that we are in a *serious* business. (Miller, in his letter about my D-con piece, said that he would not have bothered to discipline me were it not that the issues involved were so "deadly serious."[11] *Deadly serious*? As in an essay in a policy-oriented journal on a critical fad?)

I suggest that we shift terms from Greek to Latin. The Latin word, *ludus*, is roughly the equivalent of the Greek *agon*, but its connotations are "play," "game," even — and obviously — "inter*lude*." It suggests that we are in a *delightful* business.

I said earlier that most of what we do is trivial. That was an obvious half-truth, or I wouldn't be here. We *are* trivial when, accepting the covenant of Apollo or Samael, we posture as if what we did *matters*; but we *matter*— and matter in ways poor Samael can't see — when we admit — and giggle about it, too — that all our canons and borderlines and frontiers are there just so we can cross them. "The sons of Hermes love to play," but "Apollo's children ... have to think/Their work important."[12] I would nominate Auden as our patron saint, were that itself not just too Apollonian, and were not he already, I am sure, enjoying another and more exalted tenure.

So let me turn from Auden to Roland Barthes, another of the critics, along with Blackmur, Burke, Frye, and Bloom, to whose memory and achievement every day I light a candle in the quiet room of my heart. The line from Barthes I quoted earlier is from his inaugural lecture in 1977 as Professor at the Collège de France. The lecture is a short and stunning explication of what he thinks it means to be a teacher and writer, and I think it is a holy thing. All language is the inscription of power, he argues (his friend, that brilliant and vile man, Foucault, is obviously in the wings here); all literature is an inscription of power, and all university systems are ditto. *Except* for the act of teaching — which subsumes the act of writing criticism. And that is a performance whose glory is its *powerlessness*. It is *ludus*, not *agon*, the free space of discourse where the Contingent cedes to the plenum. I translate his conclusion, with apologies for violating his prose: "That experience has, I think, an ancient and currently unfashionable name, which I will dare to say here in the full complexity of its etymology: *Sapientia*, no power, a little knowledge, a little wisdom, and the greatest possible delight."[13]

14. Seven Types of Chopped Liver   143

At this point, with Barthes as my shield, let me begin to conclude. I have referred throughout this chapter to what we all do for a living as both a profession and a racket. If it is *only* what we do for a living, then it *is* only a profession or a racket. It's the chopped liver syndrome again. "Profession" and "racket" are the same thing, except the guys in the racket don't have to claim so much of their income for the I.R.S.

But neither of these terms really applies to anyone here; otherwise you, like me, wouldn't *be* here. Think about the word, *vocation*. It means "calling," but it also means "called." It is pretty close to the concept of "shaman," and to the Hebrew word for prophet, *navi*, and a galaxy away from anything like the concept of "priest," "minister," or "authority."

It's what you are. It isn't a profession, it's a habit of, and compulsion to, the highest level of play. It is not useful or practical, and there is no sane reason for society to support it, except that society is smart enough to realize that *it* would go mad without it. It is anarchic and sloppy and, at its best, it can't really tell the difference between Henry James and Robert A. Heinlein, and boy do the priests ever hate *that*, but it wears the smile of Dionysus and the priests dare not approach too close. It will not cure racism or urban crime or gender-discrimination because it knows Auden was right when he said, "Poetry makes nothing happen,"[14] but without it everybody would forget why they *wanted* to do those things. It is as sublimely useless and silly as religion itself. Maybe it is religion itself: the catch in the breath of a dying animal at the opening sentence of *Neuromancer* or Berryman's last "Dream Song" or Magic Johnson almost anytime. *Sapientia*, says Barthes. The Fool in *Lear*, say I. What Moses heard from the burning bush.

Or, maybe, just — teacher.

Science fiction — which, we now all agree, is not really a genre at all — provides two salient examples of the chances for the ultimate outcome of the any challenge to authority: Wells's *The Time Machine* (1895) and Arthur C. Clarke's *Childhood's End* (1953).

In Wells, the Eloi, the Children of Light, are allowed to play and gambol in a fruitarian Disneyland to their hearts' content, but always with the suppressed awareness that the Morlocks, the un-men who run the machines that keep the world alive, are maintaining them only eventually to devour them. (No one who has lived with the administration of the University of California recently can fail to find this scenario uncannily familiar.)

In Clarke, on the other hand, the Overlords, outworld beings only *superficially* Satanic, dominate and micromanage human society, but only so that the humans themselves may eventually evolve into purely spiritual beings and join the cosmic community of *other* purely spiritual beings from which the Overlords, sorrowing servants of the plenum, are forever excluded. (No one who has listened to the self-justification of the University of California recently can fail to find *this* scenario uncannily familiar.)

Both Wells and Clarke are wrong. The true story would be a union of the two, but such an act of subtlety and visitation of grace that can come, if at all, only in the playing-out of a life and not in the telling of a tale. We are teachers, shamans. And our vocation is to teach courses in "Science Fiction," courses in "The Novel," courses in "Shakespeare," because that is what Samael needs us to do to keep the records straight. But our *vocation* is to teach science fiction, *and* the novel, *and* Shakespeare, and the early recordings of Miles Davis, if we feel like it, because that is what we need to stay alive. That is Barthes's *Sapientia*—which, need I say it, is the Latin for the gnostic Sophia.

I am delighted by the Joseph D. Miller essay that titularly refers to "The Grails of Science Fiction"—because I have long thought that the whole activity of criticism, and therefore of teaching, is a belated version of the Grail Quest. In Wolfram von Eschenbach's *Parzival*, the earliest fully developed Grail narrative, Parzival finds himself in the Grail Castle and witnesses the mystery of the Grail. He is not sure what is going on, and being a shy lad, asks no questions about what he has seen. He is berated for his failure to ask: if he had only asked the right questions, he is told, the Grail would have been redeemed and the wounded Grail-King would have been saved. He leaves the Castle in disgrace, and spends most of the remainder of the book learning what he should have known when he first entered the Castle. Finally, at the end of his walkabout, he comes back to the Castle, asks the right questions, and the king and the land are healed.

Take Parzival as the reader—you, me, our students—and take the Grail as the Book (I will *not* say "text"), and take the Castle as the edifice of authority, forbidding and even a little adversarial, that both needs the mystery completed, and yet is anxious about it being too well completed: for when the mystery of the Grail *is* done, then the Castle of the Grail declines to irrelevance. And you have our collective autobiography.

We all—we and our students and our colleagues—were at one time or another surprised by the radiance of Story, and found ourselves in thrall. And we entered the Castle of the mystery, only to find that the Castle was inhospitable unless we learned the right questions. And learn them we did, if we were lucky and canny, and ask them we did, and we regained our first joy of the Grail, as the Castle, now no longer necessary, evanesced around us.

But it is still a real Castle for our students. And *our* quest, unless it was all just a bad joke, which it could have been and still could be, should have turned into a vocation.

That vocation, at least as I see it, is to teach that authority is the least of things to worry about, to keep an eye fixed steady on the Grail itself, and to obey the rules of the Castle even as we inculcate the questions that will end the Castle. And, one last thing, always to ask those questions with the smile of Dionysus on our lips. There's so *much* at stake.

15

The Missionary Physician, from Asclepius to Kevorkian

In confronting the topic of "disease and medicine in science fiction and fantasy," I am reminded of the title of J.D. Bernal's classic book, *The World, the Flesh, and the Devil* (1929), all three of those terms being understood as the entrapments of history — money, sex, and sheer cussedness, say — that impede the soul in its ascent to the purity of union with godhead.

Now, that's a classically gnostic notion, implying absolute contempt for society, for the life of the body, and for the passions — what else can "the devil" mean? — in favor of a spiritual, immortal essence of the self, in eternal congress with what the Kabballah calls the "Ain-Sof," the Gnostics call "The Father" or "The Pleroma," and Paul Tillich calls "The Ground of All Being."

And that's pretty heady stuff. It can feel right, on a day when the sun is shining, the check is in the mail, you're convinced she really loves you, and your shoes don't hurt. Gnosticism, in other words, is a helluva good religion if you feel great. And if you *don't* feel great, it's got a lot of ways of convincing you that you actually *do*. Pain is only a delusion: the Buddhist *samsara* as opposed to *nirvana* (copies to Kurt Cobain, founder of the group with the latter name and suicide); pain is "redemptive suffering," the dodge of those Christians who, like Teilhard de Chardin and Pope John Paul II, want you to believe that Uncle Ernie's lung cancer is a suffering offered up — I love that phrase, "offered up" — for the salvation of, well, the world; or pain is an impolite imposition by that underbred fellow, Satan, easily overcome by proper meditation upon the Scriptures — the answer of America's premiere writer of science fiction, Mary Baker Eddy.

Gnosticism, in other words, doesn't need doctors — or says it doesn't — just because doctors either heal or soothe the body, and gnosticism, whatever else it does, really hates the body.

15. The Missionary Physician

Christopher Hitchens, in his grand *Buchlein*, *The Missionary Position*, relates a television interview with the late hospice-founding celebrity, Mother Teresa — or, as Hitchens has termed her on television, "the ghoul of Calcutta":

> She described a person who was in the last agonies of cancer and suffering unbearable pain. With a smile, Mother Teresa told the camera what she told this terminal patient: "You are suffering like Christ on the Cross. So Jesus must be kissing you." Unconscious of the account to which this irony might be charged, she then told of the sufferer's reply: "Then please tell him to stop kissing me." There are many people in the direst need and pain who have cause to wish, in their extremity, that Mother Teresa was less free with her own metaphysical caresses and a little more attentive to actual suffering.[1]

I relate that anecdote, not only to chill you to the bone, but to make the point that what we call "mainstream" science fiction is, by and large, much more on the side of Mother Teresa than on the side of her unhappy charge. I have argued before that science fiction is essentially gnostic. I now insist, under the pressure of our common topic, that if it is a genre at all, it is so *only* because of its deep participation in the gnostic urge to be *elsewhere*: out of this time, out of this body, out of this iron chain of circumstance we call life. Jesus is kissing you. We are Men Like Gods. We are Last and First Men. We are Lazarus Long, or cowboys in the bodiless eternity of cyberspace. Or we are Thetans, spiritual beings from another dimension, entrapped in and drugged into forgetfulness by the MEST, or matter/energy/space/time lower cosmos. That is the essential teaching of Scientology, founded by an important colleague of Isaac Asimov, Frederik Pohl, and the whole Golden Age generation, and it is also, precisely, the plot of *The Pearl*, one of the earliest and finest gnostic poems. If mainstream science fiction has never noticed Mary Baker Eddy as one of its guiding spirits, it has blushed to acknowledge L. Ron Hubbard; but in all honesty, it can afford to do neither.

And these are really not visions of the future. I have always maintained that people — even that lovely man, Fred Pohl — who defend science fiction on the basis of its predictive power are missing the boat — like the guys in Vegas who fade the faders. I mean, what's the *point*? So H.G. Wells may have predicted the tank, and Hugo Gernsback described radar, and Arthur C. Clarke imagined a communications satellite. Big damn deal. Make enough wild guesses and you've got to be right some of the time. Stay at the table long enough, with a bottomless stash of cash, and you *will* roll triple sevens. That's, as the British say, a mug's game.

No. Far from being visions of the future, these are — in true gnostic fashion — anxious expressions of profound discomfort with the present. And that means profound discomfort with the body — for the body is our interface with the present. Let me explain.

Pohl once told me, jokingly, that all science fiction writers are ugly. The reason? Since they were ugly, they couldn't make friends on the playground at recess or get dates for the prom — so they had to retreat into a world of their own imagining, replete with pleasures only they could enjoy, and hence became writers of science fiction.

I don't think that was entirely a joke. Not that science fiction writers really *are* ugly — the field has, of course, matinee idols like Chip Delany and Gregory Benford — but that a certain fear and loathing of the body as the body is built into the form. Think about the heroes and heroines of classic space opera, the perfect bodies of Flash Gordon and Dale Arden or of the moon-voyaging couple in the film *Things to Come* (1936), or of the statuesque male and female *Hitler Jugend* who adorned virtually every cover of *Amazing Stories* and *Planet Stories* during the fifties. Granted, those covers, along with the covers of my grandfather's *Police Gazette*, were my own personal introduction to the brave new world of eroticism, and as such are remembered with sincere, nay Proustian, affection. But isn't the "perfect body" precisely the fatal will-o'-the-wisp of those who hate the body — the opiate of the anorexics?

"Anorexia" is derived from two Greek words: the prefix *an*, a privative meaning "not," and the verb *oregomai*, "I desire." It means, in other words, "desirelessness" — *not* simply aversion to food — rather like the state of *nirvana* or the state of perfect, disinterested contemplation aspired to by the gnostics. It is anti-life, and it is notoriously difficult to treat.

It's difficult to treat — actually, it's damned near impossible to treat — for the same reason that science fiction, on the whole, has such a difficult time dealing with the idea of the doctor. (And you thought I'd never get around to the topic at hand, didn't you?)

According to the *Oxford English Dictionary*, the first use of the term "anorexia" was in 1588 — before William Shakespeare wrote *Romeo and Juliet*. Astonishingly, the first use of the word "anorexic" is not until 1907 — twelve years after Wells invented those passionless, dreamy stoners, the Eloi, in *The Time Machine* (1895). The condition was identified, that is, four hundred years before it was necessary to come up with a name for the sufferers of that condition.

Why?

Because, I think, before the end of the nineteenth century, there simply weren't enough anorexics around to be worth the naming. And now, as anyone with access to a tv set knows, there are enough of them to populate the talk shows — all the talk shows — for a whole season; and, more heartrendingly, to populate all the campuses at which we teach. And what's that got to do with science fiction? Everything.

Think about Case, the problematic hero of William Gibson's *Neuromancer* (1984). Like all cyberspace buccaneers, he entertains complete contempt for the body — for what he calls "the meat." (I am informed by some of my more advanced computer-weenie students, by the way, that it is common enough among them to refer to real-world, interpersonal encounters as merely "meat space" — the poor bastards!) At the beginning of the novel Case has been exiled from cyberspace, having been caught stealing information from the net. Surgically disabled from interfacing with the net, he is exiled to the punk hell of Chiba City. There he is visited by Molly, a beautiful, dangerous woman who enlists him on a risky enterprise, the reward for which will be his reinstatement as a cyberspace voyager, free again from exile in the mere dark wood or *selva oscura* of "the meat." They move to the Sprawl, the purgatorial mega-city extending from Boston to Atlanta, where Case is assigned a helper, the computer-generated personality construct of the "Dixie Flatline," the now-dead, greatest cyberspace jockey in history. Eventually Case, Molly, and Dixie ascend to the fabulous orbiting colony, Straylight, where the mission is successful. And the mission's ultimate purpose? To bring about the union of Neuromancer and Wintermute, two gigantic mainframes whose union — yin and yang — produces the ultimate Artificial Intelligence, able to connect with other AI's throughout the universe. And Case is returned to full health, his liver, spleen, kidneys replaced, free as promised to cruise the net and indulge his contempt for "the meat."

Now, it should be obvious that, splendid as Gibson's novel is, in all conscience he owes thirty percent of his royalties to the estate of Dante Alighieri. *Neuromancer* is a dark book (George Slusser has written brilliantly about the extent of its darkness); but it is dark just because it is — not an inversion — but a gnostic skewing of *The Divine Comedy*, perhaps the most *anti*-gnostic poem in the Western Canon. Case is Dante the pilgrim, Molly his Beatrice, and the Dixie Flatline his eminent precursor in the art, his Virgil. But the end of *this* comedy is not to behold the Multifoliate Rose of the Godhead and return to life *in* the body, *in* time, but rather to witness the birth of the purely abstract deity, Neuromancer/Wintermute, and return to the infinitely replaceable, therefore time-free body which is, really, only a vehicle to allow the mind to escape forever into cyberspace — not all that different, really, from the fata morgana "perfect body" of the anorexics. Man at his worst, as Kenneth Burke once observed, is separated from his proper life by instruments of his own devising, and rotten with the spirit of perfection.

In the world of the anorexic, doctors are sublimely irrelevant because the body is not a thing to be healed, or nurtured, but rather punished into ideality (which is to say, into abstraction). In the world of *Neuromancer* — and, I'd say, in science fiction altogether — doctors are relevant *only* because of what they can do, not *for*, but *to* the body.

As the *OED*, again, tells us, it's only comparatively recently that the word "doctor" came to mean, almost exclusively, "medical practitioner," with all the attendant mojo. (Here's an experiment you can try at home for fun. When I call the phone company to complain about a charge and identify myself as "Frank McConnell," the guy at the other end always responds, "Well, Frank, our records show...." When I identify myself as "Doctor Frank McConnell," though, it's always, "Well, yes, Doctor McConnell, just let me check our records here...." Dig? And I don't think he gives me the honorific and the politesse because he thinks I may be a Ph.D. in English Literature.)

"Doctor" comes from the Latin *doceo*, "I teach." So to be *doctus* is to be one who has been taught, and to be a *doctor* is to be a teacher: an expert, a professional, a *technician*: rather as to be a gnostic (Greek *gnosis*, "knowledge") is to be a guy in the know, a technocrat of the transcendent.

And to be that is to regard the body as a thing to be either overcome or improved upon — but *not* as something to be comfortable in on its own terms. Remember the opening voiceover of *The Six Million Dollar Man*: "Steve Austin, astronaut. We can *make him* stronger — faster." (I always want to add "hornier" — but that's precisely what the gnostic/medical orientation *doesn't* allow.)

It's an old delusion, the mind/body split, and it's probably all Plato's fault — although, as Friedrich Nietzsche understood, Plato didn't really *mean* to cause such a mess; really, now, no one who venerated Socrates can be all that opposed to horniness. Nonetheless, it's part of the bedrock of our culture, and it's been growing apace — if bedrock can grow — since William Harvey discovered in 1616 that blood is just lubricant and the heart is just a pump, since René Descartes in 1645 argued, epochally, that the body is just a machine with a bored spirit at the control panel, and since Luigi Galvani passed an electric current through vermicelli, causing his little dead worms to boogie, thereby inspiring not only Walt Whitman ("I sing the body electric") but the first ever authentic science fiction novel (written, significantly, by a woman).

Victor Frankenstein is surely the *capo* of all sf doctors. And what, precisely, *is* his real, unforgivable sin? This is like asking, what is the essential crime of Oedipus? Or what is at the core of Hamlet's *angst*? All three characters are so crucially, authentically mythic that they give us back an infinite array of answers to those questions, depending upon the angle of attack with which we *ask* them ("them" meaning the characters *and* the questions, since the characters *are* the questions).

In the present context — doctors, sf, and that old thing, the meaning of the universe — here's what I think about Victor Frankenstein's sin. He lost his beloved, madonna-like mother at an early age. He was raised with the family's adopted daughter, Elizabeth, as if she were his loving sister but also with the tacit understanding that she eventually would be his betrothed. And that's a kind of hygienic incest — incest, whatever else it is, being a passionate denial that the body of the beloved can be *other*—can, in fact, really be a "body" ("somebody") at all. He fed his young imagination on the works of Paracelsus, Cornelius Agrippa, and the other gnostic/alchemists, went to University at Ingolstadt, and heard from his kindly tutor in chemistry, M. Waldman, that the guesses of the mystics were becoming realities in the researches of the new scientists: the philosopher's stone could be achieved, after all: the transmutation of lead (body) into gold (spirit). So Victor set about to discover the secret of life, did so, and in the hope of creating a race of greater men, animated a giant body stitched together from corpses. And as soon as the animated creature opened his eyes, and stared at his creator, his creator stared back and, repulsed by the ugliness of his creation, fled.

And that's the sin: not to create life, but to be repulsed by the life you have created: to give symbolic birth to a "new man" and then to reject that birth, in a grotesque parody of parturition, because it is still a *body*. Think about Wells's Dr. Moreau; Robert Louis Stevenson's Dr. Jekyll; Rotwang in Fritz Lang's *Metropolis* (1927); the bloodless, passionless Dr. Susan Calvin of Asimov's overrated robot stories; the disinterested experimenters who make retarded Charlie Gordon a genius only to have him fall back into a worse retardation in the *really* best sf story ever, Daniel Keyes's "Flowers for Algernon"; or Ash, in Ridley Scott's *Alien* (1979), himself an android, contemptuous of the flesh and in love with the purity of the inhuman. To be "incarnate" means, precisely, to be "made flesh," to be of woman born, to live *in* time, in what W.B. Yeats calls "the frog spawn of a blind man's ditch"[2]; and in that sense the gnostic urge is, precisely, anti-incarnational. It does not want the Word to be *made* flesh, but rather for the flesh to burn away so that the Word can conquer, and by conquering escape, the world. At its terminus is the exaltation of the anorexic, the loathsome faith of Mother Teresa — at its terminus is the "dream begotten by the hatred of death upon the fear of true immortality, fondled in secret by thousands of ignorant men and hundreds who are not ignorant."

That last bit isn't me, by the way. It's C.S. Lewis, describing the folly of science fiction in his own great science fiction novel, *Perelandra*.[3] And Lewis helps us see how, while sf participates essentially in the gnostic urge, it also, by a blessed swerve of bad faith, refutes the doctrine. (This should surprise no one, since storytelling is always wiser than doctrine.)

As that crucial thinker and vile man, Michel Foucault, tells us, post–Enlightenment medicine ("sf" medicine, for our purposes) is, in its obsession with the improvement of the body, another objectification of the body, another inscription of power, another benevolent—or *faux*-benevolent—manifestation of the need to control. Philippe Ariès, in *Western Attitudes Toward Death* (1960), makes the same point, less shrilly than Foucault: the fact that we die now, by and large, in the antiseptic anonymity of hospital rooms rather than in our own homes is actually a technological blasphemy, a denial of the reality and dignity of death itself. The missionary physicians, who would save us from our own corporeality, have done great things, but they have also depleted what Alfred North Whitehead called the *enjoyment* of the very body they wish to exalt and refine. Really: aren't we the first culture in history who count calories, spot-check cholesterol, and make love with the sole purpose of not dying? We *are* a gnostic culture. Even our national obsession with pornography is a sign of it, since pornography—the fantasy of the "perfect body" again—defines the flesh as a purely objectified, scented, depillatoried scene of gratification—a "meat puppet," in Gibson's brilliant phrase—that, since it cannot respond, is as disposable as a condom and as insignificant as a wet dream. We glorify our intellectuality by making sexuality a trivialized commodity. Our pornographers are not lyricists of the flesh. They are Anabaptists with Leicas.

But notice. All the missionary physicians from sf I enumerated are failures, their gnostic voyages wrecked on the shoals of the intransigent flesh. They discover that we *are* mortal if we are to be human, and that our life is, must be, in Alexander Pope's astonishing phrase, only—only!—"this long disease."[4] Science fiction at its profoundest denies the very gnosticism for which it yearns, and that conflictedness is its great value for our increasingly conflicted era, and its inestimable gift to such almost-sf writers as William Burroughs, Thomas Pynchon, Don DeLillo, and Jonathan Lethem.

For sf—mythology, not theology—cannot forget what Whitehead, again, calls "the witness of the body."[5] And since it cannot forget, it is forced to remember another kind of medicine, another kind of doctor, who existed before doctors usurped the term.

Pharmakos is the Greek word for what I mean, and though masculine in declension, it is taken to be feminine in syntax. The source of our "pharmacy" and "pharmacology," it is usually translated as "witch." But that is a male imposition upon the history of female healing. *Pharmakon* means, equally, "drug," "medicine," and "poison." So a *pharmakos* is, basically, a "wise woman," skilled (*not* learned) in the life and death of the body, or, simply, a "healer." In Mexico today — if you know the right people — you can find a *Curandera* — a healer, almost always a woman — who will give you roots and teas for your pain, not to deny it or transcend it, but to soothe it so you may reenter your own life.

Mind you: I would not go to a *Curandera* about a broken tooth or an attack of gout. But I would also not go to a doctor — or, to be realistic, an HMO — to be reassured about my possession of *my* body, *my* own life. I'm simply discussing alternate, and essential, attitudes towards life in time. And mind also: I do not wish to be called a "feminist" any more than I wish to be called a "Marxist," say, or a "Rosicrucian." All firm opinions, as the divine Oscar should have said and certainly believed, are vulgarities.

Nevertheless, it is undeniable that the tradition of the healer — the *yin* side of the circle — has been overshadowed by the exploratory, experimentalist, *yang* heritage. Ever live in a small town and try to find a female ob-gyn? Woman — the women's tradition of medicine — knows birth as no male ever can and therefore understands death as no male ever can. Men are puzzled and frightened by both, and therefore are driven to transcend or deny the riddle: "You nurse the kids, honey — I've got to go slay a dragon." As Thorstein Veblen suggested long ago, that may be the heart of all male narratives.

Thus, the god of healing, Asclepius, is really more on the *yin* side of things. His power is to guide the body through its dying life to a human death, accepting the body as, not the carapace of the self, but the self *it*self. And thus Jack Kevorkian — whom I regard as a rather heroic fellow — is a legitimate heir of Asclepius, defending the right of humans to possess their lives and their lives' ends away from the desiccation of life-support plumbing and so-called "heroic measures." It's a different kind of medicine, a different kind of mission. Like storytelling itself, it seeks to lead you into, rather than away from, your life. It's why Socrates's last words, in the *Phaedo*, are a reminder to make a sacrifice to Asclepius: for a life well and truly lived.

Science fiction boasts less healers than it does doctors, just because its concern is — whether it recognizes it or not — with the anxiety, the inescapable *malaise*, of the gnostic urge. Fleeing the body, it always returns to the body. And that paradox is not just its real glory, but its connection with the central myths of our culture. As G.K. Chesterton says, there are two ways of getting home, and one of them is to stay there. Science fiction, gorgeously, takes the long way round. Let me conclude with two texts without comment.

The last written, and my least favorite, of the Gospels, that of John (circa 120 C.E.) gives us a gnostic Jesus, a strange visitor from another planet, who would be quite at home in sf. John's Jesus is a luminous being, hardly *there* save for his *obiter dicta*: in John's Last Supper, there isn't even a sharing of the bread and wine among the twelve, just a long, rather tedious monologue by the Christ. Food, after all, is a tawdry thing for the true gnostic to muck about with. John's Jesus, effectively, is a resurrected being even before the resurrection.

In the Gospel of Luke (circa 90–100 C.E.), on the other hand, the *most* narrative of the gospels, Jesus is a figure in and of the world, in and of the body. It is Luke alone of the evangelists who tells the birth of the babe; Luke alone who sets the Sermon on the Mount not on a Mount (an exalted place) but on a plain (a man speaking to men); and Luke alone who tells the most wonderful of the post-resurrection narratives. Listen:

The tomb has been found empty, and no one knows what that means. The next day, two disciples are walking to the town of Emmaus. A stranger — Jesus, of course — joins them, talking with them about the things of God and man, but they don't recognize him. They urge him to come to dinner with them. They recline to eat. And, in Luke's sublime phrase, "they recognized Him in the breaking of the bread": in the life of *this* body, in the body of *this* life, in the holy complexity of human time. Luke's risen Jesus is less "the Christ" than he is the ratification of our life as we live it. I think Luke's Jesus could have shared a cup or two with Plato's Socrates.

And sf — like us all — is torn between the two gospels, and fortunately falls back from John's transcendence into Luke's immanence, keeping us sane (a word which in Latin also means "healthy," in the only sense of "health" that makes sense). Early legends about Luke, of course and rightly, described him as a physician.

"The imperfect is our paradise," says Wallace Stevens.[6] The fallible, dying, and sensuous body is our only real Pleroma. And like the travellers to Emmaus, we recognize God — and ourselves — in that most gloriously mortal of activities, the breaking of the bread.

16

The Science of Fiction and the Fiction of Science

A Storytelling Animal in an Inhospitable World

I really think it's all the fault of William Wordsworth. I could be wrong, of course: since I wrote my first book, on Wordsworth's *Prelude*, I've tended to assume that a lot of what's good and almost all of what's not in the modern imagination is finally, somehow, his fault — the Ronald Reagan of our visionary climate. To paraphrase Frank Kermode on John Milton, he made it possible to write and think badly in a whole new way; and this, like inventing a really *new* sin, is a remarkable accomplishment.

But here — "here," by the way, is the whole, sublimely, inconsequential, "two cultures" debate — I've got, I think, the smoking gun. In the preface to the 1800 edition of *Lyrical Ballads*, Wordsworth — was any poet, by the way, ever more ironically named? — famously redefines the classicist idea of "poetic diction" as the mere language of ordinary men, raised to sublimity by the heightened — but universally available — perceptions of the poet himself.

Now at its overwhelming — I want to say, Shakespearian — pitch of energy, this attitude accounts for an amazing amount of the best writing in English (or must we now say "Anglophone"?) of the last two hundred years. Revising and inverting Milton in the preface to *The Excursion*, he asks why the myths of Paradise should be only unattainable memories or a "mere history of what never was?" "For," he says in what for me is his most unavoidably exalted and exalting passage:

> For the discerning intellect of Man,
> When wedded to this goodly universe

> In love and holy passion, shall find these
> A simple produce of the common day.
> — I, long before the blissful hour arrives,
> Would chant, in lonely peace, the spousal verse
> Of this great consummation: — and, by words
> Which speak of nothing more than what we are,
> Would I arouse the sensual from their sleep
> Of Death....[1]

We could be reading William Blake here — Blake who despised Wordsworth — except that Blake's language never achieved this fusion of the cosmic and the quotidian. So much becomes possible in a passage like this: Charles Dickens; Thomas Hardy; Wallace Stevens; William Carlos Williams; Thomas Pynchon; Theodore Sturgeon; Isaac Asimov; Arthur C. Clarke; *The Three Stooges Go to Mars*; *Gilligan's Island*.

Perhaps I should explain.

To reenter — actually, recapture — Eden through "words which speak of nothing more than what we are" is the crucial effort of romanticism, and by now I think we can all admit that we are still living in the romantic era. It is also, as I've written often, a variety of the ancient "heresy" of Gnosticism — the faith that this world, or this scripture — any scripture — properly understood, contains a hermetic meaning that is the key to arouse the sensual from their sleep of Death. And what we mistakenly call "science fiction" is part of the same urge — is, in fact, the furthest reach of romanticism in popular culture (as opposed, by the way, to what? *Un*popular culture?). As is, to use a word almost irrevocably degraded by current academic critics, the discourse of science. We talk about "two cultures," in other words, not because there really *are* two cultures — there aren't — but because *believing* that there are preserves our comfortable Gnostic faith in the infinite promise of the everyday, our faith that words which speak of nothing more than what we are actually do speak of something more than what we are.

Not that any of this is all that new: God, is anything? The first romantics, as far as I can discern, had names like Thales, Heracleitus, Anaximenes, and Parmenides, folks who in a stunning leap of imagination argued that world is exactly what it is and subtly not what is. Think about Ludwig Wittgenstein's famous, corrosive opening to the *Tractatus:* "the world is all that is the case."[2] Everything is really water; everything is really fire; everything is really — shades of Alan Guth — a vacuum fluctuation; everything is really — shades of Haight-Ashbury — everything, man. It can't be denied, though, that we've turned the cottage industry of pre–Eleatic speculation into a heavy industry.

16. The Science of Fiction and the Fiction of Science

But enough history of ideas, already. What do Wordsworth, Gilligan, and Stephen Hawking have to do with one another?

Well, think about the difference between Dave Bowman at the end of *2001: A Space Odyssey* (1968) and Luke Skywalker at the end of the first *Star Wars* movie (1977). In both films, technology reaches a pitch of crisis where it must either collapse in on itself or be lifted — G.W.F. Hegel's term was *aufgehoben* — into spirituality. But one *Aufhebung* is what I, Chestertonian to the core, would call "orthodox," while the other is definitively gnostic. Perpend.

Dave Bowman, on a mission to discover the source of extraterrestrial communications from Jupiter, finds himself rapt — in St. Paul's sense of "rapture" through a stargate by alien entities — just call them God — who give him a second birth as the enigmatic, embryonic, starchild orbiting Earth, in the unforgettable last shot of the film, with that quizzical smile, the inevitable end-product of an evolutionary process that began before the dawn of time. Man, through no conscious effort of his own, has become more than man: in a way, it's a Christmas story, ending with the birth of a babe.

Luke Skywalker, on the other hand, has to learn to reject technology completely, to switch off his radar or whatever and use "the Force" as he launches his bomb into the heart of the malevolent Death Star. It's the moment for which the entire film has been waiting, and it's, to risk an oxymoron, transcendently gnostic. Nature, technology, things as they are are not to be collaborated with, but to be overcome. Dave Bowman emerges as a newborn humanity; Luke emerges as a conqueror. I'm not sure about Wordsworth, but I am reasonably certain that Blake, Percy Shelley, Wolfgang Pauli, and Hawking would prefer Luke to Dave.

Now let me be clear. I find most of feminist criticism hopelessly silly. Hell, I find most of *everything* hopelessly silly. Nevertheless, there's a point to the feminist argument that post–Enlightenment science is "male" in that it assumes a rhetorical stance of dominance over and — I shudder as I write this — penetration into the secrets of Nature — a word that, by the way, takes the feminine case in all Indo-European languages.

Not, as Seinfeld would say, that there's anything wrong with that. The Pythagorean Theorem holds whether or not you have a Y chromosome; light still hits you at 186,000 miles per second; and quarks and hadrons and leptons and all their tiny tiny pals are no respecters of gender — or do you want to try and describe a quarkette?

What I'm trying to describe, rather clumsily I fear, is a habit of speech that we've all, poets and physicists alike, acquired over the last couple of centuries. And a large part of my problem is that this habit of speech is a good thing, even despite the abuses to which it has given cause. Let's call it, with a nod to George Orwell, one of this century's patron saints, gnostispeak.

And gnostispeak is precisely why some of us labor under the delusion that there are two cultures. (I am, by the way, explaining what Wordsworth, Gilligan, and Hawking have to do with one another; have a little faith, can't you?)

C.S. Lewis remarks somewhere that the Renaissance is brooded over by two contrasting figures of power, the astrologer and the alchemist. The astrologer, rooted in the age of faith, assumes the world to be comprehensible, reading, but essentially unalterable: Dave Bowman, realizing that the cosmos is going to take him precisely where it wants him to go. The alchemist, rooted in the age of inquiry, assumes that the world is his playground, to be manipulated according to the demands of his own quest for selfhood: rather like Luke Skywalker, giving himself to and then using the Force.

Now I want to suggest that these two magi, the astrologer and the alchemist, brood over not only the Renaissance but also our current thought. And I also want to suggest that their antagonism is very much the stuff—or at least the speech—our dreams are made of. Poetry—whatever "poetry" is— and science—whatever "science" is—are not "two cultures," but simply two dialects of the same language, which happens to be the discourse of our happy discontent.

In what I more and more believe to be the single most inexhaustible of poems, *King Lear,* Gloucester, the good but gullible old Earl, articulates the orthodoxy of the astrologer: "These late eclipses in the sun and moon portend no good to us. Though the wisdom of Nature can reason it thus and thus, yet nature finds itself scourged by the sequent effects." And his bastard son Edmund—an even more wonderful villain than Iago—immediately afterwards articulates the stance of the alchemist, the Cartesian to his father's Thomist: "An admirable evasion of whoremaster man, to lay his goatish disposition on the charge of a star. My father compounded with my mother under the dragon's tail and my nativity was under Ursa Major, so it follows I am rough and lecherous. Fut! I should have been that I am had the maidenliest star in the firmament twinkled on my bastardizing."[3]

Now immediately after this remarkable *Kulturkampf* another character comes on the stage: Edgar, Gloucester's legitimate son, whom Gloucester will, terribly, disown and banish and who will ultimately redeem his father and sanction (I love tradecraft words) his half-brother. Edgar is very important—perhaps even as much so as Gilligan or as, to stir one more name into the soup, Prospero. But for the moment let him rest.

The astrologer and the alchemist attack reality from distinctly different angles; yet they seem to share—they do share—one essential assumption. That assumption, to quote Wittgenstein once again, is that the world is everything which is the case. Maybe we don't realize what a world of trouble that implies.

Martin Heidegger, that brilliant and vile man, observes that the central question of metaphysics is, *Wacht ist überhaupt Seiendes und nicht vielmehr Nichts?* Why is there something instead of nothing?[4]

Seems reasonable, right?

But then consider one of the first, and most important, koans—meditative riddles—given a Zen student by his master. It's the question of *u* and *mu*: *u* means "nothing" and *mu* means "something." The question, the koan, is, simply, "Is everything nothing or something?"

Now don't worry. This is not going to turn out to be one of those wow-we-knew-it-in-the-sixties-the-wisdom-of-the-East-shall-shake-the-West-awake-and-what's-in-the-fridge? bits of hippie retrocrap. Nevertheless, you can surely hear the difference between Heidegger's question and that of the sensei. It's a difference of *timbre* as much as of thought.

Why is there something instead of nothing? Is everything nothing or something? The first question—the protognostic question, I'd say—assumes that there is something, and that it can be read and reasoned thus and thus. It's the wisdom of Gloucester and also of his bastard Edmund: reality and can be known and seized—Clarke's *Childhood's End* (1953) or Alfred Bester's *The Stars My Destination* (1956) (and is there a more definitively gnostic title anywhere?)—but reality is *there*. Something *is*: even Parmenides, the first purely theoretical physicist, had to admit that. Actually, you have to assume that—that something is—if you want to tell a story at all, whether your story is the *Mahabharata*, Charles Darwin's *On the Origin of Species* (1859), Mickey Spillane's *Kiss Me Deadly* (1952), or Albert Einstein's Special Theory of Relativity.

But what about the koan? If nothing else it gives us a new perspective—if I were looking for tenure I'd call it something like a "paradigm shift" or, worse, "episteme"—on the relation between the mind and the world of things, i.e. on the motive for both storytelling and science altogether. Let me now violate all decorum by actually trying to explain a koan.

Is everything something or nothing? The point of the question is that it really isn't a question at all; it simply will not *tolerate* a binary yes/no, on/off response. It teaches you, by its unanswerability, that "this goodly universe" and "words that speak of nothing more than what we are" can—not must, but can—be regarded not as two different things, but aspects of a single, seamless process. You've solved the question when you *get* the question. Presumably, you stare at your Zen master, your eyes light up, you say "Oh, wow. Is everything something or nothing? *Yeah!*" And he smiles, you hug and whoop and holler, and go out for a drink or something.

The riddle carries the same kind of kick as Bertrand Russell's paradox (is the set of all sets which are not members of themselves itself a member of itself?); as Kurt Goedel's Incompleteness Theorem; as Werner Heisenberg's so-often-misconstrued Uncertainty Principle; and as St. Augustine's assertion, at the beginning of the *Confessions*, that we can know God only by first calling upon him. Moment by moment, we make the world by whispers; or as Wallace Stevens titles one of his last poems, "Reality is an Activity of the Most August Imagination."[5]

Mysticism? You bet. But the splendid paradox here — and when we think about thinking, we're Hansels and Gretels all, hopelessly lost in paradox — is that mysticism of this sort is actually a good deal more realistic than realism — at least than what I've been calling gnostic "realism."

Look. This isn't a good guys/bad guys thing. But the fact is that the mystic — the guys who thinks about how he knows as much as about what he knows — is in some important ways a little more in tune with The Way Things Are than his gnostic cousin. Remember the old gag about the difference between a psychotic and neurotic. The psychotic knows, with absolute certainly, that two plus two equals five; the neurotic knows that two plus two equals four — but the fact makes him nervous. My very favorite legend of the Baal Shem Tov is this one:

"The Baal Shem Tov and his disciples were traveling. While they were riding along the road a leaf floated down and settled upon the lap of the Baal Shem Tov. A bit further on a wind came and blew the leaf from the lap of the Baal Shem Tov to the ground; and there a worm came and crawled onto the leaf and used it for shelter and food. The Baal Shem Tov stopped the wagon and called his disciples. 'Look here,' he said. 'When the world was created, even then did the Almighty decree that this leaf should fall on my lap and that a wind should come and take it from my lap and blow it onto the ground where this worm would use it for food and shelter.'"[6]

What? You want to say. That's it? Well, actually, yes: that's it. *Die Welt ist alles, was der Fall ist.* Or — the Besht goes Wittgenstein one better here — *Die Welt ist nur alles, was der Fall ist.* Dave Bowman would get it; the most gnostically named Skywalker, not.

Wordsworth really wants to rouse the sensual from their sleep of Death. And Stephen Hawking, an authentic hero of consciousness, wants, as he says in *A Brief History of Time* (1998) (wonderful title!) to know the mind of God.[7] These are both exhilarating, Promethean desires without which our culture would be impoverished. Gilligan, on the other hand, good mystic — if not outright Taoist — that he is, does not seek to know the mind of God so much as he simply wants to dwell there. Everybody else, the Skipper, the millionaire and his wife, the movie star, the professor and Mary Ann, Faustians all, sees the island of exile as a problem to be solved, a place to leave. Gilligan sees it as a place to be, at least until events take him somewhere else. Is everything nothing or something, *u* or *mu*? His response is in effect another word, perhaps the most meaning-fraught word I know: *u* or *mu*? *nu*?

A completely Gilliganized world would, of course, be hell on Earth: nothing would work (you are welcome to ask my wife about this). But how sad a world it would be without him. He's the spirit of acceptance. He's (to invoke what I think the most fascinating, maddeningly complicated character in all of Shakespeare) the Fool who cures or at least salves the madness of the King. He's the necessary angel of earth, the mystic, the teller of shaggy dog jokes — since all real mystics are tellers of shaggy dog jokes.

All fiction, which is to say all human knowledge of any conceivable value, is to be found in jokes you know. And there are only two sorts of jokes, representing, as Blake said of Innocence and Experience, two contrary states of the human soul: punch-line and shaggy dog. Which type of joke you prefer is a rather strong indication of what sort of person you are, what sort of stories you like, and whether you think the "two cultures" debate is a serious issue or just another pretext for a conference.

The punch line joke implies that the universe is ordered, and either knowable or controllable. Whether it's "to get across the road" or the law of inverse squares, the punch line explains why there is something rather than nothing. Punch line folks like chess and bridge and Wolfgang Amadeus Mozart and books like *Childhood's End*. Shaggy dog folks, at home with the concept of indeterminacy, like poker and backgammon and Charles Mingus and books like Lewis's *Perelandra* (1944).

And if course it's clear that everybody — at least everybody not certifiable — is, alternately, both sorts of person. Some years ago I asked a friend of mine from Tokyo what his religion was (after the third sake you can ask that sort of thing). He laughed. "It depends," he said. "If things are going well for me, I'm a Confucian. If I'm confused, I'm a Taoist. And some day — well, some days I'm almost a Christian."

Sir Arthur Eddington once summarized quantum theory in the observation that "*Something unknown is doing we don't know what.*"[8] At the moment of that utterance Eddington was being a shaggy dog person — Eddington, who usually was one of the most punch line people of the century. Einstein's more celebrated saying — "The Lord God is subtle, but he is not malicious"[9] —

comes close to this but, for me at least, just misses the force of the final, definitive shrug: *nu*? But then Einstein, the definitive gnostic of the age, was notoriously distressed at quantum mechanics, spending his later years in quest of the Grail, the Philosopher's Stone of the Universal Constant that would put everything back in place again.

The point of the shaggy dog view of the world, though, is that there *is* no Grail; that the point of the quest is just getting back to where you started from. In my favorite, really really favorite tale, Sir Gawain journeys into the other world and confronts the daunting Green Knight only to find out that it's been an elaborate practical joke all along. And in my second favorite story, Gilgamesh, the anti–Dante, voyages into the otherworld questing for a cure for mortality only to find that there is none, that the world is — well — everything which is the case. The same sensibility permeates what is certainly one of the best sf novels written, Walter M. Miller, Jr.'s *A Canticle for Leibowitz* (1959), as well as, as well as I understand chaos theory, chaos theory.

I must confess that, until I began to contemplate this topic, it hadn't occurred to me that the quest stories I like best are the ones where the quest is a bust. The common, and inaccurate definition of the shaggy dog story is that it's a story with no point. The point of the story, in fact, is that *you listened to it*, all the way to the end. It's a model for the expectation of meaning, always deferred but always seductively there: faith, if you prefer the term, instead of certainty.

I don't want, in other words, Fermat's Last Theorem to be proved. I don't want a Grand Unified Theory. No more do I want an irrefutable demonstration of the existence of God, or to read a novel with absolutely no flaws.

Nor is this perversity. It's simply a conviction that consciousness is, as Wallace Stevens never tires of telling us, consciousness of imperfection, that the imperfect is our paradise. Two cultures? Not at all. Only one, which is, to quote Stevens again, "the poem of the mind in the act of finding/What will suffice."[10] The idea that the discourse of science and that of the humanities are growing farther apart holds true *only* if you're thinking about the compartmentalization of the modern university where people from different disciplines don't talk to one another because they never get the chance; or if you're thinking about the by-now-irreversible decline of academic literary discourse into hopelessly zero-meaning jargon. Let's face it: the prose of Fredric Jameson, J. Hillis Miller, or Gerald Graff makes the prose of science writers like Roger Penrose and Paul Davies sound positively lyrical. And then there's Ilya Prigogine.

But the professors of literature, having splendidly reduced themselves to self-parody (who would have thought one would ever long for the comparative lucidities of Kenneth Burke?) do not even deserve a voice in the debate: let them speak when they learn to speak plainly; for the rest of us, poor bastards crawling between Heaven and Earth, cosmic amphibians all, there is only the search, already doomed, for finality or, as a dear friend once wrote about scholarship, "A thrust to fill a bright gold ring/Whose challenge is its own defense."[11]

I was going to conclude with an elegant, really classy discussion of Mary Shelley's *Frankenstein* (1818): believe me, you'd have loved it. But, as the immortal phrase goes, the hand of fate stepped in. About two weeks ago, walking to our car with my wife in Santa Barbara, I tripped over an irregular piece of pavement and launched, headfirst, into the side of a parked SUV. Dislocated shoulder; thirty-two stitch gash over the left eye; concussion; and the entire torso one large bruise (actually, I looked like a giant plum with no nipples).

And there was no reason at all for it. I'd done nothing to bring it on myself, it had no antecedents or consequences — except, to be sure, considerable discomfort for me — and was my own little private demonstration that the world is everything which is the case.

And we don't like that: at least I know I don't. So we make up stories — myths or enthememes — to reassure us, in effect, that shit *doesn't* happen.

And all the while — this is the real glory of our species — we know that it does. I'd suggest that the most salient characteristic of humankind is its enormous capacity for radiant self-delusion about its own importance. Stars die, galaxies explore, Leo Tolstoy's Anna Karenina throws herself under a train, Bester's Gully Foyle finds himself the most important man in the universe. And our way is to make up tales to explain why those absurdities are not, really, absurd — as, in fact, I've just done by turning my fall in the parking lot into an intro to a theory of fiction.

We are the storytelling animal. And whether we call our stories *Principia Mathematica* or *Blade Runner* makes, finally, little difference. They are our assertions — like Lear, like Job — that we exist in an inhospitable universe but nevertheless choose to make sense of it. A tragic species, since aware of our own mortality, we have invented comedy to tell us that everything will be okay, anyway. And on that truth and on that brilliant lie are founded all the worthwhile stories — novels or theorems — ever told. They're our glory.

And they shine.

Epilogue
Memories of Frank

Paul Alkon, University of Southern California

"It has the beady eyes of a killer," Frank said, backing away. That was his response at first sight of the Keeshond Ellen and I brought along to an Eaton Conference one year. Placid little dogs of Dutch extraction, Keeshonden look like teddy bears and are about as menacing. I don't know whether Frank disliked dogs or just saw another opportunity for a comic turn. In any case it seemed a flawless performance for our benefit: the hasty backward motion, a facial expression of alarm that Laurence Olivier couldn't have improved on, and that perfectly chosen cliché, "beady eyes," that turned the encounter into a parody of itself and all those third-rate literary scenes that Frank detested and appreciated. His instinct for comedy was infallible. It made his Eaton papers the highlight of each conference, the grand finale. Even if not placed last, his was an act that simply couldn't be followed to any effect. More than delightfully funny, however, his papers were also always — I was going to say "challenging" but what I would have meant, what everyone who heard them would have understood I really meant, and what I might as well say, is "annoying." They were annoying. Not just mildly annoying either, but very annoying because almost invariably at some point they belligerently rejected those firm ideas about genre which are the stock-in-trade of literary historians like myself (and Polonius, one uncomfortably recalls).

Each of Frank's attacks on the concept of genre as indispensable to criticism was usually buried under such an avalanche of hilarious but undeniably accurate, insightful, and original comments on particular works that any attempt at refutation would be dead on arrival. I wanted to object, but felt I would come across like an academic Custer trying to raise a point of order with the Indians at Little Big Horn. Frank had me surrounded. He outnumbered me. At least I knew when to stay out of a fight. Now I'm glad I did, not only because I would have been wiped out as thoroughly as Custer though able to limp away from the defeat, but because as the years have gone by I've realized that Frank was right. Though he tended to put it in the most provocative (ok, annoying) way, his point was not that we couldn't or shouldn't usefully distinguish genres, but that most often it was less important to do so than to consider a work's qualities as story, as verbal artistry, and as illumination of the human condition. These are what matter most. I can't remember whether Frank ever bolstered his case, though he certainly might have, by citing as an arch-example all the mileage Shakespeare got by mixing comedy with tragedy to blur their differences in ways that worked very nicely indeed to entertain, invite thought, and as a fringe benefit irritate all those French critics who loved to police the boundaries of genre. Recent widespread erosion of distinctions between science fiction, fantasy, and mainstream literature has also borne out Frank's sense that science fiction scholars would by choice or perforce have to get away from our early era of concern with defining what does or doesn't qualify as the genuine article, alone worthy of our attention.

Frank's showmanship and scholarship at the podium were nonpareil. Almost equally treasured during the conferences and in my memories are those moments in restaurants, bars, or lobbies when he was happy to talk with all who clustered around. Many always did. He was witty, learned, willing to listen as well as talk, and as much a showman offstage as on. The performances were not performances in any bad senses of that term, however. They were him. He knew a lot and was glad to share what he knew in amusing rather than lugubrious ways. I think he saw the social world, especially its academic aspects, as comic, and human life as tragic. Only after he died, too soon and unexpectedly, did I get copies of *Murder Among Friends* and *Blood Lake*. Wonderfully manifested in them are his eye for social comedy and his ear for the kind of dialogue wanted by detective story fans. Whatever Frank's caveats about genre during Eaton conferences, he showed in these novels that he could perfectly understand and (what's harder) conform in practice to the conventions that define a genre and satisfy its aficionados. These two novels are splendid detective stories — or, as I hear Frank's ghost urging me to say, splendid stories. Their excellence — which I admit I didn't really expect — intensified my grief at his departure. If only there had been more! And more scholarship! What remains, however, is no small comfort. Just before being invited to write a few words for this volume, I reread, and recommended to a grad student as indispensable for her thesis, Frank's 1981 Oxford book *The Science Fiction of H.G. Wells*. This was among the pioneering works that first brought science fiction studies into the realm of major university presses and thus respectable scholarship. This time around, as initially, I found perceptive analysis lucidly expressed in ways that avoid the jargon that so much bedevils literary criticism and so quickly sends most of it down the memory hole when fashions change. Frank's book on Wells and his other studies are that rarest of all scholarly achievements, an enduring legacy that will continue to attract and instruct.

Gregory Benford, University of California, Irvine

Talking with Frank. I recall through the years I knew Frank McConnell a thread beneath his ideas and humor. He and I both sensed in our country, and much of the world, a gathering pessimism and cynical attitude toward the institutions of government that should deal with problems. It's easy to do in the perpetual campaign mode of our politics.

So Frank and I discussed The Cynic's Conundrum — that while a cynic might prefer that others believe an idealistic theory of his cynical mood ("cynics like us have high standards," he once said), his own beliefs should lead him to believe a cynical theory of his own cynical mood. That is, cynics should think that complainers tend to be losers, rather than altruists who gave away free, useful advice about a cruel world.

Furthermore, that meta-cynical theory we conjured up — that cynics tend to be loser whiners — seems to better explain the patterns: that cynics are often abrupt, and that people don't like to be around cynics — unless they're witty, like Frank.

If idealism correlates with more attractive features, then people and institutions should naturally try to appear more idealistic. So politicians always say positive things, even though we know they're lying. This explained much of what Frank saw in the world, and a lot of literature, too.

Of course both the idealistic and the cynical theory of cynical moods seem to accept that cynical beliefs contain a lot of truth. This fact, and the fact that more informed people tend to be more cynical, tends to favor cynical beliefs in general, and thus the cynical theory of cynicism in particular. Thus while hypocrisy and low motives probably may well be much more widespread than most people acknowledge, people who want to be liked may well be well-advised to pretend that they believe otherwise.

Knowing this made me more cynical still, but not Frank. To him science fiction was most valuable because it was both sophisticated in its ideas and yet not cynical about them, or about the future. He retained his funny, oblique view of our world, against all odds. I miss him.

Harold Bloom, Yale University

Frank and I were close friends from the time I supervised his doctoral work on Wordsworth until his death. His mind was fecund, generous, innovative, and exuberant. I was always surprised by the range of his literary and human interests. He was one of those former students with whom I exchanged influences and I have felt diminished since his departure. If I could see him and talk with him just once more I would tell him how much his affection and his intellectual support had meant to me. Remarkable as his achievements were, he was cut off before what I believed would be his major phase. In these days of our waning humanism, Frank remains for me a luminous instance of what has made a lifetime in teaching worthwhile.

Sheila Finch, El Camino College

It was impossible not to like Frank. He was so full of life and energy, dominating any session of the Eaton Conference in which he took part with his wise and witty comments. His sense of humor rescued many an afternoon otherwise destined to dryness. He could be profound and uproariously funny by turns, poking fun at the most serious topic, but he was never mean-spirited. I came to look forward to the Eaton Conferences because Frank would be there.

There was a kindness to Frank, a concern for the well-being of those less important to the conference than he was. He remembered my name from the first meeting at UC Riverside, and always had time to ask what I'd been doing lately, or to compliment me on a story of mine that he'd somehow found out about and read. I hadn't published much when I first met him, and many of the big name participants found me invisible when it came time for the social hour at the end of the day; I would find myself standing alone in the room, feeling awkward, while conversation swirled around me. Then a hand would touch my arm, and Frank would offer a place to sit with his group; he'd insist

I take a plate of hors d'oeuvres he'd gathered, and in no time he'd have me laughing.

The Eaton Conference was not the same without its royal jester.

Carl Freedman, Louisiana State University

Frank McConnell, R.I.P.: An Eaton Memory. I once started to compose a set of correspondences between the personnel of the Eaton Conferences and the dramatis personae of the old television sitcom *Cheers.* I didn't get very far (and no, I won't tell you who, if anyone, I picked to be Sam, Carla, Diane, or Cliff), but of one thing I was certain: Frank was our Norm. He was always there, always liked by everyone, always ready to have a good time. Though I don't suppose it ever actually happened, one can easily imagine all the other conference-goers yelling, "Frank!" as he walked into the room. You knew the tavern was Cheers because Norm was sitting at the bar, and you knew the conference was the Eaton because Frank was — well, quite likely *he* was sitting at the bar, though he might also have been sermonizing in spell-binding manner from the podium, or vigorously walking around the perimeter of the audience, cane in hand, as someone else talked.

Of course, the analogy between Norm and Frank, like all analogies, breaks down at some points. Norm, however likeable, was a lazy failure, and Frank was anything but. His *bon vivant* manner, his eagerness to let the good times roll, didn't prevent him from also working extremely hard. He taught literally thousands upon thousands of students — more, it is said, than any other professor at his university — and I've never heard of a teacher who was more popular with his students or more supportive and nurturing of them (and he was just the same way with many other young people whom he informally mentored but never formally taught). Frank also produced more good written work — criticism, scholarship, fiction — than most of us could manage in several lifetimes.

There were few colleagues around the profession with whom I more enjoyed exchanging ideas and laughs than Frank — even though, or maybe partly because, we were in exact agreement on practically nothing (except the towering greatness of Charlie Parker). In many ways, Frank was everything a colleague ought to be: outgoing, generous, intelligent, full of good humor, and perfectly secure in his own views while always ready to engage, respectfully, the views of others. Seeing him was always one of the high points of the Eaton; and shortly before the 1999 Eaton I was disappointed to hear that he was in hospital and would be unable to deliver his keynote address in person. But it didn't occur to me that there was any danger, and I looked forward to seeing him at the 2000 conference.

As things turned out, the 20th Eaton (one of the best ever, by the way) will always be associated in my mind (and in the minds of many others) with Frank. His death came on the conference's final day, January 17th, 1999. I remember Andy Gordon accosting me in a bathroom with the news; he noted that it was, at least, fortunate that so many of us who loved Frank could be together at such a time. I remember George Slusser making the formal announcement, barely able to hold back tears but also rightly maintaining that Frank, the unsurpassed academic showman, would have been the first to insist that the show must go on. Above all, I remember Joe Miller reading Frank's keynote address immediately after George's announcement. Joe had known for several days that he would be subbing for Frank — a daunting enough task in any case, but one made almost unimaginably hard by Frank's death. Yet Joe did the job superbly. He made no attempt to imitate Frank's style; that, of course, would have been a mistake, since Frank was inimitable. Instead, Joe read the paper in his own voice, with just a hint, I thought, of Frank's mischievously witty manner; and he thereby conveyed, to those of us who knew Frank, a powerful sense of what he would have sounded like delivering the address himself. It was, really, Frank's final Eaton performance, and it ended with a meditation on human mortality. Could he have somehow guessed the truth? Could he have possibly suspected the circumstances in which his paper would be delivered? In any case, no one ever out-performed Frank at the podium, and it was wholly fitting that, just a few hours after his death, he should have given us the supreme performance of his own obituary.

But it's still difficult to believe that we'll really never see him again.

Howard V. Hendrix, California State University, Fresno

Out of the Ghetto, Endlessly Grokking: A Toast to Frank McConnell. Yeah, I remember Frank. Hard guy to forget, even if you wanted to. I never wanted to.

I knew him, as much as I could. Heard he was already doing the detective-novel gig in his other life by '84, but that was the year I first met him. At the Eaton, talking about Orwell's yearbook. Meant as a warning, taken as a blueprint, all that.

Frank was stand-up shamaning about what he called boring dates in the apocalypse game. Riffing on Prince, Petronius, Patmos John, Poe. Truffaut,

Kubrick, Mel Brooks. Blake, Genet. Wells, Bradbury, Ellison. Casting his net almost apophenically wide. Follow me and ye shall become fishers of authors. If you dare.

A force of nature. F equals MC^2. A leprechaun hipped to gnosis and good whiskey. Trickster. Eccentric. Rebel. Anarch. Iconoclast. Jester. Fool. Dissenter. Protester. Atavistic witchmanchild. A struggler with words against words. A man who could say "Dig?" and mean it.

Frank knew well as anyone that what's true is not always popular, and what's popular is not always true, but he never shunned searching for truths in the pop cult ghettos. Places like science fiction, fantasy, horror, mystery, detective, western, romance. All the funkier neighborhoods of the High Lit City, where the Arch Priests feared to tread. Where Frank turned his collar 'gainst the cold and damp and didn't slum, but lived — and could teach others so well to appreciate and understand the myths. If you don't believe me, check out his "Seven Types of Chopped Liver: My Adventures in the Genre Wars."

I remember him in 1990, lame — walking and throwing down his cane to do "'Turn That Shit Down!': Or, How To Market an Underground" for the year of *Science Fiction and Market Realities*. Dancing the words on Charlie Parker and Allen Ginsberg. Franz Kafka and Phil Dick. Dave Brubeck and Paul Desmond. Norman Mailer and Pete Townshend. Harlan Ellison and Herbert Marcuse. Mona Lisa and E.E. "Doc" Smith. Isaac Asimov and Judy Garland. Fred Pohl and Edgar Rice Burroughs. Joe Siegel and Jerry Shuster. Superman and Walt Whitman and Tarzan the Apeman. Andy Warhol and Stanley Fish. Barry Malzberg and Harold Bloom. David Bowie and William Gibson. Orson Scott Card and Robert Lowell. All somehow surviving over the rainbow of God's will.

The Frank who could belt out "The Missionary Physician, from Asclepius to Kevorkian" in *No Cure for the Future*, rapping about J.D. Bernal and L.Ron Hubbard, Mary Baker Eddy and Mother Teresa, Arthur C. Clarke and Victor Frankenstein, C.S. Lewis and G.K. Chesterton — or whose "You Bet Your Life: Death and the Storyteller" in *Immortal Engines* ends with a list of "heroes of consciousness" to which I would add Frank's name — alas, Frank and his Frankness were gone before someone did the 911 and called in the police state.

Frank would certainly puzzle the Nothing-To-Hide Nothing-To-Fear folks of our vaterland sicherheits world today. They would be forced to consult their predictably dependable experts and dependably predictable professors, who would see, in Frank's reality-tweaking, parallels to Loki. Coyote. Anansi. Legba. Their search engines and data prospectors (allowed more quirky and idiosyncratic chains of association than their learned users themselves) might go so far as to suggest that Frank was an N+1 dimensional being in an N dimensional world.

None of these parallels quite intersect with the reality of Frank and his Frankness, a fact which might understandably bother the Individuality-Is-A-Socially Constructed-Illusion crowd. As the kind of hero he was, however, Frank knew that privacy is critically important to the existence of the happy disorder known as individual consciousness.

Given the march of electronically mediated social networking, it has perhaps now become inevitable that, as the virtual is being realized, the real is also being virtualized. Perhaps Frank would give an impish grin to see how we are forging ahead steadily toward that day (great to some, loathsome to others) when the event horizon of the Transparent Singularity is crossed at last — when the true Panopticon of universal surveillance is achieved — when, impatient of Big Brother's slowness, we thoroughly and completely surveil ourselves — until the last walls of our final Fortress of Solitude are breached, all our most private spaces turned inside out, and our lives like cyberspace become places where all the depth is irrevocably on the surface — all individual consciousness gone, a most profound Superficiality descending upon the world like the coming of some Disneytopian Kingdom of Heaven.

Seeing that screen-lit dark age come upon the world, Frank's spirit would, I fully expect, reincarnate itself in a Harlequin disrupting such a tick-tock planet. Frank was an idiosyncratic individual in the best sense, and the danger such an individual poses to the Grand Superficiality is always profound.

Frank McConnell was in some ways the opposite of an escape artist — not an Extricationist, but an Intricationist. Someone whose thought and words emphasized our entangled situation as human beings, not so we might pull off the magic trick of extricating ourselves from complexity and intricacy and entanglement, but rather that we might more fully learn the subtler magic of appreciating and understanding our complex, intricate, and entangled existence.

Watching Frank's performances was like watching a car-surfer or ghost-rider jump out from behind the wheel of a vehicle while it was still moving, seeing him leap onto the hood and then the roof, dancing and stunting wildly on the car while it rolled on, driverless. Frank in his presentations and teaching always seemed to be pushing in that gnoatic direction for which the driverless car (with the driver still dancing atop it) is only a metaphor. Yet he wasn't about exiting the vehicle the way the Heaven's Gate folks were, Comet Hale-Boppin' their way to the Next Level. Frank always returned us to the body and the world — always brought us back into the car that it was our responsibility to operate so as to do no harm to others — no matter how much fun we might have had with the vehicle in the meantime.

In a world and time where, in pleasuring ourselves to death, we are auto-erotically asphyxiating the current iteration of the biosphere, we could do worse than recalling that arc back to the body and physical reality to which Frank's work always called us. It beats hell out of looking for Mister Goodjazz and ending up a species lost to accidental suicide, or suicidal accident.

Bruce Kawin, University of Colorado

Frank McConnell, May 20, 1942 – January 17, 1999. Frank McConnell was a Romantic and a lover, a lover of people and words and jazz, a teacher, a mystic, a closet Catholic and an honorary Jew. He was the most learned man I ever met, and the most generous. He was my brother, my teacher, my reader, my nephew, my rabbi, and my confessor. And he told the best jokes. He would ask the big questions and in the next breath start to answer them. He would do anything for the people he loved. He would play you any piece you hadn't heard.

In his spirit, here is a question: Does everything make sense or just go on till it ends? From jokes, from jazz, from his spirit, and from my heart, here comes the start of an answer. In the last piece he wrote, in terrible pain, Frank said there were only two kinds of jokes, punchline and shaggy dog. The issue, then, is What kind of joke is life? If death is its punch line, a wallop in the heart, a summing up that gives it a twist and makes it all make sense, then life is a practical joke. Or if life is the perfect setup for the definitive payoff, we can admire its logic but be forgiven if we don't find it funny. But I do not think that Frank's life was explained, given a twist, or knocked into wondrous perspective by his death. I think his life was a shaggy-dog story, because its end was only where it stopped, and its point was that we listened to it, all the way to the end. All of us did, every one of us here, listened to it, loved it, every minute of it, and every minute of him. When you can't get enough of someone — that's love.

On the other hand, however, there is always room for the possibility that the world makes sense and that death makes sense of life, the way a door explains a doorway. In that same last essay, Frank told his favorite story of a wise Jewish man known as the Baal Shem Tov:

> The Baal Shem Tov and his disciples were traveling. While they were riding along the road a leaf floated down and settled upon the lap of the Baal Shem Tov. A bit further on a wind came and blew the leaf from the lap of the Baal

Shem Tov to the ground; and there a worm came and crawled onto the leaf and used it for shelter and food. The Baal Shem Tov stopped the wagon and called his disciples. "Look here," he said. "When the world was created, even then did the Almighty decree that this leaf should fall on my lap and that a wind should come and take it from my lap and blow it onto the ground where this worm would use it for food and shelter."

It is, as Frank would say, a punchline joke, a tale from an ordered universe. And if that is the way things are, then from the beginning of the world it was ordained by the Almighty that Frank should die, like all the other leaves, and that we should use his memory for food and shelter. If a punchline story comes to its end, THE end, a shaggy-dog story comes, like jazz, to AN end.

Frank was a spiritual man and a carnal one, a man who talked and listened. If all his questions are answered now, he is certainly making up new ones.

So this guy walks into Heaven. And because his name is written in the Book of God, they let him in, and he gets an audience with the Big Guy. He's ready to ask a million questions, and even before he gets an answer, the whole shebang becomes clear to him; he realizes he got it a long time ago, maybe when he was quoting Stevens to his students — and you know what he says. That isn't a question: you know. He says, "Nu?"

[Note: An earlier version of this was delivered as Frank McConnell's eulogy and published in *Sniper Logic*, 7 (Winter–Fall, 1999), pp. 118-119.]

Joseph D. Miller, Ph.D., University of Southern California

Remembering Frank. Lately I have been re-reading Frank McConnell's Eaton Conference essays published over the last twenty-five years or so. And they scintillate! Hilarious, brilliant, outrageous, often all at the same time. And yet the essays are not the half of it. Frank was the best speaker I have ever heard. His presentations at the Eaton were events, rather than talks. The worst position one could be in at these conferences was to be the speaker following Frank! I believe what success I have had as a teacher is directly attributable to what I cribbed from Frank in terms of Story, Theatre and purest Showmanship.

I want to talk about conversation and conspiracy (reconstructed and deconstructed as best I can) I engaged in with Frank which I think revealed different facets of this gem of a man. The first must have been around April, 1992 at the Eaton Conference on Life Extension and Immortality. In the bar, where the best conversations always took place, I remember asking Frank if he could ever accept immortality with the usual caveats of the body and mind of a twenty year old, but all memories to date intact. And Frank said "No way!"

It has taken me another fifteen years to really understand what he meant. Frank's concern was "the burden of mortality" or what Hamlet calls "the calamity of so long life." I don't think this is something most can grasp at age thirty or even forty. It is Lear's realization, "I am not ague-proof," but it is really the ague of memory of which I speak. "The heartache and the thousand natural shocks" with no closure, resolution or surcease. Alfred Bester's story title comes to mind: "Hell Is Forever."

I said to Frank, "But wouldn't that be the response of a Cro Magnon at the venerable age of twenty or perhaps a man of the eighteenth century at the end of his average forty year span, when confronted with the possibility of living to age seventy-five, the average now for our society?" And Frank said "Just differences in quantity. Real immortality is indefinite, to the heat death of the universe or longer. The thing is, human stories end. Indefinite existence isn't human."

And that was the crux. For Frank, indefinite existence is the escape into gnosis, a state in which life means nothing since death means nothing, a state in which you are, finally, ague-proof, but at the cost of your humanity. There is but one way to avoid this—"You go into the magic forest and dance with the masquers there precisely so you can come back, healed and refreshed and wisely innocent, to the world where agues and gravity — the closure that makes us real — claim their due." (McConnell, "You Bet Your Life: Death and the Storyteller") At that point I said "Well, what about some sort of induced partial amnesia, just to remove the most painful memories?" And Frank said, approximately, "If you have a complete memory wipe, then you are for all intents and purposes again an infant and an innocent in the quotidian realm. And if you only eliminate those painful, ague-ridden memories, then again you have abrogated your humanity."

And so on a personal level Frank rejected gnosis, at least of the perpetual variety. Frank was not agnostic, his concern was *nostos* or homecoming *from* that gnostic state (*ibid*).

But I wasn't quite done. I said "Well, why not just try immortality for a few centuries and see how it works out. You still have the thanatic option. Heinlein said, at the end of *Methuselah's Children*, "Ask me again in about five hundred years." I don't recall Frank's reply, but in the Heinlein Centennial edition of *Locus* (August, 2007, page 57) there is a recollection by Spider Robinson of the attempts by the Alcor Foundation to convince Heinlein to have himself cryogenically frozen, a kind of hedge on the development of a future longevity technology. Heinlein refused. According to Jim Baen, the reason for Heinlein's refusal is summed up in his question to Baen: "How do I know it wouldn't interfere with rebirth?" And so Frank posthumously illuminates even the Dean of science fiction!

But in the end I am a biologist and Frank was a humanist. My view of the human condition is that it has been and will continue to change and evolve. I do not see sufficient perfection in that condition to eschew a journey into gnosis. In fact, I suspect that to be a condition for our survival.

On a much lighter note I must mention a scheme Frank and I once cooked up for an Eaton Conference. I was going to be talking on time travel or some such when Frank would burst through the doors, dressed in disheveled rags, muddy and woebegone, glance around wildly and ask in the most heart-rending of voices, "Can anyone tell me what year this is?" Sadly our scheme foundered on logistical details, but I have always found comfort in the thought that somewhen in the multiverse Frank and I generated a little *frisson* in the participants of some alternate Eaton conference. It occurs to me that we never specified whether that Traveler was coming home to the quotidian realm of Riverside, CA or whether Riverside was indeed his gnostic destination from some far past or future. But that uncertain journey between the sublime and the mundane was Frank's philosophical condition and perhaps the condition of us all.

Eric S. Rabkin, University of Michigan

My Brother Frank. The evening of the day I first met Frank McConnell, he called me brother. It was an Eaton Conference weekend and earlier we had each given papers, two native Easterners stuck that day indoors. I had come from wintry Ann Arbor, Michigan, and would have loved to be outside in the hazy February sunshine of Riverside, California; Frank had moved to Santa Barbara, but, so far as I could see that day or any other for the rest of his too brief life, he never broke through. True Southern Californians, no matter where they are raised, have a different idea about doors and windows and buildings than I grew up with. Their bedrooms and living rooms and sometimes even kitchens and bathrooms have sliding glass walls that as often as not just sit open, obviating the immemorial fence between inside and outside, human and natural, controlled and contingent. Southern Californians don't huddle; they roam the room, the deck, and the world equally, like buffalo in the song, but still with air conditioning and Chardonnay ever handy in case the mood strikes. In their world, boundaries reduce to signs of boundaries and crossing them with apparent thoughtlessness is a spiritual indulgence of their faith that the whole world belongs to them. Frank never had that faith, although, as with his Roman Catholicism, he always struggled with it and the struggle marked him. The world was always a problem. The boundaries, real and necessary, fueled in him a deep, glorious, tormenting ambivalence.

I had been smart that day; he had been coruscating. Frank entertained brilliantly whenever he chose; he didn't win his University's students' award as the very best teacher on campus accidentally. You couldn't take your eyes off him, or your ears. He was under medium height but outsized in every other way. On stage, his jacket threatened to pop its buttons. His eyes could blaze or deepen into sudden sadness. His rhetoric was outrageous. He told his audience of science fiction scholars that there was no such thing as science fiction, that the category was bogus, the boundary didn't exist, but there he was anyway, explaining the boundary, roaming not across it but along it, not so much like a tightrope artist as like a man suddenly abandoned who, unmoored, now commits himself to walk a dangerous ledge. Did that man know all along that he would draw a crowd? Did the presence of that crowd ever undo his sense of abandonment?

Between talks, we went outside, I in the short sleeves of a Midwestern fugitive, Frank still in his straining sport coat. He smoked in the fresh air. We talked. We really talked. In my decades-long and ever wonderful experience of him, Frank always really talked. He wanted connectedness and freely gave humor, insight, honesty, and love. Always.

"What do you think of Bakhtin?" I once heard a student ask him from the floor of a lecture hall.

"I would never trust a critic who sounds like an antiseptic."

Of course not. What is the point of criticism if it kills the grit of life?

At a conference-arranged cocktail party that first evening, he and I wound up exchanging jokes. That sort of exchange, especially among people who pride themselves on their intellects, often descends into a barely clothed competition. Not for us, that night or ever. We were like the characters in the old joke who know so many old jokes so well that each can say just a number and they laugh together. The point isn't the joke, or its number, but the order of the jokes, the exchange of the jokes, the use of those barbs against the world to build a home of conversation to share with a sympathetic soul.

People watched us with ready laughter. Frank made me feel proud.

He could do that for people. He did do that for people.

I stayed sometimes in Frank and Celeste's home. Have you ever seen a man in pajamas and a buttoned up sport coat?

I recall one late morning at Frank's breakfast table, the newspaper comic section spread before us. Frank explained to me in his typical way — giving, seeking, ironic, mischievous, deadly serious — that *Calvin and Hobbes* was brilliant in part because Hobbes was precisely the right philosopher for whom to name this comic strip character. Thomas Hobbes believed that people needed to be controlled for their own good. The comic strip boy Calvin had an adult-sized companion in his imaginary friend, Hobbes the tiger, who burned bright for him and, although gently superegotistical, always ultimately fostered Calvin and set him free. Calvin, the real John Calvin, promulgated a strict Christianity that still constrains American culture, but imagination could free it.

For Frank, as for the hand-drawn Calvin, imagination freed one only for moments here or there. Hobbes too often becomes just a stuffed animal. A parent or teacher too often wrenches Calvin's alter-ego, Spaceman Spiff, back into the mundane and bound.

Frank loved that comic strip. It was his real breakfast.

Along with *Garfield*.

He had a thing for tiger-striped cats.

Dinner, when he hosted me, often began with a single malt Scotch. He wanted purity, pleasure, and spirits, and he wanted to share them.

He asked me once at another party if I knew about this great new religion, Frisbyterianism. I didn't. "Frisbyterians have only one belief: when you die, your soul gets stuck on the roof." Everyone around us burst into laughter.

Frisbyterians, it seems, can't really escape the Earth, but perhaps that is because, despite their flying-saucer-shaped souls, their motive power is the hand and eye that set them spinning. Frank McConnell set people spinning, but their souls soaring, when he was with us and now when he soars, too. I still hear you, brother. And I always will.

Mark Rose, University of California, Santa Barbara

It was in 1986, I think, the year that *Aliens* came out. In Santa Barbara *Aliens* opened at an old-style moving picture palace. The moment the monster — double jawed and vile — appeared on the giant screen producing the predictable gasps, a clear tenor voice soared like a virtuoso over the soundtrack and the huge audience: "I betcha this one ain't going to phone home!" Shock turned to laughter and the hall exploded in guffaws. It was of course

Frank McConnell sitting somewhere up front, fearless and irreverent, gifted with a species of wit that in a comic flash could make connections that only seem obvious once they have been achieved. That moment in the Arlington Theatre remains with me some twenty years later as an epiphany in which the essence of Frank's insouciant genius — a very public genius because he was, above all, a brilliant performer in person as well as in print — revealed itself. In ways big and small Frank added, as Ursula K. Le Guin might say, to the positive sum of human consciousness.

George Slusser, University of California, Riverside

Frank McConnell the Jazzman. I first met Frank at the 1982 Eaton Conference in Riverside. The Eaton Conference was only four years old at that time. The topic, science fiction and fantasy, was scoffed at by many pundits. The theme of this year's conference, SF and Fantasy in Film, nonetheless drew a number of major film scholars. Frank was among them. I had read *The Spoken Seen*, and found it fascinating in the breadth of its argument. Its focus was what Frank would return to again and again in later writings: story. The year 1982 saw the beginnings of the invasion of French theory in American academia, and the corruption of academic discourse. Frank's approach was the opposite: he had a *big* idea, and approached it with the subtlety and complexity that emerges from sensitive analysis of specific works. Great stories, whether told in prose, poetry, film, or science fiction, held an eternal mystery for him.

But meeting Frank in 1982 was most memorable because of the man and his physical presence on stage. He was immensely funny, yet dead serious about what he was saying. He was not afraid to enter the territory of SF, and to link its treasure to stories to the vast trove of literature, beginning with Gilgamesh and the Bible, and going god knows where. Every one of his talks at subsequent Eaton Conferences, and there were many, was a delight and an intellectual adventure. One of my more jaded colleagues, listening to Frank speak, said: My God, this is what an academic should be. He is a *teacher* in the strongest sense of the word. I agree, he taught many of us that there is life in the academic profession. He also taught us that there is courage, that no topic is unworthy of serious attention, that there are no boundaries to an inquiring mind.

As befits a seeker, Frank had a restless mind. He wrote a distinguished book on Wordsworth. Then he wrote several significant books on film and the visual imagination. He then wrote what, for me, is the best study of H.G. Wells. Then, as if tiring of the academic press format, he produced his series of Eaton essays, in which he took the form back to its roots in the word "to try," to reach for the stars in realm after realm of modern thought. Alongside that, Frank wrote excellent mystery novels, a genre that he particularly liked. And of course Frank remained a teacher, beloved of his students, a man able to convey wisdom to restless generations during the 1970s and 1980s. His model was his mentor Harold Bloom, and Frank carried that torch into uncharted areas.

I knew Frank on all fronts, due to his longtime connection with Eaton. But I think that where we really hit it off the most was in our love of jazz. We used to discuss what were the greatest achievements of American culture in the 20th century. Our common list was: film noir, science fiction, and jazz, jazz of the 1950s and early 1960s. How do two fans like us talk about jazz? They dig. They go to the phonograph (yes, the technology was quaint then), put on some sides, and dig how Bud Powell straddles two worlds in "I Should Care," how Lee Konitz tears apart "Sweet and Lovely," how the rhythm section excels in "Dear Old Stockholm." What about Jack Sheldon's screaming high C in "Grooveyard," or the Bob Zieff tunes with Chet Baker and Richard Twardzik in Europe 1954, the lost recordings somehow found? We knew that the early Coltrane, the Davis years, or even the Impulse recordings such as "Inchworm," were superior to the later Coltrane of "A Love Supreme." We saw the multicultural wonder that was jazz, the greatest musical expression since Mozart, develop, then dissipate somehow in the later culture wars.

I thought I knew jazz till I met Frank. He had simply dug everything, from standards to Ornette Coleman. He could hum the riffs. We were alike in that we loved something we could not play, and sought to work our way into it by sheer empathy. We often talked about doing a book together: the history of jazz. That book will never be written. And often in the privacy of my late night living room, as I listen to Coltrane playing "Slow Dance," or Miles's "Blue in Green," I think of Frank and all of his great improvisations on life, culture, story, and finally, on jazz. Like the great improvisations of jazz, Frank's riffs were "stolen moments," words stolen from the void, and alive again only when music awakens an inner voice.

Rest in peace, Frank.

Chapter Notes

Chapter 1

1. Lord Byron, *Don Juan*, Canto II, Stanza 212, in *The Oxford Authors: Byron*, edited with an introduction and notes by Jerome J. McGann (Oxford and New York: Oxford University Press, 1986), 486.
2. Mary Shelley, *Frankenstein*, in Leonard Wolf, editor, *The Annotated Frankenstein* (New York: Clarkson N. Potter, 1977), 15.
3. Shelley, *Frankenstein*, 15.
4. Harold Bloom, "*Frankenstein, or The New Prometheus*," *Partisan Review*, 32 (1965), 611–618.
5. Thomas Pynchon, *The Crying of Lot 49* (Philadelphia and New York: Lippincott, 1966), 129.
6. Zosimus the Panopolitan. At this time, I have been unable to locate a source for this quotation.
7. *Frankenstein*. Edison, 1910. [Editor's note: The film was rediscovered after this essay was written.]
8. C.G. Jung, "Transformation Symbols in the Mass," in *Psyche and Symbol: A Selection from the Writings of C.G. Jung*, edited by Violet S. de Laszlo (Garden City, NY: Doubleday, 1958), 148–224.
9. W.B. Yeats, "Sailing to Byzantium," in *The Collected Poems of W.B. Yeats* (New York: Macmillan, 1956), 224.

Chapter 2

1. Roy Huss and T.J. Ross, editors, *Focus on the Horror Film* (Englewood Cliffs, New Jersey: Prentice-Hall, 1972).
2. Raymond Durgnat, "The Wedding of Poetry and Pulp — Can They Live Happily Ever After and Have Many Beautiful Children?," in *Films and Feelings* (Cambridge, Massachusetts: M.I.T. Press, 1967), 251–267.
3. Robert Lowell, "Skunk Hour," in *Selected Poems* (New York: Farrar, Straus and Giroux, 1976), 96.

Chapter 3

1. H.G. Wells, *The Time Machine*, in *Three Prophetic Science Fiction Novels of H.G. Wells*, selected and with an introduction by E.F. Bleiler (New York: Dover, 1960), 322.
2. I have been unable to locate a source for this Ernest Barker quotation. Wells did make a similar observation about his epitaph in the 1941 preface to *The War in the Air, and Particularly How Mr. Bert Smallways Fared While It Lasted* (1908): "Is there anything to add to that preface now? Nothing except my epitaph. That, when the time comes, will manifestly have to be: 'I told you so. You *damned* fools.' (The italics are mine.)" (Cited in Gary Westfahl, *Science Fiction Quotations: From the Inner Mind to the Outer Limits* [New Haven, Connecticut: Yale University Press, 2005], 135.)
3. H.G. Wells, *The Fate of Homo Sapiens: An Unemotional Statement of the Things That Are Happening to Him Now, and of the Immediate Possibilities Confronting Him* (London: Secker and Warburg, 1939), 2.
4. Norman and Jeanne MacKenzie, *The Time Traveller: The Life of H.G. Wells* (London: Weidenfeld & Nicolson, 1973), 225.
5. Van Wyck Brooks, *The World of H.G. Wells* (New York: Mitchell Kennerley, 1915), 62.
6. H.G. Wells, *Kipps* (London: Macmillan, 1905), 392.
7. H.G. Wells, *The War of the Worlds*, in *Seven Famous Novels by H.G. Wells* (New York: Alfred A. Knopf, 1934), 349.
8. Wells, *The Time Machine*, 335.
9. I have examined the most likely source for this quotation — the chapter on "H.G. Wells" in Christopher Caudwell, *Studies in a Dying Cul-*

ture (London: John Lane, 1938) — and although there are passages conveying the idea that Wells was overly spiritual in his thinking, I did not locate this precise word. It is possible, of course, that he applied the term to Wells in another publication.

10. I have been unable to locate a source for this C.S. Lewis quotation.

11. H.G. Wells, *When the Sleeper Wakes*, in *Three Prophetic Science Fiction Novels of H.G. Wells*, selected and with an introduction by E.F. Bleiler (New York: Dover, 1960), 170.

Chapter 4

1. H.G. Wells, *The Time Machine*, in *Three Prophetic Novels of H.G. Wells*, selected and with an introduction by E.F. Bleiler (New York: Dover, 1960, 330–331.

2. H.G. Wells, *The First Men in the Moon*, in *Seven Famous Novels by H.G. Wells* (New York: Alfred A. Knopf, 1934), 429.

3. Joseph Conrad, letter to H.G. Wells, December 4, 1898, in *The Collected Letters of Joseph Conrad, Volume 2: 1898–1902*, edited by Frederick R. Karl and Laurence Davies (Cambridge: Cambridge University Press, 1986), 126.

4. H.G. Wells, *The Invisible Man*, edited by MacDonald Daly (London: J.M. Dent, 1995), 35.

5. Graham Greene, review of *Rhythm on the Range*, in *The Pleasure Dome: The Collected Film Criticism 1935-40*, by Graham Greene, edited by John Russell Taylor (London: Secker & Warburg, 1972), 94.

6. H.G. Wells, *A Modern Utopia*, introduction by Mark R. Hillegas (Lincoln, Nebraska: University of Nebraska Press, 1967), 2.

7. H.G. Wells, "Mr. Wells Reviews a Current Film: He Takes Issue with This German Conception of What the City of One Hundred Years Hence Will Be Like," *The New York Times*, April 17, 1927, *The New York Times Magazine*, 4,22. [Editor's note: the actual quotation provided by McConnell was "Quite the silliest film," which is the version of the quotation most commonly found; however, I examined both the 1927 newspaper version of the review, noted above, and its republication as "The Silliest Film: Will Machinery Make Robots of Men?" in Harry Geduld, editor, *Authors on Film* (Bloomington: Indiana University Press, 1972), and in both cases there was no "Quite" to be found.]

8. Robert Browning, "Pippa Passes," in *The Oxford Authors: Robert Browning*, edited by Adam Roberts, introduction by Daniel Karlin (Oxford and New York: Oxford University Press, 1997), 65.

9. H.G. Wells, *The History of Mr. Polly* (New York: Press of the Readers Club, 1941), 261.

Chapter 5

1. Herbert N. Schneidau, *Sacred Discontent: The Bible and Western Tradition* (Baton Rouge: Louisiana State University Press, 1976).

2. Keszek Kolakowski, *Religion: If There Is No God — On God, the Devil, Sin, and Other Worries of the So-Called Philosophy of Religion* (New York and Oxford: Oxford University Press, 1982), 57–58.

3. Jules Verne, cited in Gary Westfahl, editor, *Science Fiction Quotations: From the Inner Mind to the Outer Limits* (New Haven: Yale University Press, 2005), 324.

4. Harold Bloom, *The Flight to Lucifer: A Gnostic Fantasy* (New York: Farrar, Straus and Giroux, 1979), 25.

5. Søren Kierkegaard, *The Sickness Unto Death*, in *Fear and Trembling and The Sickness Unto Death*, translated with an introduction and notes by Walter Lowrie (Garden City, NY: Doubleday, 1954), 168, 170.

6. William Blake, "The Marriage of Heaven and Hell," in *The Poetry and Prose of William Blake*, edited by David V. Erdman, commentaries by Harold Bloom (Garden City, NY: Doubleday, 1970), 29.

7. G.K. Chesterton, "Introduction: The Plan of This Book," in *The Everlasting Man* (London: Hodder and Stoughton, 1925), 9.

8. Thomas Hanzo, "The Past of Science Fiction," in *Bridges to Science Fiction*, edited by George Slusser, George R. Guffey, and Mark Rose (Carbondale and Edwardsville: Southern Illinois University Press, 1980), 131–147.

9. Olaf Stapledon, *Star Maker*, in *Last and First Men and Star Maker* (New York: Dover, 1968), 262.

10. Stapledon, *Star Maker*, 300.

Chapter 6

1. George Orwell, *Nineteen Eighty-Four* (New York: Harcourt, Brace, 1949), 28–29.

2. Peter Stansky and William Abrahams, *The Unknown Orwell* (New York: Alfred A. Knopf, 1972), and *Orwell, The Transformation* (London: Constable, 1979).

3. Harlan Ellison, "Introduction: Revealed at Last! What Killed the Dinosaurs! And You Don't Look So Terrific Yourself," in *Strange Wine: Fifteen New Stories from the Nightside of the Imagination* (New York: Harper & Row, 1978), 7.

4. George Steiner, *Language and Silence* (New York: Atheneum, 1967).

5. Karl Marx, "Theses on Feuerbach," translated by C. Dutt and C.P. Magill, in Karl Marx and Friedrich Engels, *The German Ideology: Part One*, edited with an introduction by

C.J. Arthur (London: Lawrence & Wishart, 1970), 122.

Chapter 7

1. Albert Einstein, cited in J.M. Cohen and M.J. Cohen, compilers, *The Penguin Dictionary of Twentieth-Century Quotations* (New York: Penguin, 1980), 115.
2. Tom Robbins, *Jitterbug Perfume* (Toronto and New York: Bantam Books, 1984), 110.
3. William Shakespeare, *King Lear*, Act IV, scene 1, lines 38–39, edited by R.A. Foakes (London: Thomas Nelson, 1997), 306.
4. Shakespeare, *King Lear*, Act V, scene 3, line 235, 383.
5. Shakespeare, *King Lear*, Act V, scene 3, line 255, 385.
6. John Simon, cited in Jerome Agel, editor, *The Making of Kubrick's 2001* (New York: Signet, 1970), 244.
7. Wallace Stevens, "Sunday Morning," In *The Collected Poems of Wallace Stevens* (New York: Alfred A. Knopf, 1954), 70.
8. John Ashbery, "I Had Thought Things Were Going Along Well," in *As We Know: Poems* (New York: Viking Press, 1979), 94.
9. Leszek Kowakowski, *Religion: If There Is No God—On God, the Devil, Sin, and Other Worries of the So-Called Philosophy of Religion* (New York and Oxford: Oxford University Press, 1982), 40.

Chapter 8

1. Wallace Stevens, "The Man with the Blue Guitar," in *The Collected Poems of Wallace Stevens* (New York: Alfred A. Knopf, 1954), 165.
2. Emile Benveniste, *Problems in General Linguistics*, translated by Mary Elizabeth Meek (Coral Gables, FL: University of Miami Press, 1971), 227, 218.
3. Arthur Rimbaud, *Lettres du Voyant (13 et 15 Mai 1871)*, éditées et commentées par Gérald Schaeffer, including *La Voyance avant Rimbaud* par Marc Eigeldinger (Paris: Librarie Minard, 1975), 113.
4. Jacquetta Hopkins Hawkes, *Prehistory and the Beginnings of Civilization* (New York: Harper & Row, 1963).
5. Sigmund Freud, *The Psychopathology of Everyday Life*, translated by Alan Tyson, edited with an introduction and additional notes by James Strachey (New York: W.W. Norton, 1965), 48.
6. F. Scott Fitzgerald, *The Great Gatsby* (1925; New York: Charles Scribner's Sons, 1953), 94.
7. Stanislaw Lem, "Philip K. Dick: A Visionary Among the Charlatans," *Science-Fiction Studies*, 2 (March 1975), 59.

Chapter 9

1. Wallace Stevens, "The Man with the Blue Guitar," in *The Collected Poems of Wallace Stevens* (New York: Alfred A. Knopf, 1954), 165.
2. *Patton* (20th Century–Fox, 1970).
3. Sir Arthur Eddington, "Beyond the Veil of Physics," in Ken Wilber, editor, with the research assistance of Ann Niehaus, *Quantum Questions: Mystical Writings of the World's Great Physicists* (Boston: Shambhala, 2001), 193.
4. Lord Byron, *Don Juan*, Canto II, Stanza 212, in *The Oxford Authors: Byron*, edited with an introduction and notes by Jerome J. McGann (Oxford and New York: Oxford University Press, 1986), 486.
5. William Shakespeare, *Hamlet*, Act II, Scene 2, edited by Harold Jenkins (London: Methuen, 1982), 254.
6. Alexander Pope, "The Rape of the Lock," Canto III, lines 45–46, in *Alexander Pope's Collected Poems*, edited with an introduction by Bonamy Dobrée (London: Dent, 1956), 85; italics added.
7. Gaston Bachelard, *The Poetics of Space* (New York: Orion Press, 1964).
8. William Shakespeare, *King Lear*, Act III, Scene 4, edited by R.A. Foakes (London: Thomas Nelson, 1997), 272.
9. At this time, I have been unable to locate the source of this quotation.
10. *Beowulf*, author unknown, in *Beowulf: A Prose Translation: Background and Contexts; Criticism*, Second Edition, translated by E. Talbot Donaldson, edited by Nicholas Howe (New York and London: W.W. Norton, 2002), 37.
11. John Hough, *The Conduct of the Game* (San Diego: Harcourt Brace Jovanovich, 1986), 175.
12. Stefan Zweig, "The Royal Game," in *The Royal Game and Other Stories*, translated by Jiff Sutcliffe, introduction by John Fowles (London: Jonathan Cape, 1981), 8.
13. Karl Rahner, *The Practice of Faith: A Handbook of Contemporary Spirituality* (New York: Crossroad, 1983), 3–4.
14. F. Scott Fitzgerald, *The Great Gatsby* (1925: New York: Charles Scribner's Sons, 1953), 2.
15. Ernest Hemingway, "Soldier's Home," in *The Complete Short Stories of Ernest Hemingway: The Finca Vigia Edition* (New York: Simon & Shuster, 1987), 117.

Chapter 10

1. George Slusser, "Who's Afraid of Science Fiction?," *Foundation: The Review of Science Fiction*, No. 42 (Spring 1988), 5–20.
2. J.R.R. Tolkien, "On Fairy Stories," in

The Monster and the Critics and Other Essays, edited by Christopher Tolkien (Boston: George Allen & Urwin, 1983), 116, 135, 156–157. Essay originally published in 1947.
3. Thomas Hanzo, "The Past of Science Fiction," in *Bridges to Science Fiction*, edited by George Slusser, George R. Guffey, and Mark Rose (Carbondale and Edwardsville: Southern Illinois University Press, 1980), 131–147.
4. David Lindsay, *A Voyage to Arcturus* (1920; London: Allison and Busby, 1965), 277.
5. Marie Louise von Franz, *The Interpretation of Fairy Tales*, Revised Edition (Boston: Shambhala, 1996).

Chapter 11

1. Allen Ginsberg, "Howl," in *British and American Poets, Chaucer to the Present*, edited by W. Jackson Bate and David Perkins (San Diego: Harcourt Brace Jovanovich, 1986), 968.
2. Philip K. Dick, *The Man in the High Castle* (1962; New York: Berkley, 1986), 182–183.
3. Dick, *The Man in the High Castle*, 164.
4. Theodor Adorno, "Perennial Fashion—Jazz," in *Prisms*, translated by Samuel and Shierry Weber (London: Spearman, 1967), 132.
5. Robert Lowell, "The Quaker Graveyard at Nantucket," in *Selected Poems* (New York: Farrar, Straus and Giroux, 1976), 10.

Chapter 12

1. Samuel R. Delany, *Babel-17* (New York: Ace Books, 1966), 160.
2. Norman Spinrad, *The Void Captain's Tale* (1983; New York: Pocket Books, 1984), 71.
3. Wallace Stevens, "Sunday Morning," in *The Collected Poems of Wallace Stevens* (New York: Alfred A. Knopf, 1954), 69.
4. William Gibson, "The Gernsback Continuum," in *Burning Chrome* (1986; New York: Ace Books, 1988), 32–33.
5. Thomas Pynchon, "Introduction," *Slow Learner: Early Stories* (Boston: Little, Brown, 1984), 5.
6. Jean Anthelme Brillat-Savarin, *Physiologie du Gout*, Edition Mise en Ordre et Annoteé, avec une Lecture de Roland Barthes (Paris: Hermann, 1975), 37; McConnell's translation.
7. Douglas Adams, *The Hitchhiker's Guide to the Galaxy* (1979; New York: Pocket Books, 1981), 215.
8. Roland Barthes, introduction to Brillat-Savarin's *Physiologie du Gout*, 9; McConnell's translation.
9. John Berryman, "Dream Song 308: An Instructions to Critics" [title sic], in *His Toy, His Dream, His Rest: 308 Dream Songs* (New York: Farrar, Straus and Giroux, 1968), 240.

10. Roland Barthes, introduction to Brillat-Savarin's *Physiologie du Gout*, 12; McConnell's translation.
11. Roland Barthes, introduction to Brillat-Savarin's *Physiologie du Gout*, 14; McConnell's translation.
12. At this time, I have been unable to locate a source for this Graham Greene quotation.
13. Ludwig Wittgenstein, *Tractatus Logico-Philosophicus*, translated by D.F. Pears and B.F. McGuinness, introduction by Bertrand Russell (London and New York: Routledge, 1974), 5.
14. Wallace Stevens, "The Man with the Blue Guitar," in *The Collected Poems of Wallace Stevens*, 184.

Chapter 13

1. William Shakespeare, *King Lear*, act 4, scene 6, edited by R.A. Foakes (London: Thomas Nelson, 1997), 334–335.
2. Karl Rahner, *The Practice of Faith: A Handbook of Contemporary Spirituality* (New York: Crossroad, 1983).
3. Henri Bergson, *Laughter*, translator unidentified, in *Comedy*, edited by Wylie Sypher (Garden City, NY: Doubleday, 1956), 84.
4. Wallace Stevens, "Esthétique du Mal," in *Transport to Summer* (New York: Knopf, 1951), 52–53.
5. Stevens, "Esthétique du Mal," 53.
6. Thomas Pynchon, "Introduction," *Slow Learner* (Boston: Little, Brown, 1984), 5.
7. William Wordsworth, "The Recluse," in *Selected Poems and Prefaces*, edited by Jack Stillinger (Boston: Houghton Mifflin, 1965), 46.

Chapter 14

1. Harold Bloom, "Introduction," *The Book of J*, translated by David Rosenberg, interpreted by Harold Bloom (New York: Random House, 1990), 13.
2. Oscar Wilde, "Preface," *The Picture of Dorian Gray*, in *The Complete Works of Oscar Wilde, Volume IV*, introduction by Coulson Kernahan, review by Walter Pater (New York: Wise, 1927), 5.
3. Alexander Pope, "An Epistle to Dr. Arbuthnot," in *Alexander Pope's Collected Poems*, edited by Bonamy Dobrée (London: Everyman's Library, 1956), 262.
4. W.H. Auden, "Under Which Lyre," in *Selected Poems*, New Edition, edited by Edward Mendelson (New York: Random House, 1979), 180.
5. John Barth, "*The Ocean of Story*," in *The Friday Book: Essays and Other Nonfiction* (New York: G.P. Putnam's Sons, 1984), 84–90, and elsewhere.

6. Frank D. McConnell, "Will Deconstruction Be the Death of Literature?" *Wilson Quarterly*, 14 (Winter 1990), 99–109.
7. J. Hillis Miller, "Defending Deconstruction" [letter], *Wilson Quarterly*, 14 (Summer 1990), 143.
8. Roland Barthes, *Leçon: Leçon Inaugurale de la Chaire de Sémiologie Litéraire du Collège de France, Prononcée le 7 Janvier 1977* (Paris: Editions du Seuil, 1978), 15; McConnell's translation.
9. C.M. Cioran, *Precis de Decomposition* (Paris: Galliland, 1949), 13; McConnell's translation.
10. Ludwig Wittgenstein, cited in Norman Malcolm, *Ludwig Wittgenstein: A Memoir* (London: Oxford University Press, 1958), 93.
11. Miller, 143.
12. Auden, "Under Which Lyre," 179.
13. Barthes, [46]; McConnell's translation.
14. Auden, "In Memory of W.B. Yeats," *Selected Poems*, 82.

Chapter 15

1. Christopher Hitchens, *The Missionary Position: Mother Teresa in Theory and Practice* (London and New York: Verso, 1995), 41–42.
2. W.B. Yeats, "A Dialogue of Self and Soul," in *The Collected Poems of W.B. Yeats* (1933; New York: Macmillan, 1956), 232.
3. C.S. Lewis, *Perelandra* (1944; New York: Macmillan, 1964), 82.
4. Alexander Pope, "Epistle to Dr. Arbuthnot," in *Alexander Pope's Collected Poems*, edited by Bonamy Dobrée (London: Everyman's Library, 1956), 257.
5. Alfred Lord Whitehead, *Process and Reality*, Corrected Edition, edited by David Ray Griffin and Donald W. Sherburne (New York: Free Press, 1978), 5.

6. Wallace Stevens, "The Poems of Our Climate," in *The Collected Poems of Wallace Stevens* (New York: Alfred A. Knopf, 1954), 144.

Chapter 16

1. William Wordsworth, "The Recluse," in *Selected Poems and Prefaces*, edited by Jack Stillinger (Boston: Houghton Mifflin, 1965), 46.
2. Ludwig Wittgenstein, *Tractatus Logico-Philosophicus*, translated by D.F. Pears and B.F. McGuinness, introduction by Bertrand Russell (London and New York: Routledge, 1974), 5.
3. William Shakespeare, *King Lear*, Act I, Scene 2, edited by R.A Foakes (London: Thomas Nelson, 1997), 185–187.
4. Martin Heidegger, *Einführung in die Metaphysik* (Tübingen: Max Neimeyer Verlag, 1957), 1; McConnell's translation.
5. Wallace Stevens, "Reality Is an Activity of the Most August Imagination," in *Collected Poetry and Prose* (New York: Library of America, 1997), 471–472.
6. Jerome R. Mintz, *Legends of the Hasidim: An Introduction to Hasidic Culture and Oral Tradition in the New World* (Chicago and London: University of Chicago Press, 1968), 337.
7. Stephen Hawking, *A Brief History of Time* (New York: Bantam, 1998).
8. Sir Arthur Eddington, *The Nature of the Physical World* (1928; Cambridge: Cambridge University Press, 1953), 291; author's italics.
9. Albert Einstein, cited in J.M. Cohen and M.J. Cohen, compilers, *The Penguin Dictionary of Twentieth-Century Quotations* (New York: Penguin, 1980), 115.
10. Wallace Stevens, "Of Modern Poetry," in *The Collected Poems of Wallace Stevens* (New York: Alfred A. Knopf, 1954), 239.
11. At this time, I have been unable to locate a source for this quotation.

A Bibliography of the Works of Frank McConnell

Scholarly Books Authored

The Confessional Imagination: A Reading of Wordsworth's Prelude. Baltimore: Johns Hopkins University Press, 1974. 211 pp.
Four Postwar American Novelists: Bellow, Mailer, Barth, and Pynchon. Chicago: University of Chicago Press, 1977. 206 pp.
The Science Fiction of H.G. Wells. New York: Oxford University Press, 1981. 235 pp.
The Spoken Seen: Film and the Romantic Imagination. Baltimore: Johns Hopkins University Press, 1975. 195 pp. Translated into Spanish and republished as *El Cine y la Imaginación Romántica.* Versión castellana y revisión filmográfica por Ramon Font. Revisión bibliográfica por Joaquim Romaguera i Ramió. Barcelona: Editorial Gustavo Gili, 1977. 204 pp. Reprinted in 2004.
Storytelling and Mythmaking: Images from Film and Literature. New York: Oxford University Press, 1979. 303 pp.

Scholarly Books Edited

The Bible and the Narrative Tradition. Edited by Frank McConnell. New York: Oxford University Press, 1986. 152 pp.
Byron's Poetry: Authoritative Texts, Letters and Journals, Criticism, Images of Byron. By Lord Byron. Selected and edited by Frank McConnell. New York: W.W. Norton, 1978. 484 pp.
The Time Machine; The War of the Worlds: A Critical Edition. By H.G. Wells. Edited by Frank McConnell. New York: Oxford University Press, 1977. 455 pp.

Fiction (Detective Novels and Short Story)

Blood Lake. New York: Walker, 1987. 237 pp.
The Frog King. New York: Walker, 1990. 226 pp.
Liar's Poker. New York: Walker, 1993. 214 pp.
Murder Among Friends. New York: Walker, 1983. 186 pp.
"They Won't Get Hodge." *Ellery Queen's Mystery Magazine,* 101:1 (January 1993), 110–121.

Eaton Conference Essays

"Alimentary, My Dear Watson: Food and Eating in Scientific and Mystery Fiction." In *Foods of the Gods: Eating and the Eaten in Fantasy and Science Fiction*. Edited by Gary Westfahl, George Slusser, and Eric S. Rabkin. Athens: University of Georgia Press, 1996, 200–212. Originally presented at the 13th Annual J. Lloyd Eaton Conference on Science Fiction and Fantasy Literature, Riverside, California, 1991.

"Boring Dates: Reflections on the Apocalypse Game." In *Storm Warnings: Science Fiction Confronts the Future*. Edited by George Slusser and Colin Greenland. Carbondale: Southern Illinois University Press, 1987, 232–240. Originally presented at the 6th Annual J. Lloyd Eaton Conference on Science Fiction and Fantasy Literature, Riverside, California, 1984.

"Born in Fire: The Ontology of the Monster." In *Shadows of the Magic Lamp: Fantasy and Science Fiction in Film*. Edited by George Slusser and Eric S. Rabkin. Carbondale: Southern Illinois University Press, 1985, 231–237. Originally presented at the 4th Annual J. Lloyd Eaton Conference on Science Fiction and Fantasy Literature, Riverside, California, 1982.

"Frames in Search of a Genre." In *Intersections: Fantasy and Science Fiction*. Edited by George Slusser and Eric S. Rabkin. Carbondale: Southern Illinois University Press, 1987, 119–130. Originally presented at the 7th Annual J. Lloyd Eaton Conference on Science Fiction and Fantasy Literature, Riverside, California, 1985.

"From Astarte to Barbie and Beyond: The Serious History of Dolls." In *Aliens: The Anthropology of Science Fiction*. Edited by George Slusser and Eric S. Rabkin. Carbondale: Southern Illinois University Press, 1987, 199–207. Originally presented at the 8th Annual J. Lloyd Eaton Conference on Science Fiction and Fantasy Literature, Riverside, California, 1986.

"The Missionary Physician, from Asclepius to Kervorkian." In *No Cure for the Future: Disease and Medicine in Science Fiction and Fantasy*. Edited by Gary Westfahl and George Slusser. Westport, CT: Greenwood Press, 2002, 23–30. Originally presented at the 18th Annual J. Lloyd Eaton Conference on Science Fiction and Fantasy Literature, Riverside, California, 1996.

"The Playing Fields of Eden." In *Mindscapes: The Geographies of Imagined Worlds*. Edited by George Slusser and Eric S. Rabkin. Carbondale: Southern Illinois University Press, 1989, 78–87. Originally presented at the 9th Annual J. Lloyd Eaton Conference on Science Fiction and Fantasy Literature, Riverside, California, 1987.

"The Science of Fiction and the Fiction of Science: A Storytelling Animal in an Inhospitable World." In *Sniper Logic*, 7 (Winter-Fall 1999), 113–120. Originally presented posthumously at the 20th J. Lloyd Eaton Conference on Science Fiction and Fantasy Literature, Riverside, California, 1999.

"Seven Types of Chopped Liver: My Adventures in the Genre Wars." In *Science Fiction, Canonization, Marginalization, and the Academy*. Edited by Gary Westfahl and George Slusser. Westport, CT: Greenwood, 2002, 25–36. Originally presented at the 16th Annual J. Lloyd Eaton Conference on Science Fiction and Fantasy Literature, Riverside, California, 1994.

"Sturgeon's Law: First Corollary." In *Hard Science Fiction*. Edited by George Slusser and Eric S. Rabkin. Carbondale: Southern Illinois University Press, 1986, 14–23. Originally presented at the 5th Annual J. Lloyd Eaton Conference on Science Fiction and Fantasy Literature, Riverside, California, 1983.

"'Turn That Shit Down!' Or, How to Market an Underground." In *Science Fiction and Market Realities*. Edited by Gary Westfahl, George Slusser, and Eric S. Rabkin. Athens: University of Georgia Press, 1996, 101–110. Originally presented at the 12th Annual

J. Lloyd Eaton Conference on Science Fiction and Fantasy Literature, Riverside, California, 1990.

"You Bet Your Life: Death and the Storyteller." In *Immortal Engines: Life Extension and Immortality in Science Fiction and Fantasy*. Edited by George Slusser, Gary Westfahl, and Eric S. Rabkin. Athens: University of Georgia Press, 1996, 221–230. Originally presented at the 14th Annual J. Lloyd Eaton Conference on Science Fiction and Fantasy Literature, Riverside, California, 1992.

Other Essays

"Black Words and Black Becoming." *Yale Review* 63 (1974): 193–210.

"Byron's Reductions: 'Much Too Poetical.'" *Journal of English Literary History* 37:3 (September 1970): 415–432.

"A Conversation: McConnell, Goff, Sherman." By Frank McConnell, Robert Goff, and Rosalyn S. Sherman. *Soundings: An Interdisciplinary Journal* 53 (1970): 281–292. McConnell's section was entitled "Effective Lies."

"The Corpse of the Dragon: Notes on Postromantic Fiction." *Tri-Quarterly* 33 (1975): 273–303. Republished in *The New Romanticism: A Collection of Critical Essays*. Edited by Eberhard Alsen. New York: Garland, 2000, 233–260.

"'Death Among the Apple Trees': *The Waves* and the World of Things." *Bucknell Review: A Scholarly Journal of Letters, Arts and Sciences* 16:3 (1968): 23–39. Republished in *Virginia Woolf: A Collection of Critical Essays*. Edited by Claire Sprague. Englewood Cliffs, NJ: Prentice-Hall, 1970, 117–129. Republished, slightly revised, with added "Comment by the Author" in *Makers of the Twentieth-Century Novel*. Edited by Harry R. Garvin. Lewisburg, PA: Bucknell University Press, 1977, 49–61.

"*Felicite, Passion, Ivresse*: The Lexicography of Madame Bovary." *Novel: A Forum on Fiction* 3 (1970): 153–166.

"Film and Writing: The Political Dimension." *Massachusetts Review: A Quarterly of Literature, the Arts and Public Affairs* 13 (1972): 543–562.

"Film as Antipedagogy: Laughing at *Laura*, Cackling at *Kane*." *Massachusetts Review: A Quarterly of Literature, the Arts and Public Affairs* 19 (1978): 571–584.

"Graham Greene." *The Wilson Quarterly* 5:1 (Winter 1981): 168–186.

"H.G. Wells: Utopia and Doomsday." *The Wilson Quarterly* 4:3 (Summer 1980): 176–186.

"Ishmael Reed's Fiction: Da Hoodoo Is Put on America." In *Black Fiction: New Studies in the Afro-American Novel since 1945*. Edited by A. Robert Lee. New York: Barnes & Noble, 1980, 136–148.

"It's Only a Paper Moon: Fantasy and the Professors." In *Genre at the Crossroads: The Challenge of Fantasy*. Edited by George Slusser and Jean-Pierre Barricelli. Riverside, CA: Xenos, 2003, 21–31.

"Meeting Mr. Eliot." *The Wilson Quarterly* 12:2 (Spring 1988): 152–163.

"Noam Chomsky: The Linguist as Anti-Hero." *Soundings: An Interdisciplinary Journal* 53 (1970): 266–280.

"Northrop Frye and *Anatomy of Criticism*." *Sewanee Review* 92:4 (Fall 1984): 622–629. Republished in *The Critics Who Made Us: Essays from Sewanee Review*. Edited by George Core. Columbia and London: University of Missouri Press, 1993, 290–299.

"Notes, Reviews, Speculations: The Chicago Conspiracy Trial: *Explication de Texte*." *Epoch* 20:3 (Spring 1971): 315–324.

"*Pickup on South Street* and the Metamorphosis of the Thriller." *Film Heritage* 8:3 (Spring 1973): 9–18.

"Realist of the Fantastic: H.G. Wells about/in/on the Movies." In *H.G. Wells: Reality and Beyond: A Collection of Critical Essays Prepared in Conjunction with the Exhibition and

Symposium on H.G. Wells. Edited by Michael Mullin. Champaign, Illinois: Champaign Public Library and Information Center, 1986, 23–32.

"Recent Trends in American Films: A Mythology Grows Up." *National Forum: The Phi Kappa Phi Journal* 60:4 (Fall 1980): 8–9.

"Reconsideration: *The End of the Affair.*" *The New Republic* 178:10 (March 11, 1978): 35–37.

"Reconsideration: The Poetry of Richard Wilbur." *The New Republic* 179:5 (July 29, 1978): 37–39.

"Rock and the Politics of Frivolity." *Massachusetts Review: A Quarterly of Literature, the Arts and Public Affairs* 12 (1971): 119–134.

"Romanticism, Language, Waste: A Reflection on Poetics and Disaster." *Bucknell Review: A Scholarly Journal of Letters, Arts and Sciences* 20:3 (1972): 121–140.

"Rough Beasts Slouching: A Note on Horror Movies." *Kenyon Review* 32:1 (1970): 109–120. Republished in *Focus on the Horror Film*. Edited by Roy Huss and T.J. Ross. Englewood Cliffs, NJ: Prentice-Hall, 1972, 24–35.

"'Sensible Talk' about Catholic Novels." *National Catholic Reporter* 17:3 (November 7, 1980): 9–10.

"Shelleyan 'Allegory': *Epipsychidion.*" *Keats-Shelley Journal: Keats, Shelley, Byron, Hunt, and Their Circles* 20 (1971): 100–112.

"Sherlock Holmes: Detecting Order Amid Disorder." *The Wilson Quarterly* 11:2 (Spring 1987): 172–183.

"Song of Innocence: *The Creature from the Black Lagoon.*" *Journal of Popular Film* 2 (1973): 15–28. Republished in *HAL in the Classroom: Science Fiction Films*. Edited by Ralph J. Amelio. Dayton, Ohio: Pflaum Publishing, 1974, 90–102. Republished in *Movies As Artifacts: Cultural Criticism of Popular Film*. Edited by Michael T. Marsden, John G. Nachbar, and Sam L. Grogg, Jr. Chicago: Nelson-Hall, 1982, 208–217.

"Stalking Papa's Ghost: Hemingway's Presence in Contemporary American Writing." In *Ernest Hemingway: New Critical Essays*. Edited by A. Robert Lee. London: Vision, and Totowa, NJ: Barnes & Noble, 1983, 193–211. Republished in *The Wilson Quarterly* 10:1 (New Year's 1986): 160–172.

"The Suburbs of Camelot." *The Wilson Quarterly* 7:3 (Summer 1983): 80–93.

"Television and American Culture." By Douglas Gomery, Todd Gitlin, and Frank McConnell. *The Wilson Quarterly* 17:4 (Fall 1993): 40–65. McConnell's section was entitled "Seeing Through the Tube."

"*The Time Machine* and *The War of the Worlds*: Parable and Possibility in H.G. Wells." By Samuel L. Hynes and Frank McConnell. In *The Time Machine; The War of the Worlds: A Critical Edition*. By H.G. Wells. Edited by Frank McConnell. New York: Oxford University Press, 1977, 345–366.

"To Stand in the Fire." *Notre Dame Magazine* 20:4 (Winter 1991/1992): 14–15.

"Toward a Lexicon of Slogans." *Midwest Quarterly: A Journal of Contemporary Thought* 13 (1971): 69–90.

"Toward a Syntax of Fiction." *College English* 36:2 (Fall 1974): 147–160.

"Uncle Tom and the Avant-Garde." *Massachusetts Review: A Quarterly of Literature, the Arts and Public Affairs* 16 (1975): 732–745.

"Understanding Wallace Stevens." *The Wilson Quarterly* 8:3 (Summer 1984): 160–169.

"Vietnam and 'Vietnam': A Note on the Pathology of Language." *Soundings: An Interdisciplinary Journal* 51 (1968): 195–207.

"We Are Not Alone." *The Wilson Quarterly* 2:3 (Summer 1978): 110–114. Republished in *American Media: The Wilson Quarterly Reader*. Edited by Philip S. Cook, Douglas Gomery, and Lawrence Wilson Lichty. Washington, D.C.: Wilson Center, 1989, 133–137. Republished in *Media in America: The Wilson Quarterly Reader*. Revised Edition. Edited by Douglas Gomery. Washington, D.C.: Wilson Center, 1998, 156–159.

"Welcome Back, Zonker." *In These Times* 10:2 (November 1985): 23–24.
"Will Deconstruction Be the Death of Literature?" *The Wilson Quarterly* 14:1 (Winter 1990): 99–109. Republished in *The Best of the Wilson Quarterly* [special issue of *The Wilson Quarterly*], undated [1992], 52–61.
"William Burroughs and the Literature of Addiction." *Massachusetts Review: A Quarterly of Literature, the Arts and Public Affairs* 8 (1967): 91–101. Republished in *The American Literary Anthology 2: The Second Annual Collection of the Best from the Literary Magazines*. Edited by George Plimpton and Peter Ardery. New York: Random House, 1969, 367–378. Republished in *William S. Burroughs at the Front*. Edited by Jennie Skerl and Robin Lydenberg. Carbondale, Illinois: Southern Illinois University Press, 1991, 91–101.
"Words and the Man: The Art of James Joyce." *The Wilson Quarterly* 6:1 (Winter 1982): 176–187.

Commonweal *Columns and Articles*

[Note: Most McConnell columns were published under the heading of "Media"; a few which dealt with topics unrelated to the media were published as articles. McConnell book reviews published in *Commonweal* are listed under Reviews.]

"Ads and Addiction: Booze on the Tube." *Commonweal* 110:22 (December 16, 1983): 689–692.
"Art Is Dangerous: 'Beavis and Butthead,' for Example." *Commonweal* 121:1 (January 14, 1994): 28–30. At http://findarticles.com/p/articles/mi_m1252/is_n1_v121/ai_14979779.
"Bebop Takes a Hard Shot: Dizzy Gillespie, R.I.P." *Commonweal* 120:3 (February 12, 1993): 17–18. At http://findarticles.com/p/articles/mi_m1252/is_n3_v120/ai_13434701.
"Cathedral to Octoplex: Remembering the Movies." *Commonweal* 119:10 (May 22, 1992): 13–14.
"The Chat Show: From Steve Allen to Oprah." *Commonweal* 119:3 (February 14, 1992): 18–19.
"Comic Relief: From 'Gilgamesh' to 'Spiderman.'" *Commonweal* 119:4 (February 28, 1992): 21–22.
"Death on Trial: PBS's 'Before I Die.'" *Commonweal* 124:8 (April 25, 1997): 20–21. At http://findarticles.com/p/articles/mi_m1252/is_n8_v124/ai_19997914.
"Desecrating Literature: Reading the *PMLA*." *Commonweal* 123:7 (April 5, 1996): 24, 26–27. At http://findarticles.com/p/articles/mi_m1252/is_n7_v123/ai_18181676.
"Dimming of the Private Eye: From Fr. Brown to Fr. Dowling." *Commonweal* 118:9 (May 3, 1991): 296–297.
"Documenting a Revolution: Reflections on Vatican II." *Commonweal* 125:15 (September 11, 1998): 31–33. At http://findarticles.com/p/articles/mi_m1252/is_n15_v125/ai_21148207.
"Downhill and Slippery: CBS Goes to the Olympics." *Commonweal* 121:6 (March 25, 1994): 18–19. At http://findarticles.com/p/articles/mi_m1252/is_n6_v121/ai_14960810.
"The Elephant in the Room: *Moyers on Addiction: Close to Home*." *Commonweal* 125:6 (March 27, 1998): 20–21. At http://findarticles.com/p/articles/mi_m1252/is_n6_v125/ai_20520534.
"Eloise Knapp Hay, R.I.P.: I've Lost a Sparring Partner." *Commonweal* 123:14 (August 16, 1996): 21–22. At http://findarticles.com/p/articles/mi_m1252/is_n14_v123/ai_18600905.

"Epic Comics: Neil Gaiman's 'Sandman.'" *Commonweal* 122:18 (October 20, 1995): 21–22. At http://findarticles.com/p/articles/mi_m1252/is_n18_v122/ai_17446772.

"Eric Clapton's Genius: A Mensch Who Plays the Blues." *Commonweal* 119:5 (March 13, 1992): 25–26.

"Expecting Visitors?: Aliens from Inner Space." *Commonweal* 123:20 (November 22, 1996): 21–22. At http://findarticles.com/p/articles/mi_m1252/is_n20_v123/ai_19022281.

"Faith and Doubt on the Tube." *Commonweal* 124:17 (October 10, 1997): 23–24. At http://findarticles.com/p/articles/mi_m1252/is_n17_v124/ai_20039479.

"The First 'Murray Awards': Winners and Losers." *Commonweal* 118:10 (May 17, 1991): 325–326.

"Follow That Moose: 'Northern Exposure's Pedigree.'" *Commonweal* 120:19 (November 5, 1993): 18–20. At http://findarticles.com/p/articles/mi_m1252/is_n19_v120/ai_14553650.

"Foodscam: Only the Fat Are Free." *Commonweal* 117:14 (August 10, 1990): 458–459.

"Frank and Celeste and Dan: The Unthinkable 'Murphy Brown.'" *Commonweal* 119:13 (July 17, 1992): 19–20.

"Future Perfect: 'Welcome to Paradox.'" *Commonweal* 125:21 (December 4, 1998): 18–19. At http://findarticles.com/p/articles/mi_m1252/is_21_125/ai_53450452.

"Games People Watch: Unsportsmanlike Products." *Commonweal* 117:21 (December 7, 1990): 724–725.

"The Games We Play: Data Into Dollars." *Commonweal* 118:14 (August 9, 1991): 482–484.

"'Genesis': PBS Does a Mitzvah." *Commonweal* 123:17 (October 11, 1996): 17–18. At http://findarticles.com/p/articles/mi_m1252/is_n17_v123/ai_18783817.

"'Genesis' II: Redactor Missing in Action." *Commonweal* 123:18 (October 25, 1996): 19–20. At http://findarticles.com/p/articles/mi_m1252/is_n18_v123/ai_18937956.

"Go Ahead, Take a Peek: Fox's 'X-Files.'" *Commonweal* 121:15 (September 9, 1994): 15–17. At http://findarticles.com/p/articles/mi_m1252/is_n15_v121/ai_15822962.

"Goliath Swallows Leviathan: *Conglomerates and the Media.*" *Commonweal* 124:19 (November 7, 1997): 17–18. At http://findarticles.com/p/articles/mi_m1252/is_n19_v124/ai_20227038.

"How *Seinfeld* Was Born: Jane Austen Meets Woody Allen." *Commonweal* 123:3 (February 9, 1996): 19–20. At http://findarticles.com/p/articles/mi_m1252/is_n3_v123/ai_17985539. Republished under the title "Seinfeld" in *Common Culture: Reading and Writing about American Popular Culture*. Second Edition. Edited by Michael Petracca and Madeleine Sorapure. Upper Saddle River, NJ: Prentice Hall, 1998, 244–247.

"In a Galaxy Far, Far Away: Lucas's 'Star Wars.'" *Commonweal* 124:9 (May 9, 1997): 16–17. At http://findarticles.com/p/articles/mi_m1252/is_9_124/ai_58400664.

"Infant Art: The Video Is Born." *Commonweal* 111:7 (April 6, 1984): 212–214.

"It's Not Hell, Just Limbaugh: Excellence in Bombast." *Commonweal* 120:13 (June 4, 1993): 20–22. At http://findarticles.com/p/articles/mi_m1252/is_n11_v120/ai_13828252.

"It's Time to Take Sides: Catholicism, Yes; Popular Culture, No." By John D. Hagen, Jr., Richard Alleva, and Frank McConnell. *Commonweal* 122:16 (September 22, 1995): 19–23. At http://findarticles.com/p/articles/mi_m1252/is_n11_v120/ai_13828252.

"Just a Moment: The Logic of Nintendo." *Commonweal* 117:8 (April 20, 1990): 256–257.

"Just Doing It: Stephen King's Craft." *Commonweal* 118:2 (January 25, 1991): 57–59.

"A Killer Serial: Chris Carter's 'Millennium.'" *Commonweal* 124:13 (July 18, 1997): 19–20. At http://findarticles.com/p/articles/mi_m1252/is_13_124/ai_58400698.

"Let's Dance: The Democracy of 'Swing.'" *Commonweal* 125:17 (October 9, 1998): 18. At http://findarticles.com/p/articles/mi_m1252/is_n17_v125/ai_21227665.

"'Live Long and Prosper': The Trek Goes On." *Commonweal* 118:19 (November 8, 1991): 652–654.

"The McConnell Quakes: The Electronic Hearth Blazes." *Commonweal* 121:3 (February 11, 1994): 18–19. At http://findarticles.com/p/articles/mi_m1252/is_n3_v121/ai_14824106.

"Music to Have Fun By: Gerry Mulligan and His Baritone Sax." *Commonweal* 123:5 (March 8, 1996): 17–18. At http://findarticles.com/p/articles/mi_m1252/is_n5_v123/ai_18093491.

"A Name for Loss: Memorials of Vietnam." *Commonweal* 112:14 (August 9, 1985): 441–442.

"A Nation of Standups: Starring in Our Own Scripts." *Commonweal* 120:4 (February 26, 1993): 20–21. At http://findarticles.com/p/articles/mi_m1252/is_n4_v120/ai_13609403.

"Nintendo from Hell: The Gulf War on the Tube." *Commonweal* 118:4 (February 22, 1991): 134–136.

"No Fall Classic: Burns's 'Baseball.'" *Commonweal* 121:20 (November 18, 1994): 31–32. At http://findarticles.com/p/articles/mi_m1252/is_n20_v121/ai_15879434.

"No Way to Exit?: *Seinfeld* as Sartre." *Commonweal* 125:11 (June 5, 1998): 20–21. At http://www.encyclopedia.com/doc/1G1-20825330.html.

"A Nun's 'Story': Sister Wendy on PBS." *Commonweal* 124:18 (October 24, 1997): 19–21. At http://findarticles.com/p/articles/mi_m1252/is_n18_v124/ai_20159022.

"O'Malley of Notre Dame." *Commonweal* 118:16 (September 27, 1991): 543–547.

"On the Road Again: Willie Nelson's Sprezzatura." *Commonweal* 112:17 (October 4, 1985): 532–534.

"Our Town: Lynch's *Twin Peaks*." *Commonweal* 117:10 (May 18, 1990): 320–322.

"Perfect Fools: Lenny, George, Richard and Frank." *Commonweal* 119:18 (October 23, 1992): 18–19. At http://findarticles.com/p/articles/mi_m1252/is_n18_v119/ai_12806789.

"A Perfect Match: CDs and Jazz." *Commonweal* 119:16 (September 25, 1992): 21–22. At http://findarticles.com/p/articles/mi_m1252/is_n16_v119/ai_12702903.

"The Prince of Darkness: Miles Davis, R.I.P." *Commonweal* 118:18 (October 25, 1991): 616–617.

"'Real' Cartoon Characters: *The Simpsons*." *Commonweal* 117:12 (June 15, 1990): 389–390.

"The Right Hand of God: PBS Looks at the Political Prophets." *Commonweal* 123:16 (September 27, 1996): 21–22. At http://findarticles.com/p/articles/mi_m1252/is_n16_v123/ai_18732960.

"A Rock Poet: From Fitzgerald to Springsteen." *Commonweal* 110:14 (August 12, 1983): 431–433.

"Self-Hugging Parables: Boiling the Irish Catholic Pot." Review of *The Cardinal Sins* and *Thy Brother's Wife* by Andrew Greeley, presented as an article. *Commonweal* 109:11 (June 4, 1982): 342–343.

"Shelf-Indulgence: Marketing Boom, Literary Bust." *Commonweal* 112:21 (November 29, 1985): 676–677.

"Smart, Hip and Real: Bochco's 'NYPD Blue.'" *Commonweal* 120:17 (October 8, 1993): 20–21. At http://findarticles.com/p/articles/mi_m1252/is_n17_v120/ai_14555659.

"Something Gained — and Lost: What Reunification Feels Like: Report from Germany." *Commonweal* 117:18 (October 26, 1990): 598–600.

"Soothing Music: For Those in a Coma." *Commonweal* 121:9 (May 6, 1994): 18–19. At http://findarticles.com/p/articles/mi_m1252/is_n9_v121/ai_15256009.

"Southern Baptists on PBS: Lipscomb's 'Battle for the Minds.'" *Commonweal* 124:11 (June 6, 1997): 21–22. At http://findarticles.com/p/articles/mi_m1252/is_n11_v124/ai_19962935.

"Sunday with David: A Sabbath of Sorts." *Commonweal* 118:6 (March 22, 1991): 195–196.

"Superpersons: 'Lois and Clark.'" *Commonweal* 121:12 (June 17, 1994): 22–23. At http://findarticles.com/p/articles/mi_m1252/is_n12_v121/ai_15546532.

"Take My Wife — Please: Good (Deeds) to the Last Drop." *Commonweal* 121:4 (February 25, 1994): 18–19. At http://findarticles.com/p/articles/mi_m1252/is_n4_v121/ai_14880472.
"The Trials of Television: The McMartin Case." *Commonweal* 117:6 (March 23, 1990): 189–190.
"The Trials of TV Acting: The Triumph of Sharon Gless." *Commonweal* 118:1 (January 11, 1991): 19–20.
"Truly Dishonest: And Joe Six-Pack Knows It." *Commonweal* 120:2 (January 29, 1993): 14–16. At http://findarticles.com/p/articles/mi_m1252/is_n2_v120/ai_13370504.
"Twice-Told Tales: Why 'Law and Order' Works." *Commonweal* 121:19 (November 4, 1994): 19–20. At http://findarticles.com/p/articles/mi_m1252/is_n19_v121/ai_15892213.
"The Values Things: It's Noonan Again in America." *Commonweal* 122:5 (March 10, 1995): 16–17. At http://findarticles.com/p/articles/mi_m1252/is_n5_v122/ai_16646037.
"The Vanishing Family: Mirroring the Successful Self." *Commonweal* 110:3 (February 11, 1983): 85–86.
"A Very Good 80 Years: Frank Sinatra's Birthday." *Commonweal* 122:22 (December 15, 1995): 18–19. At http://findarticles.com/p/articles/mi_m1252/is_n22_v122/ai_17932538.
"Watching Talk: Donahue as Diet Cola." *Commonweal* 110:8 (April 22, 1983): 245–247.
"What Hath Phil Wrought? A Coarsening of Culture." *Commonweal* 123:6 (March 22, 1996): 20–21. At http://findarticles.com/p/articles/mi_m1252/is_n6_v123/ai_18150274.
"Who's on First: The Greatest Rock Band." *Commonweal* 122:1 (January 13, 1995): 16–18. At http://findarticles.com/p/articles/mi_m1252/is_n1_v122/ai_16028001.
"Young for His Age: The Tube, the Music and the Shadow." *Commonweal* 119:20 (November 20, 1992): 19–20. At http://findarticles.com/p/articles/mi_m1252/is_n20_v119/ai_12911719.

Introductions

"Foreword." In *Telling It Again and Again: Repetition in Literature and Film*. By Bruce Kawin. Niwot: University Press of Colorado, 1989, ix–xviii. Book originally published without McConnell foreword in 1972.
"Introduction." In *The Sandman, Volume 9: The Kindly Ones*, by Neil Gaiman. New York: Time Warner, 1996, [6–11]. Translated into German and republished in *Sandman*. Translator unknown. Bad Tölz: Tilsner, 2002. Unseen; pages unknown.
"Introduction." In *The Time Machine; The War of the Worlds: A Critical Edition*. By H.G. Wells. Edited by Frank McConnell. New York: Oxford University Press, 1977, 3–10.
"Preface." In *The Sandman: Book of Dreams*. Edited by Neil Gaiman and Edward E. Kramer. New York: HarperPrism, 1996, 1–6.

Interviews

"Interview: Frank McConnell." Interviewer Ellen Nehr. *Mystery Scene* No. 10 (1987): 22.
"John Gardner: The Art of Fiction LXXIII." Interview. Interviewers Paul F. Ferguson, John R. Maier, Sara Matthiessen, and Frank McConnell. *The Paris Review* 75 (Spring, 1979): 36–74. At http://www.parisreview.org/media/3394_GARDNER.pdf. Republished as "John Gardner" in *Writers at Work: The Paris Review Interviews: Sixth Series*. Edited by George Plimpton. Introduction by Frank Kermode. New York: Viking, 1984, 375–410. Republished in *Conversations with John Gardner*. Edited by Allen Chavkin. Jackson: University Press of Mississippi, 1990, 143–171.

Bibliography of the Works of Frank McConnell 195

"Sir Arthur C. Clarke: A Telephone Conversation." Interview. Interviewer Eric S. Rabkin with questions from Paul A. Carter, Gary Kern, Frank McConnell, Daryl F. Mallett, Melissa Mannion, Joseph D. Miller, and Gary Westfahl. In *Space and Beyond: The Frontier Theme in Science Fiction.* Edited by Gary Westfahl. Westport, CT: Greenwood, 2000, 185–190.

Reviews

"Alas, Gargantua: In 'The Tunnel,' the Rabelaisian William Gass Has Produced a Vast, Shimmering Heap of Postmodern Rubble." Review of *The Tunnel,* by William Gass. *Boston Sunday Globe,* February 26, 1995, B14, B16.

"Angels in the Burial Ground." Review of *Decorations in a Ruined Cemetery* by John Gregory Brown. *San Francisco Chronicle,* May 29, 1994, Review Section, 4.

"Authors and Books." Review of *A Gentle Madness: Bibliophiles, Bibliomanes, and the Eternal Passion for Books,* by Nicholas A. Basbanes, *Writers' Houses,* by Erica Lennard and Francesca Premoli-Droulers, *Who's Writing This?: Notations on the Authorial I, with Self Portraits,* edited by Daniel Halpern, *The Oxford Companion to English Literature,* edited by Margaret A. Drabble, *The Oxford Companion to American Literature,* edited by James D. Hart and Phillip W. Leininger, *Science Fiction: The Illustrated Encyclopedia,* by John Clute, and *The Cambridge Encyclopedia of the English Language,* by David Crystal. *San Jose Mercury News,* December 3, 1995, "Books," 3–4.

"The Bard's Primal Scene." Review of *Shakespeare and the Goddess of Complete Being* by Ted Hughes. *Commonweal* 119:19 (November 6, 1992): 31–33. At http://findarticles.com/p/articles/mi_m1252/is_n19_v119/ai_12843677.

"Barth Reviewed: The Novel's Intricate Turnings Articulate the Human Depth and Pathos Underlying All Stories." Review of *Letters,* by John Barth. *Books and Arts* 1:4 (October 26, 1979): 6–7.

"Behind the Walls: A Middle-Aged Teacher Finds Himself, and a New Germany." Review of *Novemberfest,* by Theodore Weesner. *San Jose Mercury News,* November 27, 1994, "Books," 1, 2.

"Black Humor: Out of Oppression Has Come a Powerful, Healing Weapon." Review of *On the Real Side: Laughing, Lying and Signifying: The Underground Tradition of African-American Humor That Transformed American Culture from Slavery to Richard Pryor,* by Mel Watkins. *Boston Sunday Globe,* February 20, 1994, B36, B39.

"Bloom's Gnostic Doodling: Literature's Great Curmudgeon Takes on Angels, Apocalypse and the Notion of God." Review of *Omens of Millennium: The Gnosis of Angels, Dreams, and Resurrection* by Harold Bloom. *Boston Sunday Globe,* September 1, 1996, N13, N14.

"The Boy from Tupelo: One for the Money, Two for the Show Three to Get Ready Now Go, Cat, Go." Review of *Last Train to Memphis: The Rise of Elvis Presley,* by Peter Guralnick. *San Jose Mercury News,* October 2, 1994, "Books," 1, 5.

"Capital or Casbah, Seedbed or Jungle?: Max Eastman and His Compatriots Occupy a Special but Contradictory Place in the Mythology of the American Left." Review of *Children of Fantasy: The First Rebels of Greenwich Village,* by Robert E. Humphrey, and *The Last Romantic: A Life of Max Eastman,* by William L. O'Neill. *The Chronicle of Higher Education* 17:23 (February 20, 1979), *The Chronicle Review,* 4–5.

"The Century Marked: One Journalist Talks to Himself; Another Listens to Others." Review of *A Diary of the Century: Tales from America's Greatest Diarist, 1927–1995,* by Edward Robb Ellis, and *Coming of Age: The Story of Our Century by Those Who've Lived It,* by Studs Terkel. *San Jose Mercury News,* September 3, 1995, "Books," 1–2.

"Crichton's 'Lost World' Is Predictable, Preachy." Review of *The Lost World*, by Michael Crichton. *Atlanta Journal-Constitution*, September 20, 1995, B2.

"The Critic as Romantic Hero." Review of *Andre Bazin*, by Dudley Andrew. *Quarterly Review of Film Studies* 5:1 (Winter 1980): 109–113.

"Critics' Choices for Christmas." By Sara Maitland, Robert Coles, Rembert G. Weakland, Suzanne Keen, Frank McConnell, Alane Mason, and Ron Hansen. *Commonweal* 121:21 (December 2, 1994): 15, 24–30. McConnell's reviews at http://findarticles.com/p/articles/mi_m1252/is_n21_v121/ai_15958832, http://findarticles.com/p/articles/mi_m1252/is_n21_v121/ai_15958834, and http://findarticles.com/p/articles/mi_m1252/is_n21_v121/ai_15958836.

"A Declaration of Love: Novels Get to the Heart of the Exaltation and Madness." Review of *Riven Rock*, by T.C. Boyle, and *Enduring Love*, by Ian McEwan. *San Jose Mercury News*, February 15, 1998, "Books," 3, 5.

"Defining Sci-Fi: Controversy Shouldn't Keep Readers from Norton Book Anthology." Review of *The Norton Book of Science Fiction*, edited by Ursula K. Le Guin and Brian Attebery. *Atlanta Journal-Constitution*, September 11, 1994, N10.

"'Derby Dugan's' Daily Dilemmas Recap Days Gone By." Review of *Derby Dugan's Depression Funnies*, by Tom De Haven. *Atlanta Journal-Constitution*, June 30, 1996, L8.

"Difficult Visions: In Its Arrogant, Demanding Density, 'A Frolic of His Own' Is Vintage William Gaddis: Tough Work, but Full of Intricate Rewards." Review of *A Frolic of His Own*, by William Gaddis. *Boston Sunday Globe*, January 9, 1994, B44–B45.

"Disunited States of America." Review of *Peckinpah: The Western Films*, by Paul Seydor. *Quarterly Review of Film Studies* 6:2 (Spring 1981): 217–221.

"The Divided Mind Made Whole." Review of *The Divided Mind: Ideology and Imagination in America, 1898–1917*, by Peter Conn. *American Quarterly* 36:5 (Winter 1984): 700–704.

"Dizzy with Ecstacy." Review of *Reading Jazz: A Gathering of Autobiography, Reportage, and Criticism*, edited by Robert Gottlieb. *Commonweal* 124:6 (March 28, 1997): 23–24. http://findarticles.com/p/articles/mi_m1252/is_n6_v124/ai_19517804.

"Down Wonder: The Story of a Quest, Told in a Rich Australian Voice." Review of *The Riders*, by Tim Winton. *San Jose Mercury News*, July 16, 1995, "Books," 1, 3.

"The Dream State: How America Invented California." Review of *Big Dreams: Into the Heart of California*, by Bill Barich. *San Jose Mercury News*, June 5, 1994, "Books," 1, 3.

"Everything Banished by Love." Review of *Doctor Fischer of Geneva*, by Graham Greene. *Commonweal* 107:12 (June 20, 1980): 375–376.

"Fabulous, Fabulous California." Review of *Vineland*, by Thomas Pynchon. *The Los Angeles Times*, December 31, 1989, Book Review Section, 1, 7. At http://vineland.pynchonwiki.com/wiki/index.php?title=LA_Times_Review_-_Frank_McConnell. Republished under the title "'Vineland' Makes World More Tolerable: American Voice of Late 20th Century Rings Out After 17-Year Silence." *The Deseret News*, January 14, 1990, E5. Translated into German and republished as "Zu Thomas Pynchon's Neuem Roman *Weinland*." *Sonntag*, May 13, 1990. Unseen; translator unknown; pages unknown.

"Faustian Victory: What Happens to a Culture in Which All of Its Science-Fiction Wishes Come True?" Review of *The Dreams Our Stuff Is Made Of: How Science Fiction Conquered the World*, by Thomas M. Disch. *San Jose Mercury News*, May 17, 1998, "Books," 3.

"Finding Words for the Silences Between Speech and Poetry: Dispatches from the Forbidding but Fertile No Man's Land of Our Linguistic Territories." Review of *On the Margins of Discourse: The Relation of Literature to Language*, by Barbara Herrnstein

Smith. *The Chronicle of Higher Education* 18:10 (April 30, 1979): *The Chronicle Review*, 13.
"Flight of Fancy: The Brilliant and Readable, Baroque and Minimal, New Novel by Paul Auster." Review of *Mr. Vertigo*, by Paul Auster. *Boston Sunday Globe*, July 31, 1994, B25, B28.
"Genre-Bending: Two Novels with Eerie Similarities Defy Categorization." Review of *Girls*, by Frederick Busch, and *A Face in the Window*, by Dennis McFarland. *San Jose Mercury News*, "Books," March 30, 1997, 2–3.
"Get Shorties: Collections of Neglected Craft That Shine." Review of *The Least You Need to Know: Stories*, by Lee Martin, *Batting Against Castro: Stories*, by Jim Shepard, *Emerald City: Stories*, by Jennifer Egan, *Legacies: Stories*, by Starling Lawrence, *Cruising Paradise: Tales*, by Sam Shepard, *Asking for Love and Other Stories*, by Roxana Robinson, and *Sudden Fiction (Continued): 60 New Short-Short Stories*, edited by Robert Shapard and James Thomas. *San Jose Mercury News*, June 2, 1996, "Books," 4–5.
"Glass Bead Games: Two Defenses of Apocalypse." Review of *Closing Time*, by Norman O. Brown, and *The Garden and the Map: Schizophrenia in Twentieth-Century Literature and Culture*, by John Vernon. *Contemporary Literature* 15 (1974): 406–414.
"Good and Plenty." Review of *Mason and Dixon*, by Thomas Pynchon. *Commonweal* 124:14 (August 15, 1997): 20–22. At http://findarticles.com/p/articles/mi_m1252/is_n14_v124/ai_20148160.
"Harold Bloom Reminds Us What Matters: Shakespeare's the Greatest — and Other Things That Should Go Without Saying, but Don't." Review of *The Western Canon: The Books and School of the Ages*, by Harold Bloom. *Boston Sunday Globe*, September 18, 1994, A14, A16.
"Hope in the Big Easy: Burke's Latest Reflects Shining Vitality of Private-Eye Novels." Review of *Dixie City Jam*, by James Lee Burke. *Atlanta Journal-Constitution*, August 14, 1994, N8.
"In Dubious Battles: John Steinbeck's Struggle for Acceptance." Review of *John Steinbeck: A Biography*, by Jay Parini. *San Jose Mercury News*, February 5, 1995, "Books," 1–2
"In from the Otherworld: Delusions, Real Life Duel in 'Daimonic Reality.'" Review of *Daimonic Reality: A Field Guide to the Otherworld*, by Patrick Harper. *Atlanta Journal-Constitution*, April 16, 1995, K11.
"Into the Science-Fiction Heart of Fantasy." Review of *Amnesia Moon*, by Jonathan Lethem, and *Wicked: The Life and Times of the Wicked Witch of the West*, by Gregory Maguire. *San Jose Mercury News*, November 19, 1995, "Books," 5.
"A Letter-Perfect Endeavor: Scholarly Look at Alphabet Is Eminently Readable." Review of *The Alphabetic Labyrinth: The Letters in History and Imagination*, by Johanna Drucker. *Atlanta Journal-Constitution*, August 13, 1995, L10.
"Literature and Its Discontents." Review of *The Death of Literature*, by Alvin Kernan, and *Before Novels: The Cultural Contexts of Eighteenth-Century English Fiction*, by J. Paul Hunter. *The Wilson Quarterly* 15:1 (Winter 1991): 89–91.
"A Lost Generation: Doctrinaire Self-Loathing Defrauds Today's Literature Students." Review of *Literature Lost: Social Agendas and the Corruption of the Humanities*, by John M. Ellis. *San Jose Mercury News*, October 19, 1997, "Books," 2.
"Medium with a Message." Review of *Marshall McLuhan: Escape into Understanding: A Biography*, by W. Terrence Gordon. *Commonweal* 125:4 (February 27, 1998): 24–26. At http://findarticles.com/p/articles/mi_m1252/is_n4_v125/ai_20492653.
"Of Faith and Forgiveness." Review of *Atticus*, by Ron Hansen. *San Jose Mercury News*, February 11, 1996, "Books," 1–2.
Review of *Alexander Pope: A Life*, by Maynard Mack. *The Wilson Quarterly* 10:3 (Summer 1986): 132–133.

Review of *The Challenge of the Mahatmas* and *Dreams of Adventure, Deeds of Empire*, both by Martin Green. *The New Republic* 181:13 (September 29, 1979): 34–37.
Review of *The Collected Poems of Howard Nemerov*, by Howard Nemerov. *The Wilson Quarterly* 3:1 (Winter 1979): 144.
Review of *Day by Day*, by Robert Lowell. *The Wilson Quarterly* 2:1 (Winter 1978): 154–155.
Review of *Discipline and Punish: The Birth of the Prison*, by Michel Foucault, and *Violence and the Sacred*, by René Girard. *The New Republic* 178:13 (April 1, 1978): 32–34.
Review of *Energy and Entropy: Science and Culture in Victorian Britain*, edited by Patrick Brantlinger, and *One Culture: Essays in Science and Literature*, edited by George Levine. *Victorian Studies* 33:3 (Spring 1990): 496–497.
Review of *The Executioner's Song*, by Norman Mailer. *The New Republic* 181:17 (October 27, 1979): 28–30.
Review of *Film and the Narrative Tradition*, by John L. Fell. *Style* 9 (1975): 533–536.
Review of *The Flight to Lucifer: A Gnostic Fantasy*, by Harold Bloom. *The New Republic* 180:20 (May 19, 1979): 32–34.
Review of *H.G. Wells: Aspects of a Life*, by Anthony West. *The Wilson Quarterly* 8:5 (Winter 1984): 128–129.
Review of *Henry Thoreau: A Life of the Mind*, by Robert D. Richardson, Jr. *The Wilson Quarterly* 10:5 (Winter 1986): 130–131.
Review of *Janus: A Summing Up*, by Arthur Koestler. *The New Republic* 178:19 (May 13, 1978): 34–36.
Review of *Lord Byron's Strength: Romantic Writing and Commercial Society*, by Jerome Christensen. *Rocky Mountain Review of Language and Literature* 48:1 (1994): 90–92.
Review of *Mathematics Today: Twelve Informal Essays*, edited by Lynn Arthur Steen. *American Mathematical Monthly* 86:10 (December 1979): 871–873.
Review of *Myths of Modern Individualism: Faust, Don Quixote, Don Juan, Robinson Crusoe*, by Ian Watt. *Rocky Mountain Review of Language and Literature* 50:2 (1996): 210–212.
Review of *Narrative Form in History and Fiction: Hume, Fielding, and Gibbon*, by Leo Braudy. *Philological Quarterly* 50:3 (July 1971): 376–378.
Review of *Narrative Strategies: Original Essays in Film and Prose Fiction*, edited by Syndy M. Conger and Janice R. Welsch. In *Yearbook of Comparative and General Literature* No. 31 (1981): 97–98.
Review of *The Natural History of H.G. Wells*, by John R. Reed. *Victorian Studies* 27.1 (Autumn 1983): 116–118.
Review of *Narrative Form in History and Fiction: Hume, Fielding, and Gibbon*, by Leo Braudy. *Philological Quarterly* 50:3 (July 1971): 376–378.
Review of *Vision and Revision: Coleridge's Art of Immanence*, by Jean-Pierre Mileur. *Wordsworth Circle* 14:3 (Summer 1983): 133–135.
Review of *Samuel Beckett*, by Deirdre Bair. *The Wilson Quarterly* 2:4 (Winter 1978): 152.
Review of *Trouble Downtown*, by Henry Bedord. *Nation's Cities* 16:8 (August 1978): 30–31.
Review of *Yankee Blues: Musical Culture and American Identity* by MacDonald Smith Moore. *The Wilson Quarterly* 10:2 (Spring 1986): 134–136.
"Riding High on Frontier Nights: Two Novels Join in Restitching the Fabric of Western Lore." Review of *The Mercy Seat*, by Rilla Askew, and *The Englishman's Boy*, by Guy Vanderhaeghe. *San Jose Mercury News*, September 7, 1997, "Books," 3.
"The Road to Tennessee: The Playwright Who Invented Himself." Review of *Tom: The Unknown Tennessee Williams*, by Lyle Leverich. San Jose Mercury News, November 5, 1995, "Books," 1–2.
"Roasting the Fools: Academic Intellectuals Skewered by Satire." Review of *The Handmaid of Desire*, by John L'Heureux, and *Lying on the Couch*, by Irvin D. Yalom. *San Jose Mercury News*, September 8, 1996, "Books," 1–2.

"Sci-Fi/Fantasy: Exploring the Demons of Life and Death: Horror Tale, Comic Book Stand Out in Any Crowd." Review of *Strange Angels,* by Kathe Koja, and *Death: The High Cost of Living,* by Neil Gaiman. *Atlanta Journal-Constitution,* June 19, 1994, N11.

"Sci-Fi/Fantasy: Storytelling Worthy of Wells: Though Futuristic, Kress' Look at Society Paints American Dilemma Today." Review of *Beggars and Choosers,* by Nancy Kress. *Atlanta Journal-Constitution,* December 11, 1994, N8.

"A Sexy Ghost Tells His Tale: Entertaining 'Servant' Ambles but Has the Right Rice Stuff." Review of *Servant of the Bones,* by Anne Rice. *Atlanta Journal-Constitution,* August 4, 1996, L8.

"Should We Trust a Cuddly Novelist?" Review of *Still Life with Woodpecker,* by Tom Robbins. *Commonweal* 108:5 (March 13, 1981): 153–155.

"The Source of Our Selves." Review of *Shakespeare: The Invention of the Human,* by Harold Bloom. *Commonweal* 125:19 (November 6, 1998): 20–22. At http://findarticles.com/p/articles/mi_m1252/is_19_125/ai_57944910.

"Stegner Without Shadows: Biographer Gives Us the Life of a Western Saint." Review of *Wallace Stegner: His Life and Work,* by Jackson J. Benson. *San Jose Mercury News,* November 3, 1996, "Books," 3.

"Stephen King's Unique New Twosome Is a Tour de Force of Horror Storytelling." Review of *Desperation* by Stephen King, and *The Regulators* by Richard Bachman. *Atlanta Journal-Constitution,* September 24, 1996, E7.

"Still a Master of the Game: Eco's One-Man 'Island' Unearths History Alive in Us All." Review of *The Island of the Day Before,* by Umberto Eco. *Atlanta Journal-Constitution,* November 19, 1995, L10.

"Strange Bedfellows." Review of *The Immediate Prospect of Being Hanged,* by Walter Walker. *The Washington Post,* June 18, 1989, "Book World," 9.

"Summer Reading." By Molly Finn, Frank McConnell, Elizabeth Kirkland Cahill, George W. Hunt, Elizabeth McCloskey, and Daniel M. Murtaugh. *Commonweal* 125:12 (June 19, 1998): 20–29.

"Transfigurations of Despair." Review of *A Flag for Sunrise,* by Robert Stone. *Commonweal* 109:5 (March 12, 1982): 153–155.

"Two Kinds of Faith." Review of *The Letters of Evelyn Waugh,* edited by Mark Amory, and *Ways of Escape,* by Graham Greene. *Commonweal* 108:1 (January 16, 1981): 21–23.

"Two Reports from Greeneland." Review of *The Life of Graham Greene, Volume II: 1939–1955,* by Norman Sherry, and *Graham Greene: The Enemy Within,* by Michael Sheldon. *The Wilson Quarterly* 19:3 (Summer 1995): 74–76.

"A Universe to Define: John Updike Launches Himself into the Future and Science Fiction." Review of *Toward the End of Time,* by John Updike. *San Jose Mercury News,* November 2, 1997, "Books," 6.

"What Aristotle Didn't Know." Review of *Myth and Tragedy in Ancient Greece,* by Jean-Pierre Vernant and Pierre Vidal-Naquet, and *Myth and Society in Ancient Greece,* by Jean-Pierre Vernant. *The Wilson Quarterly* 13:3 (Summer 1989): 92–94.

"Why William S. Burroughs Matters: Everyone from Mailer to Pynchon Owes a Debt to This Brooding, Self-Absorbed Addict." Review of *My Education: A Book of Dreams,* by William S. Burroughs. *Boston Sunday Globe,* January 22, 1995, 42, 44.

"William Golding's Sea-Fever." Review of *Fire Down Below,* by William Golding. *The Washington Post,* March 12, 1989, "Book World," 3, 9.

"A Williams Sampler." Review of *The Politics of Modernism,* by Raymond Williams, edited by Tony Kinkney. *American Book Review* 12:4 (September/October 1990): 13–14.

Reference Work Entries

"Black American Literature." In *Collier's Encyclopedia*. William D. Halsey, editorial director. Louis Shores, editor in chief. New York: Macmillan, 1977. Unseen; pages unknown.

"History of English Literature." In *Collier's Encyclopedia*. William D. Halsey, editorial director. Louis Shores, editor in chief. New York: Macmillan, 1977. Unseen; pages unknown.

"John Gardner." In *Contemporary Novelists*. Second Edition. Edited by James Vinson. Associate editor D.L. Kirkpatrick. Preface by Walter Allen. London: St. James, and New York: St. Martin's, 1972, 491–494.

"Literary Criticism." In *Collier's Encyclopedia*. William D. Halsey, editorial director. Louis Shores, editor in chief. New York: Macmillan, 1977. Unseen; pages unknown.

"Norman Mailer." In *The Reader's Companion to American History*. Edited by Eric Foner and John A. Garraty. New York: Houghton Mifflin, 1991, 693–694.

"Thomas Pynchon." In *Contemporary Novelists*. Edited by James Vinson. Preface by Walter Allen. New York: St. Martin's, 1972, 1033–1036.

"Thomas Pynchon." [Revised and updated.] In *Contemporary Novelists*. Second Edition. Edited by James Vinson. Associate editor D.L. Kirkpatrick. Preface by Walter Allen. London: St. James, and New York: St. Martin's, 1972, 1134–1136. Republished in *Contemporary Novelists*. Third Edition. Edited by James Vinson. Associate editor D.L. Kirkpatrick. Preface to the First Edition by Walter Allen. Preface to the Third Edition by Jerome Klinkowitz. New York: St. Martin's, 1982, 542–543. Republished in *Contemporary Novelists*. Fourth Edition. Edited by D.L. Kirkpatrick. Consulting Editor James Vinson. Preface to the First Edition by Walter Allen. Preface to the Third Edition by Jerome Klinkowitz. London and Chicago: St. James Press, 1986, 695–697.

Letter and Responses to Letters

"The Columnist Replies." Response to "McConnell the Nihilist," letter by Linda A. Morrow; "McConnell the Hysteric," letter by Charles C. Gallagher; "McConnell the Easterner," letter by Bob Ennis; and "McConnell the Liberal," letter by William A. Donohoe. *Commonweal* 120:19 (November 5, 1993): 38.

"Frank McConnell Replies." Response to "Defending Deconstruction," letter by J. Hillis Miller. *Wilson Quarterly* 14 (Summer 1990): 143.

"Hard as Rock." Letter, responding to Steven Moore's review of *A Frolic of His Own*, by William Gaddis. *The Nation* 258:22 (June 6, 1994): 770.

A Bibliography of Primary and Secondary Works Cited in the Text

Adams, Douglas. *The Hitchhiker's Guide to the Galaxy.* 1979. New York: Pocket, 1981.
_____. *Life, the Universe, and Everything.* New York: Harmony, 1982.
Adorno, Theodor. "Perennial Fashion — Jazz." In *Prisms.* Translated by Samuel and Shierry Weber. London: Spearman, 1967, 121–132.
Agel, Jerome, editor. *The Making of Kubrick's 2001.* New York: Signet, 1970.
Aldiss, Brian W. *Billion Year Spree: The True History of Science Fiction.* 1973. New York: Schocken, 1974.
Alien [feature film]. Twentieth-Century Fox, 1979.
Ariès, Philippe. *Western Attitudes Toward Death: From the Middle Ages to the Present.* 1960. Translated by Patricia M. Ranum. Baltimore, MD: Johns Hopkins University Press, 1974.
Aristotle. *Poetics.* Translated with an introduction and notes by Gerald F. Else. 1967. Ann Arbor: University of Michigan Press, 1970.
Ashbery, John. "I Had Thought Things Were Going Along Well." In *As We Know: Poems.* New York: Viking, 1979, 94.
Asimov, Isaac. *Foundation.* New York: Gnome, 1951.
Atwood, Margaret. *The Handmaid's Tale.* 1985. New York: Ballantine, 1987.
Auden, W.H. "In Memory of W.B. Yeats." In *Selected Poems.* New Edition. Edited by Edward Mendelson. New York: Random House, 1979, 80–83.
_____. "Under Which Lyre." In *Selected Poems.* New Edition. Edited by Edward Mendelson. New York: Random House, 1979, 178–183.
Auel, Jean M. *The Mammoth Hunters.* New York: Crown, 1985.
Augustine. *The Confessions.* Introduction, translation, and notes by Maria Boulding. Hyde Park, New York: New City, 1997.
Austen, Jane. *Pride and Prejudice.* 1813. Edited with an introduction and notes by Vivien Jones. London and New York: Penguin, 1996.
Bachelard, Gaston. *The Poetics of Space.* New York: Orion, 1964.
Barth, John. *Letters: A Novel.* New York: Putnam, 1979.
_____. "The Ocean of Story." In *The Friday Book: Essays and Other Nonfiction.* New York: G.P. Putnam's Sons, 1984, 84–90.
Barthes, Roland. *Leçon: Leçon Inaugurale de la Chaire de Sémiologie Littéraire du Collège de France, Prononcée le 7 Janvier 1977.* Paris: Editions du Seuil, 1978.

Battleship Potemkin [feature film]. Goskino, 1925.
Baudelaire, Charles. *Les Fleurs du Mal*. 1957. Paris: La Bibliothèque Française, 1947.
Beagle, Peter S. *The Last Unicorn*. New York: Viking, 1968.
The Beast from 20,000 Fathoms [feature film]. Jack Dietz, 1953.
Bellow, Saul. *Mr. Sammler's Planet*. New York: Viking, 1969.
Benveniste, Emile. *Problems in General Linguistics*. Translated by Mary Elizabeth Meek. Coral Gables, Florida: University of Miami Press, 1971.
Beowulf. Author unknown. In *Beowulf: A Prose Translation: Background and Contexts; Criticism*. Second Edition. Translated by E. Talbot Donaldson. Edited by Nicholas Howe. New York and London: W.W. Norton, 2002, 3–52.
Bergson, Henri. *Laughter*. In *Comedy*. Edited by Wylie Sypher. Translator unidentified. Garden City, NY: Doubleday, 1956, 61–190.
Bernal, J.D. *The World, the Flesh, and the Devil: An Inquiry into the Future of the Three Enemies of the Rational Soul*. 1929. Second Edition. London: Cape, 1970.
Berryman, John. "Dream Song 308: An Instructions to Critics" [title *sic*]. In *His Toy, His Dream, His Rest: 308 Dream Songs*. New York: Farrar, Straus and Giroux, 1968, 240.
Bester, Alfred. *The Demolished Man*. Chicago: Shasta, 1953.
_____. *The Stars My Destination*. 1956. New York: Berkley, 1975.
The Blackboard Jungle [feature film]. Metro-Goldwyn-Mayer, 1955.
Blade Runner [feature film]. Ladd, 1982.
Blake, William. "The Marriage of Heaven and Hell." In *The Poetry and Prose of William Blake*. Edited by David V. Erdman. Commentaries by Harold Bloom. Garden City, NY: Doubleday, 1970, 33–44.
Bloom, Harold. *Agon: Toward a Theory of Revisionism*. New York: Oxford University Press, 1982.
_____. *The Flight to Lucifer: A Gnostic Fantasy*. New York: Farrar, Straus and Giroux, 1979.
_____. "Frankenstein, or The New Prometheus." *Partisan Review* 32 (1965): 611–618.
_____. "Introduction." In *The Book of J*. Translated by David Rosenberg. Interpreted by Harold Bloom. New York: Random House, 1990, 9–16.
Le Boucher [feature film]. Euro International Film, 1970.
Bradbury, Ray. *Fahrenheit 451*. New York: Ballantine, 1953.
The Bride of Frankenstein [feature film]. Universal, 1935.
Brillat-Savarin, Jean Anthelme. *Physiologie du Gout*. Edition Mise en Ordre et Annoteé, avec une Lecture de Roland Barthes. Paris: Hermann, 1975.
Bring Me the Head of Alfredo Garcia [feature film]. Optimus Films, 1974.
Brooks, Van Wyck. *The World of H.G. Wells*. New York: Mitchell Kennerley, 1915.
Brower, Brock. *The Late Great Creature*. New York: Popular Library, 1971.
Browning, Robert. "Pippa Passes." In *The Oxford Authors: Robert Browning*. Edited by Adam Roberts. Introduction by Daniel Karlin. Oxford and New York: Oxford University Press, 1997, 53–98.
Burroughs, William S. *Naked Lunch*. 1959. New York: Ballantine, 1973.
Byron, Lord. *Childe Harold*. In *The Oxford Authors: Byron*. Edited with an introduction and notes by Jerome J. McGann. Oxford and New York: Oxford University Press, 1986, 19–206.
_____. *Don Juan*. In *The Oxford Authors: Byron*. Edited with an introduction and notes by Jerome J. McGann. Oxford and New York: Oxford University Press, 1986, 373–879.
_____. *Manfred*. In *The Oxford Authors: Byron*. Edited with an introduction and notes by Jerome J. McGann. Oxford and New York: Oxford University Press, 1986, 274–314.

Camus, Albert. *The Myth of Sisyphus.* In *The Myth of Sisyphus and Other Essays.* Translated by Justin O'Brien. New York: Vintage, 1955, 1–102.
Card, Orson Scott. *Ender's Game.* New York: TOR, 1985.
Caudwell, Christopher. "H.G. Wells." In *Studies in a Dying Culture.* London: John Lane, 1938, 73–95.
Chesterton, G.K. "Introduction: The Plan of This Book." In *The Everlasting Man.* London: Hodder and Stoughton, 1925, 9–22.
Cioran, C.M. *Precis de Decomposition.* Paris: Galliland, 1949.
Clarke, Arthur C. *Childhood's End.* 1953. New York: Ballantine, 1967.
_____. *2001: A Space Odyssey.* New York: Signet, 1968.
_____. *2010: Odyssey Two.* New York: Ballantine, 1982.
Clarke, I.F. *Voices Prophesying War, 1763–1984.* London and New York: Oxford University Press, 1966.
Close Encounters of the Third Kind [feature film]. Columbia Pictures, 1977.
Cocoon [feature film]. Twentieth-Century Fox, 1985.
Cohen, J.M., and M.J. Cohen, compilers. *The Penguin Dictionary of Twentieth-Century Quotations.* New York: Penguin, 1980.
Commins, Saxe, and Robert N. Linscott, editors. *Man and the Universe: The Philosophers of Science.* 1947. New York: Washington Square, 1969.
Conrad, Joseph. Letter to H.G. Wells, December 4, 1898. In *The Collected Letters of Joseph Conrad, Volume 2: 1898–1902.* Edited by Frederick R. Karl and Laurence Davies. Cambridge: Cambridge University Press, 1986, 126–127.
Coover, Robert. *The Universal Baseball Association, J. Henry Waugh, Prop.* New York: Random House, 1968.
The Creature from the Black Lagoon [feature film]. Universal International, 1954.
The Creature Walks Among Us [feature film]. Universal, 1956.
Crumley, James. *Dancing Bear.* 1983. New York: Vintage, 1984.
Dante Alighieri. *The Divine Comedy.* Translated by Allen Mandelbaum. Introduction by Eugenio Montale. Notes by Peter Armour. New York: Random House, 1995.
Darwin, Charles. *On the Origin of Species, by Means of Natural Selection.* 1859. Edited by Joseph Carroll. Peterborough, Ontario, and Orchard Park, NY: Broadview, 2003.
The Day the Earth Stood Still [feature film]. Twentieth-Century Fox, 1951.
Delany, Samuel R. "Aye, and Gomorrah." In *Nebula Award Stories Number Three.* Edited by Roger Zelazny. 1968. New York: Pocket, 1970, 51–61.
_____. *Babel-17.* New York: Ace, 1966.
_____. *Dhalgren.* 1974. New York: Bantam, 1975.
_____. *Nova.* Garden City, New York: Doubleday, 1968.
_____. *Stars in My Pocket Like Grains of Sand.* New York: Bantam, 1984.
Descartes, René. *Discourse on Method.* 1637. In *Discourse on Method and Related Writings.* Translated with an introduction by Desmond M. Clarke. London: Penguin, 1999, 5–54.
Dick, Philip K. "The Days of Perky Pat." In *The Minority Report and Other Classic Stories by Philip K. Dick.* With an Introduction by James Tiptree, Jr. 1987. New York: Kensington, 2002, 301–321.
_____. *The Divine Invasion.* New York: Timescape, 1981.
_____. *Do Androids Dream of Electric Sheep?* Garden City, NY: Doubleday, 1968.
_____. *The Man in the High Castle.* 1962. New York: Berkley, 1986.
_____. *Ubik.* Garden City, NY: Doubleday, 1969.
_____. *Valis.* New York: Bantam, 1981.
Dirty Harry [feature film]. Warner Bros., 1971.
Dune [feature film]. De Laurentiis, 1984.

Durgnat, Raymond. "The Wedding of Poetry and Pulp — Can They Live Happily Ever After and Have Many Beautiful Children?" In *Films and Feelings*. Cambridge, Massachusetts: M.I.T. Press, 1967, 251–267.
Earth vs. the Flying Saucers [feature film]. Clover Productions, 1956.
Eddington, Sir Arthur. "Beyond the Veil of Physics." In *Quantum Questions: Mystical Writings of the World's Great Physicists*. Edited by Ken Wilbur, with the research assistance of Ann Neihaus. Boston: Shambhala, 2001, 181–198.
_____. *The Nature of the Physical World*. 1928. Cambridge: Cambridge University Press, 1953.
The Elephant Man [feature film]. Brooksfilms, 1980.
Eliade, Mircea. *Myth and Reality*. 1963. Translated by Willard R. Trask. Prospect Heights, IL: Waveland Press, 1998.
Ellison, Harlan. "I Have No Mouth, and I Must Scream." In *Alone Against Tomorrow: Stories of Alienation in Speculative Fiction*. New York: Collier, 1971, 15–32.
_____. "Introduction: Revealed at Last! What Killed the Dinosaurs! And You Don't Look So Terrific Yourself." In *Strange Wine: Fifteen New Stories from the Nightside of the World*. New York: Harper & Row, 1978, 1–15.
_____. "'Repent, Harlequin!' Said the Ticktockman." In *Alone Against Tomorrow: Stories of Alienation in Speculative Fiction*. New York: Collier, 1971, 130–144.
Empson, William. *Some Versions of Pastoral*. London: Chatto & Windus, 1935.
Fahrenheit 451 [feature film]. Anglo Enterprises/Vineyard Film, 1966.
Fiedler, Leslie. *What Was Literature?: Class Culture and Mass Society*. New York: Simon and Schuster, 1982.
The First Men in the Moon [feature film]. Gaumont British Picture, 1919.
First Men in the Moon [feature film]. Ameran Films, 1964.
Fitzgerald, F. Scott. *The Great Gatsby*. 1925. New York: Charles Scribner's Sons, 1953.
The Food of the Gods [feature film]. American International Pictures, 1976.
Forbidden Planet [feature film]. Metro-Goldwyn-Mayer, 1956.
Frankenstein [feature film]. Edison Manufacturing, 1910.
Frankenstein [feature film]. Universal, 1931.
Frankenstein Must Be Destroyed [feature film]. Hammer Films, 1969.
Freud, Sigmund. *The Interpretation of Dreams*. 1900. Translated and edited by James Strachey. New York: Basic, 1959.
_____. *The Psychopathology of Everyday Life*. 1904. Translated by Alan Tyson. Edited with an introduction and additional notes by James Strachey. New York: W.W. Norton, 1965.
Genet, Jean. *Our Lady of the Flowers*. 1948. Translated by Bernard Frechtman. Introduction by Jean-Paul Sartre. London: Anthony Blond, 1964.
The Ghost of Frankenstein [feature film]. Universal, 1942.
Gibson, William. "The Gernsback Continuum." In *Burning Chrome*. 1986. New York: Ace, 1988, 23–35.
_____. *Neuromancer*. New York: Ace, 1984.
Gilgamesh: A New English Version. Author unknown. Translated by Stephen Mitchell. New York: Free Press, 2004.
Ginsberg, Allen. "Howl." In *British and American Poets, Chaucer to the Present*. Edited by W. Jackson Bate and David Perkins. San Diego, CA: Harcourt Brace Jovanovich, 1986, 922–927.
Goethe, Johann Wolfgang von. *Faust*. 1808, 1862. Translated by Barker Fairley. Toronto: University of Toronto Press, 1970.
Goldman, William. *The Princess Bride: S. Morgenstern's Classic Tale of True Love and High Adventure: The "Good Parts" Version, Abridged*. New York: Harcourt Brace Jovanovich, 1973.

Grahame, Kenneth. *The Wind in the Willows*. London: Methuen, 1908.
Greene, Graham. Review of *Rhythm on the Range*. In *The Pleasure Dome: The Collected Film Criticism 1935–40*. Edited by John Russell Taylor. London: Secker & Warburg, 1972, 93–94.
Haldeman, Joe. *The Forever War*. New York: St. Martin's, 1974.
Hanzo, Thomas. "The Past of Science Fiction." In *Bridges to Science Fiction*. Edited by George Slusser, George R. Guffey, and Mark Rose. Carbondale and Edwardsville: Southern Illinois University Press, 1980, 131–147.
The Haunted Palace [feature film]. American International, 1963.
Hawkes, Jacquetta Hopkins. *Prehistory and the Beginnings of Civilization*. New York: Harper & Row, 1963.
Hawking, Stephen. *A Brief History of Time*. New York: Bantam, 1998.
Hawkins, Anthony Hope. *The Prisoner of Zenda*. 1894. New York: H. Holt, 1896.
Heidegger, Martin. *Einführung in die Metaphysik*. Tübingen: Max Neimeyer Verlag, 1957.
Heinlein, Robert A. *The Puppet Masters*. Garden City, NY: Doubleday, 1951.
_____. *Starship Troopers*. New York: Putnam, 1959.
_____. *Stranger in a Strange Land*. New York: Putnam, 1961.
Hemingway, Ernest. "Big Two-Hearted River." In *The Complete Short Stories of Ernest Hemingway: The Finca Vigia Edition*. Foreword by John, Patrick, and Gregory Hemingway. Preface by Charles Scribner, Jr. New York: Simon & Shuster, 1987, 163–169, 173–180.
_____. "Soldier's Home." In *The Complete Short Stories of Ernest Hemingway: The Finca Vigia Edition*. Foreword by John, Patrick, and Gregory Hemingway. Preface by Charles Scribner, Jr. New York: Simon & Shuster, 1987, 111–116.
_____. *The Sun Also Rises*. New York: Scribner, 1926.
Herbert, Frank. *Dune*. 1965. New York: Ace, 1966.
Hitchens, Christopher. *The Missionary Position: Mother Teresa in Theory and Practice*. London and New York: Verso, 1995.
Hofstadter, Douglas. *Gödel, Escher, Bach: An Eternal Golden Braid*. 1979. New York: Vintage, 1989.
Homer. *The Iliad*. Translated by W.H.D. Rouse. 1938. New York: New American Library, 1962.
_____. *The Odyssey*. Translated by W.H.D. Rouse. 1937. New York: New American Library, 1962.
Hough, John. *The Conduct of the Game*. San Diego, CA: Harcourt Brace Jovanovich, 1986.
House of Usher [feature film]. American International, 1960.
Huizinga, Johan. *Homo Ludens: A Study of the Play-Element in Culture*. 1938. Boston: Beacon, 1955.
Huss, Roy, and T.J. Ross, editors. *Focus on the Horror Film*. Englewood Cliffs, NJ: Prentice-Hall, 1972.
Huxley, Aldous. *Brave New World*. 1932. London: Chatto & Windus, 1938.
Invasion of the Body Snatchers [feature film]. Walter Wanger, 1956.
The Invisible Man [feature film]. Universal, 1933.
The Island of Dr. Moreau [feature film]. American International, 1977.
Island of Lost Souls [feature film]. Paramount Pictures, 1932.
I Spit on Your Grave [*Day of the Woman*] [feature film]. Cinemagic Pictures, 1978.
Jung, C.G. "Transformation Symbols in the Mass." In *Psyche and Symbol: A Selection from the Writings of C.G. Jung*. Edited by Violet S. de Laszlo. Garden City, NY: Doubleday, 1958, 148–224.
Kafka, Franz. "Leopards in the Temple." In *Parables and Paradoxes*. 1958. New York: Schocken, 1971, 93.

———. *The Metamorphosis*. 1915. Translated by A.L. Lloyd. London: Parton, 1937.
———. *The Trial*. Translated by Willa and Edwin Muir. Revised, and with additional materials by E.M. Butler. New York: Modern Library, 1956.
Keyes, Daniel. "Flowers for Algernon." In *The Hugo Winners, Volume I*. Edited by Isaac Asimov. 1962. New York: Fawcett Crest, 1973, 249–276.
Kierkegaard, Søren. *Fear and Trembling*. In *Fear and Trembling and The Sickness Unto Death*. Translated with an introduction and notes by Walter Lowrie. Garden City, NY: Doubleday, 1954, 21–132.
———. *The Sickness Unto Death*. In *Fear and Trembling and The Sickness Unto Death*. Translated with an introduction and notes by Walter Lowrie. Garden City, NY: Doubleday, 1954, 141–262.
King Kong [feature film]. RKO Radio Pictures, 1933.
Koestler, Arthur. *The Act of Creation* New York: Macmillan, 1964.
Kolakowski, Keszek. *Religion: If There Is No God—On God, the Devil, Sin, and Other Worries of the So-Called Philosophy of Religion*. New York and Oxford: Oxford University Press, 1982.
Larsen, Stephen. *The Shaman's Doorway: Opening the Mythic Imagination to Contemporary Consciousness*. New York: Harper & Row, 1976.
Lefebvre, Henri. *Le Langage et la Société*. Paris: Galllimard, 1966.
Lem, Stanislaw. *The Cyberiad*. 1967. Translated by Michael Kandel. New York: Seabury, 1974.
———. *Microworlds: Writings on Science Fiction and Fantasy*. Edited by Franz Rottensteiner. San Diego: Harcourt Brace Jovanovich, 1984.
———. "Philip K. Dick: A Visionary Among the Charlatans." *Science-Fiction Studies* 2 (March, 1975): 54–67.
———. *Solaris*. 1961. Translated by Joanna Kilmartin and Steve Cox. London: Faber and Faber, 1971.
Lévi-Strauss, Claude. *The Raw and the Cooked*. Translated by John and Doreen Weightman. New York: Harper & Row, 1969.
Lewis, C.S. *Perelandra*. 1944. New York: Macmillan, 1964.
Lindsay, David. *A Voyage to Arcturus*. 1920. London: Allison and Busby, 1965.
Longus. *Daphnis and Chloe*. Translated by George Moore. New York: Brazilier, 1977.
Lovejoy, Jack. *Outworld Cats*. New York: DAW, 1994.
Lowell, Robert. "The Quaker Graveyard at Nantucket." In *Selected Poems*. New York: Farrar, Straus and Giroux, 1976, 6–10.
———. "Skunk Hour." In *Selected Poems*. New York: Farrar, Straus and Giroux, 1976, 95–96.
Lucretius. *De Rerum Natura: The Poem on Nature*. Translated by C.H. Sisson. Manchester, England: Carcanet New Press, 1976.
McCaffrey, Anne. *Dragonsong*. New York: Atheneum, 1976.
McConnell, Frank D. "Will Deconstruction Be the Death of Literature?" *Wilson Quarterly* 14 (Winter 1990): 99–109.
MacKenzie, Norman, and Jeanne MacKenzie. *The Time Traveller: The Life of H.G. Wells*. London: Weidenfeld & Nicolson, 1973.
The Mahabharata. Translated and edited by J.A.B. van Buitenen. Three volumes. Chicago: University of Chicago Press, 1973.
Mailer, Norman. *The Armies of the Night: History as a Novel, the Novel as History*. New York: New American Library, 1968.
———. *The Executioner's Song*. Boston: Little, Brown, 1979.
———. *Why Are We in Vietnam?* New York: Putnam, 1967.
Malcolm, Norman. *Ludwig Wittgenstein: A Memoir*. London: Oxford University Press, 1958.

Malzberg, Barry N. *Galaxies.* New York: Pyramid, 1975.
The Man from Planet X [feature film]. Sherrill C. Corwin Productions/Mid Century Film Productions, 1951.
Marcuse, Herbert. *One-Dimensional Man: Studies in the Ideology of Advanced Industrial Society.* 1964. Boston: Beacon, 1966.
Marx, Karl. "Theses on Feuerbach." Translated by C. Dutt and C.P. Magill. In *The German Ideology: Part One.* By Karl Marx and Friedrich Engels. Edited with an introduction by C.J. Arthur. London: Lawrence & Wishart, 1970, 121–123.
Metropolis [feature film]. Universum Film, 1927.
Miller, J. Hillis. "Defending Deconstruction" [letter]. *Wilson Quarterly* 14 (Summer 1990): 142–143.
Miller, Joseph D. "Popes or Tropes: Defining the Grails of Science Fiction." In *Science Fiction, Canonization, Marginalization, and the Academy.* Edited by Gary Westfahl and George Slusser. Westport, CT: Greenwood, 2002, 79–87.
Miller, Walter M., Jr. *A Canticle for Leibowitz.* 1959. New York: Bantam, 1968.
Milton, John. *Paradise Lost.* 1667. Edited by Alastair Fowler. London and New York: Longman, 1998.
Mintz, Jerome R. *Legends of the Hasidim: An Introduction to Hasidic Culture and Oral Tradition in the New World.* Chicago and London: University of Chicago Press, 1968.
Modern Times [feature film]. Charles Chaplin Productions, 1936.
Nabokov, Vladimir. *Lolita.* 1955. New York: Putnam, 1958.
Newton, Isaac. *The Principia: Mathematical Principles of Natural Philosophy.* Translated by I. Bernard Cohen and Anne Whitman assistd by Julie Budenz. Berkeley: University of California Press, 1999.
1984 [feature film]. Holiday Films, 1956.
Niven, Larry. *The Flight of the Horse.* New York: Ballantine, 1973.
_____. "Neutron Star." In *Stories from The Hugo Winners, Volume 2.* Edited by Isaac Asimov. 1971. Greenwich, CT: Fawcett Crest, 1973, 301–318.
_____. *Protector.* New York: Ballantine, 1973.
_____. *The Ringworld Engineers.* New York: Holt, Rinehart and Winston, 1980.
Not of This Earth [feature film]. Allied Artists, 1957.
Nowlan, Philip Francis. *Armageddon 2419 A.D.* 1928. New York: Ace, 1962.
Orwell, George. *Homage to Catalonia.* 1938. New York: Harcourt, Brace, 1952.
_____. *Nineteen Eighty-Four.* New York: Harcourt, Brace, 1949.
_____. "Politics and the English Language." In *A Collection of Essays.* Garden City, NY: Doubleday, 1957, 162–177.
Patton [feature film]. 20th Century–Fox, 1970.
Pearl. Author unknown. Edited by E.V. Gordon. Oxford: Clarendon, 1953.
Pickup on South Street [feature film]. Twentieth-Century Fox, 1953.
Plato. *Phaedo.* Translated with introduction and commentary by R. Hackforth. Cambridge, England: Cambridge University Press, 1955.
Poe, Edgar Allan. "The Masque of the Red Death." In *Selected Writings of Edgar Allan Poe.* Edited by Edward H. Davidson. Boston: Houghton Mifflin, 1956, 174–180.
Pohl, Frederik. *The Way the Future Was: A Memoir.* New York: Ballantine, 1978.
Pohl, Frederik, and C.M. Kornbluth. *The Space Merchants.* New York: Ballantine, 1953.
Pope, Alexander. "Epistle to Dr. Arbuthnot." In *Alexander Pope's Collected Poems.* Edited by Bonamy Dobrée. London: Everyman's Library, 1956, 252–264.
_____. "The Rape of the Lock." In *Alexander Pope's Collected Poems.* Edited with an introduction by Bonamy Dobrée. London: Dent, 1956, 76–96.
Pound, Ezra. "Hugh Selwyn Mauberly (Life and Contacts)." In *Collected Shorter Poems.* London: Faber and Faber, 1968, 203–222.

The Private War of Major Benson [feature film]. Universal International, 1955.
Pynchon, Thomas. *The Crying of Lot 49*. Philadelphia and New York: Lippincott, 1966.
———. *Gravity's Rainbow*. New York: Viking, 1973.
———. "Introduction." In *Slow Learner: Early Stories*. Boston: Little, Brown, 1984, 1–23.
———. *V.* 1963. New York: Perennial Library, 1986.
Rahner, Karl. *The Practice of Faith: A Handbook of Contemporary Spirituality*. New York: Crossroad, 1983.
Return of the Jedi [feature film]. Lucasfilm, 1983.
Revenge of the Creature [feature film]. Universal, 1955.
Richardson, Samuel. *Pamela, or Virtue Rewarded*. Edited with explanatory notes by Thomas Keymer and Alice Wakely. Introduction by Thomas Keymer. London and New York: Oxford University Press, 2001.
Rimbaud, Arthur. *Lettres du Voyant (13 et 15 Mai 1871)*. Éditées et commentées par Gérald Schaeffer. Includes *La Voyance avant Rimbaud*. Par Marc Eigeldinger. Paris: Librarie Minard, 1975.
Robbins, Tom. *Even Cowgirls Get the Blues*. Toronto and New York: Bantam, 1977.
———. *Jitterbug Perfume*. Toronto and New York: Bantam, 1984.
Sanders, Lawrence. *The First Deadly Sin*. New York: Putnam, 1973.
———. *The Seduction of Peter S*. New York: Putnam, 1983.
Sartre, Jean-Paul. *Being and Nothingness: An Essay on Phenomenological Ontology*. Translated and with an introduction by Hazel E. Barnes. New York: Philosophical Library, 1956.
Schneidau, Herbert N. *Sacred Discontent: The Bible and Western Tradition*. Baton Rouge: Louisiana State University Press, 1976.
Shakespeare, William. *Hamlet*. Edited by Harold Jenkins. London: Methuen, 1982.
———. *As You Like It*. Edited by S.C. Burchell. New York: Yale University Press, 1954.
———. *King Lear*. Edited by R.A. Foakes. London: Thomas Nelson, 1997.
———. *Macbeth*. Edited by G.K. Hunter. Harmondsworth, England: Penguin, 1967.
———. *A Midsummer Night's Dream*. Edited by Stanley Wells. Harmondsworth, England: Penguin, 1967.
———. *Romeo and Juliet*. Edited by Brian Gibbons. London and New York: Methuen, 1980.
———. *The Tempest*. Edited by Frank Kermode. London and New York: Methuen, 1983.
———. *The Winter's Tale*. Edited by Stephen Orgel. New York: Oxford University Press, 1996.
The Shape of Things to Come [feature film]. CFI Investments/SOTTC Film Productions, 1979.
Shelley, Mary. *Frankenstein, or The Modern Prometheus*. 1818. In *The Annotated Frankenstein*. Edited by Leonard Wolf. New York: Clarkson N. Potter, 1977, 1–332.
Shelley, Percy. "Alastor." In *The Complete Poetical Works of Percy Bysshe Shelley*. Edited by Thomas Hutchinson. London, New York, and Toronto: Oxford University Press, 1905, 14–30.
———. "Mont Blanc." In *The Complete Poetical Works of Percy Bysshe Shelley*. Edited by Thomas Hutchinson. London, New York, and Toronto: Oxford University Press, 1905, 532–535.
Silent Movie [feature film]. Crossbow Productions, 1976.
Sir Gawain and the Green Knight. Author unknown. Edited by J.R.R. Tolkien and E.V. Gordon. Second Edition revised by Norman Davis. Oxford, England: Clarendon Press, 1967.
Slusser, George. "Who's Afraid of Science Fiction?" *Foundation: The Review of Science Fiction* No. 42 (Spring 1988): 5–20.
Smiles, Samuel. *Self-Help: With Illustrations of Character, Conduct, and Perseverance*. 1859. Chicago: Bedford, Clarke, 1881.

Smith, Barbara Herrnstein. *On the Margins of Discourse: The Relation of Literature to Language.* Chicago: University of Chicago Press, 1978.
Smith, E.E. "Doc." *The Skylark of Space.* Providence, RI: Hadley, 1947.
Sophocles. *Oedipus Rex.* Edited by R.D. Dawe. Cambridge, England, and New York: Cambridge University Press, 1982.
Spillane, Mickey. *Kiss Me, Deadly.* New York: Dutton, 1952.
Spinrad, Norman. *The Void Captain's Tale.* 1983. New York: Pocket, 1984.
Stansky, Peter, and William Abrahams. *Orwell, The Transformation.* London: Constable, 1979.
_____. *The Unknown Orwell.* New York: Alfred A. Knopf, 1972.
Stapledon, Olaf. *Star Maker.* 1937. In *Last and First Men and Star Maker: Two Science-Fiction Novels.* New York: Dover, 1968, 247–438.
Star Wars [feature film]. Twentieth-Century Fox, 1977.
Steiner, George. *Language and Silence.* New York: Atheneum, 1967.
Stevens, Wallace. "Esthétique du Mal." In *Transport to Summer.* New York: Alfred A. Knopf, 1951, 38–53.
_____. "The Man with the Blue Guitar." In *The Collected Poems of Wallace Stevens.* New York: Alfred A. Knopf, 1954, 165–184.
_____. "Of Modern Poetry." In *The Collected Poems of Wallace Stevens.* New York: Alfred A. Knopf, 1954, 239–240.
_____. "The Poems of Our Climate." In *The Collected Poems of Wallace Stevens.* New York: Alfred A. Knopf, 1954, 193–194.
_____. "Reality Is an Activity of the Most August Imagination." In *Collected Poetry and Prose.* Selected and annotated by Frank Kermode and Joan Richardson. New York: Library of America, 1997, 471–472.
_____. "Sunday Morning." In *The Collected Poems of Wallace Stevens.* New York: Alfred A. Knopf, 1954, 66–70.
Straw Dogs [feature film]. ABC Pictures, 1971.
Sunday Bloody Sunday [feature film]. Vectia, 1971.
Tarantula [feature film]. Universal International, 1955.
Them! [feature film] Warner Bros., 1954.
The Thing (from Another World) [feature film]. Winchester Pictures, 1951.
Things to Come [feature film]. London Film Productions, 1936.
This Island Earth [feature film]. Universal International, 1955.
THX 1138 [feature film]. Warner Bros., 1971.
The Time Machine [feature film]. Galaxy Films, 1960.
Todorov, Tzvetan. *The Fantastic: A Structural Approach to a Literary Genre.* Translated by Richard Howard. Cleveland: Press of Case Western Reserve University, 1973.
Tolkien, J.R.R. "*Beowulf:* The Monster and the Critics." In *The Monster and the Critics and Other Essays.* Edited by Christopher Tolkien. Boston: George Allen & Urwin, 1983, 5–48.
_____. "On Fairy Stories." In *The Monster and the Critics and Other Essays.* Edited by Christopher Tolkien. Boston: George Allen & Urwin, 1983, 109–161.
_____. *The Lord of the Rings.* 1955–1956. Boston: Houghton Mifflin, 1974.
Tolstoy, Leo. *Anna Karenina.* Translated by Constance Garnett. Introductory essay by Thomas Mann. New York: Random House, 1939.
2001: A Space Odyssey [feature film]. Metro-Goldwyn-Mayer, 1968.
Verne, Jules. *From the Earth to the Moon.* 1965. Edited by Walter James Miller. New York: Thomas Y. Crowell, 1978.
Von Eschenbach, Wolfram. *Parzival.* Translated by Helen M. Mustard and Charles E. Passage. New York: Vintage, 1961.

Von Franz, Marie-Louise. *The Interpretation of Fairy Tales*. Revised Edition. Boston: Shambhala, 1996.
Von Harbou, Thea. *Metropolis*. London: Readers Library, 1927.
Vonnegut, Kurt, Jr. *Slaughterhouse-Five, or The Children's Crusade: A Duty-Dance with Death*. New York: Dell, 1969.
A Voyage to the Moon [feature film]. Star Films, 1902.
The War of the Worlds [feature film]. Paramount, 1953.
Wells, H.G. *Ann Veronica: A Modern Love Story*. London: T.F. Unwin, 1909.
_____. *The Fate of Homo Sapiens: An Unemotional Statement of the Things That Are Happening to Him Now, and of the Immediate Possibilities Confronting Him*. London: Secker and Warburg, 1939.
_____. *The First Men in the Moon*. 1901. In *Seven Famous Novels by H.G. Wells*. New York: Alfred A. Knopf, 1934, 391–528.
_____. *The History of Mr. Polly*. 1910. New York: Press of the Readers Club, 1941.
_____. *In the Days of the Comet*. London: Macmillan, 1906.
_____. *The Invisible Man*. 1897. Edited by MacDonald Daly. London: J.M. Dent, 1995.
_____. *The Island of Dr. Moreau*. In *Seven Famous Novels by H.G. Wells*. New York: Alfred A. Knopf, 1934, 69–157.
_____. *The King Who Was a King: The Book of a Film*. London: E. Benn, 1929.
_____. *Kipps: The Story of a Simple Soul*. London: Macmillan, 1905.
_____. *Mind at the End of Its Tether*. London: William Heinemann, 1945.
_____. "Mr. Wells Reviews a Current Film: He Takes Issue with This German Conception of What the City of One Hundred Years Hence Will Be Like." *The New York Times*, April 17, 1927, *The New York Times Magazine*, 4, 22. Republished under the title of "The Silliest Film: Will Machinery Make Robots of Men?" In *Authors on Film*. Edited by Harry Geduld. Bloomington: Indiana University Press, 1972, 59–67.
_____. *A Modern Utopia*. 1905. Introduction by Mark R. Hillegas. Lincoln, Nebraska: University of Nebraska Press, 1967.
_____. *The Outline of History; Being a Plain History of Life and Mankind*. London: George Newnes, 1920.
_____. *The Shape of Things to Come*. London: Hutchinson, 1933.
_____. *The Time Machine*. 1895. In *Three Prophetic Science Fiction Novels of H.G. Wells*. Selected and with an introduction by E.F. Bleiler. New York: Dover, 1960, 263–335.
_____. *Tono-Bungay: A Novel*. London: Macmillan, 1909.
_____. *The War in the Air, and Particularly How Mr. Bert Smallways Fared While It Lasted*. 1908. Harmondsworth, United Kingdom: Penguin, 1941.
_____. *The War of the Worlds*. 1898. In *Seven Famous Novels by H.G. Wells*. New York: Alfred A. Knopf, 1934, 265–388.
_____. *When the Sleeper Wakes*. 1899. In *Three Prophetic Science Fiction Novels of H.G. Wells*. Selected and with an introduction by E.F. Bleiler. New York: Dover, 1960, 1–187.
Westfahl, Gary, editor. *Science Fiction Quotations: From the Inner Mind to the Outer Limits*. New Haven, CT: Yale University Press, 2005.
Whitehead, Alfred Lord. *Process and Reality*. Corrected Edition. Edited by David Ray Griffin and Donald W. Sherburne. New York: Free Press, 1978.
The Wild Child [feature film]. Les Films du Carrosse, 1970.
Wilde, Oscar. "Preface." *The Picture of Dorian Gray*. In *The Complete Works of Oscar Wilde, Volume IV*. Introduction by Coulson Kernahan. Review by Walter Pater. New York: Wise, 1927, 5–7.
Wittgenstein, Ludwig. *Tractatus Logico-Philosophicus*. Translated by D.F. Pears and B.F. McGuinness. Introduction by Bertrand Russell. London and New York: Routledge, 1974.

Wordsworth, William. "Preface." *Lyrical Ballads*. By William Wordsworth and Samuel Taylor Coleridge. 1800. Edited with an introduction, notes, and appendices by R.L. Brett and A.R. Jones. London: Methuen, 1965, 211–272.
_____. *The Prelude*. Edited by J.C. Maxwell. Middlesex, England: Penguin, 1971.
_____. "The Recluse" [selection]. In *Selected Poems and Prefaces*. Edited by Jack Stillinger. Boston: Houghton Mifflin, 1965, 45–47.
Wylie, Philip. *Generation of Vipers*. 1942. New York: Rinehart, 1955.
X, Malcolm. *The Autobiography of Malcolm X*. New York: Grove, 1965.
Yeats, W.B. "A Dialogue of Self and Soul." In *The Collected Poems of W.B. Yeats*. 1933. New York: Macmillan, 1956, 270–273.
_____. "Sailing to Byzantium." *In The Collected Poems of W.B. Yeats*. 1933. New York: Macmillan, 1956, 223–224.
Young Frankenstein [feature film]. Crossbow Productions, 1974.
Zelazny, Roger. *Nine Princes in Amber*. 1970. New York: Avon, 1972.
Zweig, Stefan. "The Royal Game." In *The Royal Game and Other Stories*. Translated by Jiff Sutcliffe. Introduction by John Fowles. London: Jonathan Cape, 1981, 1–49.

Index

Abbott, Jack 58
Abrahams, William 58–59
Adams, Douglas 66, 117; *The Hitchhiker's Guide to the Galaxy* 117; *Life, the Universe, and Everything* 66
Adams, Julie 21, 23
Adorno, Theodor W. 104–105
The Adventures of Tom Sawyer (Twain) 140
Agrippa, Cornelius 151
Akiba, Rabbi 93
Alastor (Shelley) 12
Aldiss, Brian W. 17; *Billion Year Spree* 17
Alger, Horatio 33–34
Alien (film) 54, 151
Aliens (film) 177–178
Alkon, Paul 164–166
Allen, Woody 76
Amazing Stories 115, 148
Analog Science Fiction/Science Fact 92, 98, 133
Anaximenes 156
Anderson, Poul 90, 138–139
Ann Veronica (Wells) 40
Anna Karenina (Tolstoy) 101, 163
Ardrey, Robert 35
Ariès, Philippe 152
Aristotle 64, 93–94; *Poetics* 93–94
Armageddon 2419 A.D. (Nowlan) 57
The Armies of the Night (Mailer) 105
Armstrong, Louis 108
Arnold, Jack 18, 19, 25, 26
As You Like It (Shakespeare) 22, 52
Ashbery, John 72, 109; "I Had Thought Things Were Going Well" 72
Asimov, Isaac 34, 48, 51, 54, 71, 95, 107, 108, 147, 151, 156, 170; *Foundation* 48; *Foundation* trilogy 71; robot stories 151; *Second Foundation* 54
Astaire, Fred 135
Astounding Science-Fiction 115
Auden, W.H. 30, 137, 142, 143; "Under Which Lyre" 137
Auel, Jean 93, 98; *Clan of the Cave Bear* series 93; *The Mammoth Hunters* 98

Augustine, Saint 140, 141, 160; *Confessions* 160
Austen, Jane 62, 89, 94; *Pride and Prejudice* 89
The Autobiography of Malcolm X (Malcolm X) 69
"Aye, and Gomorrah" (Delany) 114

Baal Shem Tov 93, 160, 172–173
Babel-17 (Delany) 113–114, 115
Bach, Johann Sebastian 139
Bachelard, Gaston 85; *The Poetics of Space* 85
Baen, Jim 175
Baker, Chet 179
Bakhtin, Mikhail 176
Barber, Celeste McConnell 5, 7, 72, 78, 163, 176
Barker, Ernest 29, 181n
Barth, John 35, 139, 140; *Letters* 35
Barthes, Roland 77, 119–120, 141, 142–143, 144
Bate, W. Jackson 102; *British and American Poets, Chaucer to the Pres*ent (ed. with Perkins) 102–103
Batman (comic book) 107
Battleship Potemkin (film) 18
Baudelaire, Charles 119–120; *Les Fleurs du Mal* 139
Baudrillard, Jean 127, 132
Beagle, Peter S. 96, 101; *The Last Unicorn* 96
The Beast from 20,000 Fathoms (film) 20
The Beatles 27, 67
Beckett, Samuel 19–20, 53, 125
"Before the Law" (Kafka) 104
Being and Nothingness (Sartre) 121
Bellow, Saul 35, 49, 93, 98, 101, 108, 140; *Mr. Sammler's Planet* 35, 49
Benedict, Brother 139
Benford, Gregory 74, 148, 166–167
Benny, Jack 141
Benveniste, Emile 76
Beowulf 86, 93
"*Beowulf*: The Monster and the Critics" (Tolkien) 98
Bergson, Henri 126; *Laughter* 126

213

Index

Bernal, J.D. 146, 170; *The World, the Flesh, and the Devil* 146
Berryman, John 119, 136, 143; "Dream Songs" 143
Bester, Alfred 49, 96, 122, 136, 159, 163, 174; *The Demolished Man* 122; "Hell Is Forever" 174; *The Stars My Destination* 49, 96, 136, 159, 163
The Bible 95, 178
Big Town (radio program) 138
"Big Two-Hearted River" (Hemingway) 83–84
Billion Year Spree (Aldiss) 17
Bissell, Whit 24–25
The Blackboard Jungle (film) 23
Blackmur, R.P. 140, 142
Blade Runner (film) 126, 127–128, 129, 131, 137, 163
Blake, William 35, 52–53, 57–58, 103, 106, 137, 156, 157, 161, 170; "Jerusalem" 103; *Songs of Experience* 161; *Songs of Innocence* 161
Blondie (comic strip) 63
Blood Lake (McConnell) 165
"Blood's a Rover" (Oliver) 138
Bloom, Harold 12, 52, 70, 100, 109, 129–130, 134, 135, 140, 142, 167, 170, 179; *The Book of J* (with Rosenberg) 134; *The Flight to Lucifer* 52, 100
Bloom County (comic strip) 67, 68
"Blue in Green" (Davis) 179
Bohr, Niels 65
The Book of J (Rosenberg and Bloom) 134
The Book of Revelation (John of Patmos) 57
Boone, Pat 117
Borges, Jorge Luis 79, 99
"Born to Run" (Springsteen) 49
Le Boucher (film) 24
Le Bourgeois Gentilhomme (Molière) 140
Bowie, David 170
Bradbury, Ray 61, 62, 108, 170; *Fahrenheit 451* 61
Bradley, Marion Zimmer 93, 100, 101; Darkover series 100
Brave New World (Huxley) 137
Breathed, Berke 67, 68
The Bride of Frankenstein (film) 11, 14
A Brief History of Time (Hawking) 160–161
Brillat-Savarin, Jean Anthelme 117, 119–121; *Physiologie du Goût* 117, 119–120
Bring Me the Head of Alfredo Garcia (film) 60
British and American Poets, Chaucer to the Present (ed. Bate and Perkins) 102–103
Brontë, Anne 98
Brontë, Charlotte 98
Brontë, Emily 98
Brooks, Mel 14–15, 61, 169–170
Brooks, Van Wyck 30–31
Brower, Brock 18; *The Late Great Creature* 18
Browning, Robert 43; "Pippa Passes" 43
Brubeck, Dave 106, 170
Buber, Martin 108

Bultmann, Rudolf 14, 64
Bunyan, John 94
Burke, Kenneth 101, 140, 141, 142, 149, 162–163
Burroughs, Edgar Rice 52, 107, 170; *Tarzan of the Apes* 170
Burroughs, William S. 117, 122, 139, 152; *Naked Lunch* 122, 139
Butler, Octavia E. 136–137
Byron, Lord 2, 11, 12, 83, 116; *Childe Harold* 12; *Don Juan* 2; *Manfred* 11

Calvin, John 121, 177
Calvin and Hobbes (comic strip) 121, 177
Camera Obscura 138
Campbell, John W., Jr. 98, 133
Campbell, Joseph 91–92
Camus, Albert 116, 121; *The Myth of Sisyphus* 121
A Canticle for Leibowitz (Miller) 162
Card, Orson Scott 109–110, 136, 170; *Ender's Game* 109–110, 136
Carlson, Richard 21, 22, 23
Carroll, Lewis 92; *The Hunting of the Snark* 92
Cartland, Barbara 51
Cassidy, Jack 140
The Catcher in the Rye (Salinger) 102
Caudwell, Christopher 35, 181–182n; *Studies in a Dying Culture* 181–182n
Cervantes, Miguel de 135
Chabrol, Claude 24
Chandler, Raymond 2, 48–49, 133
Chaplin, Charlie 60
Cheers (TV series) 168
Cheever, John 78
Chesterton, G.K. 2, 13, 53, 76, 113, 117, 119, 125, 136, 153, 157, 170
Child, Julia 116
Childhood's End (Clarke) 50, 143–144, 159, 161
Chomsky, Noam 97
Christie, Agatha 48–49
The Chronicles of Thomas Covenant the Unbeliever (Donaldson) 49, 65, 71, 89–90, 92, 98–99
Cimino, Michael 44–45
Cioran, E.M. 141
Citizen Kane (film) 12
Clan of the Cave Bear series (Auel) 93
Clarke, Arthur C. 50, 54–55, 61, 143–144, 147, 156, 159, 170; *Childhood's End* 50, 143–144, 159, 161; *2010: Odyssey Two* 54–55, 61
Clarke, I.F. 42
The Clash 106
Close Encounters of the Third Kind (film) 37, 44
Cobain, Kurt 146
Cocoon (film) 37
Cocteau, Jean 24
Coleman, Ornette 179

Coltrane, John 179
Conan Doyle, Arthur 48–49, 51
The Conduct of the Game (Hough) 86–87
Confessions (Augustine) 160
Conklin, Groff 138
Conrad, Joseph 39
Cooper, James Fenimore 52, 65
Coover, Robert 32, 90; *The Universal Baseball Association, Inc., J. Henry Waugh, Prop.* 90
Corman, Roger 27
Corneille, Pierre 93
Cosell, Howard 86
The Creature from the Black Lagoon (film) 8, 18–28
The Creature Walks Among Us (film) 19
Critical Inquiry 104
Crumley, James 122; *Dancing Bear* 122
The Crying of Lot 49 (Pynchon) 18
Custer, George Armstrong 165
The Cyberiad (Lem) 79

Dancing Bear (Crumley) 122
Dangerous Visions (ed. Ellison) 106
Dante Alighieri 110, 149, 162; *The Divine Comedy* 110, 149
Daphnis and Chloe (Longus) 129
"Dark Star" (Grateful Dead) 74
Darkover series (Bradley) 100
Darwin, Charles 15, 32, 33, 34, 41, 159; *On the Origin of Species* 33, 159
David Copperfield (Dickens) 100
Davies, Paul 162
Davis, Jim 68, 70
Davis, Miles 144, 179; "Blue in Green" 179
The Day the Earth Stood Still (1951 film) 20
"The Days of Perky Pat" (Dick) 78–79
De Rerum Natura (Lucretius) 83
"Dear Old Stockholm" 179
Defoe, Daniel 94
Delany, Samuel R. 48, 70, 113–114, 148; "Aye, and Gomorrah" 114; *Babel-17* 113–114, 115; *Dhalgren* 48, 70; *Nova* 70, 114; *Stars in My Pocket Like Grains of Sand* 70
DeLillo, Don 152
Della Femina, Jerry 94
De Man, Paul 137
The Demolished Man (Bester) 122
Denning, Richard 21, 22
Derrida, Jacques 61, 92, 116, 137
Descartes, René 15, 128, 150
Desmond, Paul 106, 107, 170
Dhalgren (Delany) 48, 70
Dick, Philip K. 53, 75, 78, 78–79, 101, 193–105, 106, 108, 127–128, 170; "The Days of Perky Pat" 78–79; *The Divine Invasion* 79; *Do Androids Dream of Electric Sheep?* 75, 127; *The Man in the High Castle* 79, 103–105, 108; *Ubik* 79; *Valis* 79, 94
Dick Tracy (comic strip) 63
Dickens, Charles 19–20, 39, 40, 49, 62, 156; *David Copperfield* 100

Dirty Harry (film) 60
The Divine Comedy (Dante) 110, 149
The Divine Invasion (Dick) 79
Do Androids Dream of Electric Sheep? (Dick) 75, 127
Dr. Jekyll and Mr. Hyde (Stevenson) 151
Donaldson, Stephen R. 49, 65, 89–90, 92, 101; The Chronicles of Thomas Covenant the Unbeliever 49, 65, 89–90, 92, 98–99
Doonesbury (comic strip) 67, 68, 69, 70, 71
Doré, Gustave 139
Dostoyevsky, Fyodor 133
Douglass, Frederick 557
Dragnet (radio show) 138
The Dragonriders of Pern (McCaffrey) 74
Dragonriders of Pern series (McCaffrey) 94–95
Dragonsong (McCaffrey) 99
"Dream Songs" (Berryman) 143
Dryden, John 93
Dulles, John Foster 27
Dune (Herbert) 69, 95, 126, 128
Dune (1984 film) 126
Dunne, John S. 130
Durgnat, Raymond 20

Earth Versus the Flying Saucers (film) 20, 26, 27
The Earthsea Trilogy (Le Guin) 92
Eddington, Arthur 83, 101, 161
Eddy, Mary Baker 146, 147, 170
Einstein, Albert 65, 70–71, 159, 161–162
Eisenhower, Dwight 24, 27
Eisenstein, Sergei 40, 44–45
The Elephant Man (film) 15
ELH 106
Eliade, Mircea 82, 91–92; *Myth and Reality* 82
Eliot, George [Mary Ann Evans] 39, 98
Eliot, T.S. 38; "The Love Song of J. Arthur Prufrock" 103
Ellison, Harlan 48, 59, 60, 75, 93, 106, 170; *Dangerous Visions* 106; "I Have No Mouth, and I Must Scream" 48; "'Repent, Harlequin!' Said the Ticktockman" 60; *Strange Wine* 59
Empson, William 86; *Some Versions of Pastoral* 86
Ender's Game (Card) 109–110, 136
"Esthétique du Mal" (Stevens) 128
Even Cowgirls Get the Blues (Robbins) 84
Everett, Hugh 65
The Executioner's Song (Mailer) 94

Fahrenheit 451 (Bradbury) 61
Fahrenheit 451 (film) 61
Falwell, Jerry 65
The Fantastic (Todorov) 99–100
The Far Side (comic strip) 68
Farmer, Philip José 78, 95; Riverworld novels 95
The Fate of Homo Sapiens (Wells) 30

Faulkner, William 101
Faust (Goethe) 85
Fear and Trembling (Kierkegaard) 67, 100
Fermat, Pierre de 162
Feuerbach, Ludwig 62
Fiedler, Leslie 17, 101; *What Was Literature?* 101
Fielding, Henry 94
Finch, Sheila 167–168
The First Deadly Sin (Sanders) 122
The First Men in the Moon (Wells) 30, 38, 41
The First Men in the Moon (1919 film) 41
Fish, Stanley 109, 137, 170
Fitzgerald, F. Scott 88, 101; *The Great Gatsby* 78, 88, 100
Flash Gordon serials 37, 52, 95, 148
Les Fleurs du Mal (Baudelaire) 139
The Flight of the Horse (Niven) 51
The Flight to Lucifer (Bloom) 52, 100
"Flowers for Algernon" (Keyes) 151
The Food of the Gods (film) 42–43
For Better or Worse (comic strip) 67
Forbidden Planet (film) 22
Ford, Harrison 128
The Forever War (Haldeman) 54
Foucault, Michel 138, 142, 152
Foundation (Asimov) 48
Foundation trilogy (Asimov) 71
Frank, Phil 68
Frankenstein (1910 film) 13, 181n
Frankenstein (1931 film) 13, 16–17
Frankenstein (Shelley) 5, 8, 11–17, 137, 150–151, 163, 170
Frankenstein Must Be Destroyed (film) 12
Franklin, Benjamin 140
Fred Basset (comic strip) 71
Freedman, Carl 168–169
Freud, Sigmund 25, 53, 77, 78; *The Interpretation of Dreams* 77; *The Psychopathology of Everyday Life* 77
Fritz, Martha Sue 138–139
From the Earth to the Moon (Verne) 39
Frye, Northrop 93, 122, 140, 142
Fuller, Samuel 26–27

Gaiman, Neil 1–5, 7; *Sandman* (comic book) 1; *Sandman: The Kindly Ones* 2
Galaxies (Malzberg) 109
Galaxy 92
Galvani, Luigi 150
Garfield (comic strip) 64, 65, 67, 68, 69, 70, 71, 72, 177
Garfield books 98
Garland, Judy 107, 170
Garrick, David 125
Genesis 71, 84, 114, 134
Generation of Vipers (Wylie) 26
Genet, Jean 48, 170; *Our Lady of the Flowers* 58
Gernsback, Hugo 50, 134, 136
"The Gernsback Continuum" (Gibson) 115–116
Ghost (film) 127
The Ghost of Frankenstein (film) 16

Gibson, William 109–110, 115–116, 122, 136–137, 149–150, 152, 170; "The Gernsback Continuum" 115–116; *Neuromancer* 109–110, 122, 137, 143, 149–150
Gielgud, John 95–96
Gigi (film) 138
Gilgamesh 130, 136, 162, 178
Gilligan's Island (TV series) 156, 157, 158, 161
Ginsberg, Allen 102–103, 107, 109, 110, 170; *Howl* 102–103, 106, 109
Godzilla (film) 18
Goedel, Kurt 160
Goethe, Johann Wolfgang von 85; *Faust* 85
Goldman, William 96; *The Princess Bride* 96
Gordon, Andy 169
The Gospel of John 153–154
The Gospel of Luke 154
The Gospel of Mark 110
Graff, Gerald 162
Grahame, Kenneth 95, 101; *The Wind in the Willows* 91, 92
The Grateful Dead 74; "Dark Star" 74
Gravity's Rainbow (Pynchon) 35, 122, 137
The Great Gatsby (Fitzgerald) 78, 88, 100
Greene, Graham 40, 140
Gresham, Thomas 94
Gribbin, John 65
Griffith, D.W. 40
"Grooveyard" (Perkins) 179
Gulliver's Travels (Swift) 96
Guth, Alan 156

Hadas, Moses 129
Haldeman, Joe 54; *The Forever War* 54
Hamlet (Shakespeare) 83, 87, 93, 150, 174
Hammerstein, Oscar 139
Hammett, Dashiell 2, 48–49
The Handmaid's Tale (Atwood) 138
Hanzo, Thomas A. 53, 99
Harding, Tonya 132
Hardy, Thomas 156
Harry Garnish novels (McConnell) 118
Hart, Lorenz 106; "Little Girl Blue" (with Rodgers) 106
Harvey, William 128, 150
The Haunted Palace (film) 27
Hawkes, Jacquetta 76
Hawking, Stephen 157, 158, 160–161; *A Brief History of Time* 160–161
Hawkins, Anthony Hope 52; *The Prisoner of Zenda* 54
Hawks, Howard 19
Haydn, Joseph 113–114; "Surprise" symphony 113–114
Hegel, G.W.F. 77, 85, 157
Heidegger, Martin 21, 159
Heinlein, Robert A. 48, 54, 143, 174–175; *Methuselah's Children* 174; *The Puppet Masters* 54; *Starship Troopers* 48, 54; *Stranger in a Strange Land* 138
Heisenberg, Werner 50, 160

"Hell Is Forever" (Bester) 174
Hemingway, Ernest 83–84, 88, 100, 101, 108; "Big Two-Hearted River" 83–84; "Soldier's Home" 88; *The Sun Also Rises* 100
Hendrix, Howard V. 169–172
Hepburn, Katharine 115
Heraclitus 156
Herbert, Frank 69, 95, 126; *Dune* 69, 95, 126, 128
Herbert, George 18
H.G. Wells' The Shape of Things to Come (film) 42–43
The History of Mr. Polly (Wells) 40, 45
Hitchens, Christopher 147; *The Missionary Position* 147
The Hitchhiker's Guide to the Galaxy (Adams) 117
Hitler, Adolf 62, 115–116, 148; *Mein Kampf* 62
Hobbes, Thomas 122, 177; *Leviathan* 122
Hoffmann, E.T.A. 128
Hofstadter, Douglas 17
Homage to Catalonia (Orwell) 59
Homer 70, 80, 86, 88, 93, 130–131; *The Iliad* 70, 80, 86, 120, 131, 139; *The Odyssey* 67, 70, 88, 130–131, 139
Homo Ludens (Huizinga) 82
Hopkins, Gerard Manly 141
Hough, John 86–87; *The Conduct of the Game* 86–87
House of Usher (film) 27
Howl (Ginsberg) 102–103, 106, 109
Hubbard, L. Ron 147, 170
"Hugh Selwyn Mauberly" (Pound) 69
Huizinga, Johan 82; *Homo Ludens* 82
The Hunting of the Snark (Carroll) 92
Huss, Roy 19
Huxley, Aldous 137; *Brave New World* 137
Huxley, T.H. 32

I Ching 79
"I Had Thought Things Were Going Well" (Ashbery) 72
"I Have No Mouth, and I Must Scream" (Ellison) 48
"I Should Care" (Cahn, Stordahl, and Weston) 179
"I Sing the Body Electric" (Whitman) 150
I Spit on Your Grave (film) 60
The Iliad (Homer) 70, 80, 86, 120, 131, 139
In the Days of the Comet (Wells) 137
Inner Sanctum (radio show) 138
The Interpretation of Dreams (Freud) 77
Invasion of the Body Snatchers (film) 19, 20, 26
The Invisible Man (film) 41–42
The Invisible Man (Wells) 30, 39, 41–42
The Island of Dr. Moreau (1977 film) 42–43
The Island of Dr. Moreau (Wells) 30, 41, 151
The Island of Lost Souls (film) 41

Jackson, Reggie 90
James, Henry 31, 39–40, 94, 112, 143

Jameson, Fredric 107, 137, 162
JEGP 106
"Jerusalem" (Blake) 103
Jesus Christ 64, 109, 121, 147, 153–154
Jitterbug Perfume (Robbins) 69
John 153–154; The Gospel of John 153–154
John of Patmos 57, 169; The Book of Revelation 57
John Paul II 146
Johnson, Magic 143
Johnson, Samuel 68, 72
Johnston, Lynn 68
Joshua 85
Joyce, James 39–40, 40, 48, 66–67, 67, 79; *Ulysses* 67
Jung, C.G. 14, 25, 91, 95
"Jupiter" symphony (Mozart) 113–114

Kafka, Franz 19–20, 79, 89, 103, 104, 170; "Before the Law" 104; "Leopards in the Temple" 103; "The Metamorphosis" 89; *The Trial* 104
Karloff, Boris 16–17
Keats, John 60
Kennedy, John F. 27
Kermode, Frank 57, 66–67
Kettle, Arnold 94
Kevorkian, Jack 153, 170
Keyes, Daniel 151; "Flowers for Algernon" 151
Khan, Genghis 51
Kierkegaard, Søren 52–53, 54, 64, 67, 100; *Fear and Trembling* 67, 100; *The Sickness Unto Death* 52
King, Stephen 90, 101
King Kong (film) 24
King Lear (Shakespeare) 5, 67–68, 72–73, 85, 87, 90, 101, 124–125, 126, 128, 130, 131, 143, 158, 161, 174
The King Who Was a King (Wells) 43
Kingston, Maxine Hong 78
Kipps (Wells) 31, 40
Kiss Me Deadly (Spillane) 159
Koestler, Arthur 35, 66
Kolakowski, Leszek 50, 72
Konitz, Lee 179
Kornbluth, C.M. 94, 122; *The Space Merchants* (with Pohl) 94, 122
Kubrick, Stanley 17, 60–61, 126, 169–170

Lamour, Dorothy 22
Lang, Fritz 43, 151
Larsen, Stephen 91–92; *The Shaman's Doorway* 91–92
Larson, Gary 68
Last and First Men (Stapledon) 147
The Last Unicorn (Beagle) 96
The Late Great Creature (Brower) 18
Laughter (Bergson) 126
Laughton, Charles 41
Laverne and Shirley (TV series) 59
Lawrence, D.H. 30

Index

Leahy, Frank 90
Leavis, Q.D. 94
Lefebvre, Henri 97
Le Guin, Ursula K. 80, 92, 178; Earthsea Trilogy 92
Lem, Stanislaw 75, 79, 99–100; *The Cyberiad* 79; *Microworlds* 99–100; *Solaris* 79
Leonard, Sugar Ray 86
Leonardo da Vinci 94; *Mona Lisa* 106–107, 170
"Leopards in the Temple" (Kafka) 103
Lessing, Doris 92–93
Lethem, Jonathan 152
Letters (Barth) 35
Lévi-Strauss, Claude 119, 120–121
Leviathan (Hobbes) 122
Lew Archer stories (Macdonald) 118
Lewis, C.S. 30, 35, 90, 96, 97, 151–152, 157, 161, 170; Narnia series 90; *Perelandra* 151–152, 161; The Space Trilogy 96
Lewis, Jerry Lee 139
Life, the Universe, and Everything (Adams) 66
Lindsay, David 89–90, 92, 96; *A Voyage to Arcturus* 89–90, 92, 100
"Little Girl Blue" (Rodgers and Hart) 106
Little Orphan Annie (comic strip) 63
Little Richard 74; "Tutti Frutti" 74
Locke, John 128
Locus 174–175
Lolita (Nabokov) 139
Longus 129; *Daphnis and Chloe* 129
The Lord of the Rings (Tolkien) 54, 71, 74, 89–90, 96, 100, 102
Los Angeles Times 68
"The Love Song of J. Arthur Prufrock" (Eliot) 103
"The Lovers" (Picasso) 106
Lowell, Robert 27–28, 110, 170; "The Quaker Graveyard at Nantucket" 110; "Skunk Hour" 27–28
Lucas, George 59
Lucretius 83; *De Rerum Natura* 83
Lugosi, Bela 16
Lukacs, George 94
Luke 154; The Gospel of Luke 154
Lumiére, Auguste 37
Lumiére, Louis 37
Lynch, David 15, 126
Lyrical Ballads "Preface" (Wordsworth) 155

Macbeth (Shakespeare) 98–99, 135
MacDonald, John D. 48–49
MacKenzie, Jeanne 30
MacKenzie, Norman 30
The Magazine of Fantasy and Science Fiction 98
The Mahabharata 120, 159
Mailer, Norman 69, 101, 105, 116, 117, 140, 170; *The Armies of the Night* 105; *The Executioner's Song* 94; *Why Are We in Vietnam?* 69
Malcolm X 69, 140; *The Autobiography of Malcolm X* 69
Malzberg, Barry N. 109, 170; *Galaxies* 109
The Mammoth Hunters (Auel) 98
The Man from Planet X (film) 19, 20
The Man in the High Castle (Dick) 79, 103–105, 108
"The Man with the Blue Guitar" (Stevens) 76, 82–83, 122–123
Manfred (Byron) 11
Mapplethorpe, Robert 109
Marconi, Gugliemo 37
Marcus Aurelius 136
Marcuse, Herbert 106, 109, 170; *One-Dimensional Man* 106
Marlowe, Hugh 27
Martin Kane, Private Investigator (radio show) 138
Marx, Karl 13, 62, 80–81
Mary Worth (comic strip) 63
"The Masque of the Red Death" (Poe) 57, 129–130
McCaffrey, Anne 74, 93, 94–95; *The Dragonriders of Pern* 74; Dragonriders of Pern series 94–95; *Dragonsong* 99
McCarthy, Joseph 20, 26
McConnell, Frank 1–3, 5–8, 118, 141, 150, 163, 164–179; *Blood Lake* 165; Harry Garnish novels 118; *Murder Among Friends* 165; *The Science Fiction of H.G. Wells* 166, 179; *The Spoken Seen* 178
Mein Kampf (Hitler) 62
Méliès, Georges 37, 39, 41
Men Like Gods (Wells) 147
Menzies, William Cameron 43, 44
Merrick, John 15, 106–107
Merril, Judith 98, 138–139
"The Metamorphosis" (Kafka) 89
Methuselah's Children (Heinlein) 174
Metropolis (film) 43, 151
Metropolis (von Harbou) 43
Metz, Christian 39, 71
Microworlds (Lem) 99–100
A Midsummer Night's Dream (Shakespeare) 129
Mike Hammer stories (Spillane) 118
Miller, J. Hillis 141, 142, 162
Miller, Joseph D. 144, 169, 173–175
Miller, Walter M., Jr. 162; *A Canticle for Leibowitz* 162
Milton, John 68, 85, 155; *Paradise Lost* 85, 101, 140–141
Mind at the End of Its Tether (Wells) 29
Mingus, Charles 161
Mr. Sammler's Planet (Bellow) 35, 49
Mitchell, John 70
Modern Times (film) 61
A Modern Utopia (Wells) 40–41
Mona Lisa (Leonardo da Vinci) 106–107, 170
The Monkolonious 67, 71
Mont Blanc (Shelley) 11
Morin, Violette 64
Moses 86, 93, 143

Index

Mozart, Wolfgang Amadeus 67, 113–114, 161, 179; "Jupiter" symphony 113–114
Muhammad 87
Murder Among Friends (McConnell) 165
Myth and Reality (Eliade) 82
The Myth of Sisyphus (Camus) 121

Nabokov, Vladimir 79, 92; *Lolita* 139
Naked Lunch (Burroughs) 122, 139
Narnia series (Lewis) 90
Nero Wolfe stories (Stout) 118
Neuromancer (Gibson) 109–110, 122, 137, 143, 149–150
"Neutron Star" (Niven) 48
New York Times 92
New York Times Book Review 75
Newsweek 93, 104
Nietzsche, Friedrich 108, 134–135, 150
Nine Princes in Amber (Zelazny) 48
Nine Princes in Amber series (Zelazny) 70, 93
1984 (1956 film) 60
1984 (1984 film) 59
Nineteen Eighty-Four (Orwell) 57–62
"1999" (Prince) 57
Niven, Larry 48, 51, 54, 79, 80, 95; *The Flight of the Horse* 48; "Neutron Star" 48; *Protector* 54; *The Ringworld Engineers* 99; Ringworld novels 54, 95
Not of This Earth (film) 20
Nova (Delany) 70, 114
Nowlan, Philip Francis 57; *Armageddon 2419 A.D.* 57
Nyby, Christian 19

The Odyssey (Homer) 67, 70, 88, 130–131, 139
Oedipus Rex (Sophocles) 133, 150
Oliver, Chad 138–139; "Blood's a Rover" 138
Olivier, Laurence 164
"On Fairy Stories" (Tolkien) 96–97
On the Origin of Species (Darwin) 33, 159
One-Dimensional Man (Marcuse) 106
Orff, Carl 92
Orwell, George 29, 30, 44, 57–62, 85, 158, 169; *Homage to Catalonia* 59; *Nineteen Eighty-Four* 57–62; "Politics and the English Language" 62
Othello (Shakespeare) 102
Our Lady of the Flowers (Genet) 58
The Outline of History (Wells) 35
Outworld Cats (Lovejoy) 134
Overgard, William 68
Ovid 18
Oxford English Dictionary 148, 150

Pal, George 42
Pamela (Richardson) 94
Paracelsus 151
Paradise Lost (Milton) 85, 101, 140–141
Parker, Charlie 5, 102, 103, 139, 168, 170
Parmenides 156, 159
Parzival (von Eschenbach) 144

Patton (film) 83
Paul 14, 120, 157
Pauli, Wolfgang 83–84, 157
Payton, Walter 90
Peanuts (comic strip) 63, 71
Pearl 101
Penrose, Roger 162
Perelandra (Lewis) 151–152, 161
Perkins, David 102; *British and American Poets, Chaucer to the Present* (ed. with Bate) 102–103
Peters, Jean 26–27
Petronius 57, 169
Phaedo (Plato) 153
Philip Marlowe stories (Chandler) 118
Physiologue du Gout (Brillat-Savarin) 117
Picasso, Pablo 106; "The Lovers" 106
Pickup on South Street (film) 26–27
The Picture of Dorian Gray (Wilde) 108, 134–135
"Pippa Passes" (Browning) 43
Planet Stories 139, 148
Plato 70, 71, 150, 153, 154; *Phaedo* 153; *Republic* 71
PMLA 93, 106
Poe, Edgar Allan 27, 57, 129–130, 169; "The Masque of the Red Death" 57, 129–130
Poetics (Aristotle) 93
The Poetics of Space (Bachelard) 85
Pohl, Frederik 57, 94, 107, 122, 138–139, 147, 148, 170; *The Space Merchants* (with Kornbluth) 94, 122
Police Gazette 148
"Politics and the English Language" (Orwell) 62
Pope, Alexander 84, 137, 152; "The Rape of the Lock" 84, 87
Popular Mechanics 115
Potter, Beatrix 85
Pound, Ezra 69; "Hugh Selwyn Mauberly" 69
Pournelle, Jerry 71
Powell, Bud 179
The Practice of Faith (Rahner) 88
The Prelude (Wordsworth) 139
Price, Vincent 27
Pride and Prejudice (Austen) 89
Prince 57, 169; "1999" 57
The Princess Bride (Goldman) 96
Principia Mathematica (Newton) 163
Prirogine, Ilya 65, 162
The Prisoner of Zenda (Hawkins) 52
The Private War of Major Benson (film) 23
Propp, Vladimir 91–92
Protector (Niven) 54
Proust, Marcel 148
The Psychopathology of Everyday Life (Freud) 77
The Puppet Masters (Heinlein) 54
Pynchon, Thomas 5, 12, 18, 32, 35, 49, 66–67, 116–117, 122, 128–129, 137, 140, 152, 156; *The Crying of Lot 49* 18, 49; *Gravity's Rainbow* 35, 122, 137; *Slow Learner* 116–117, 128; *V* 49

"The Quaker Graveyard at Nantucket" (Lowell) 110
Queen, Ellery 133, 139

Rabelais, François 52
Rabkin, Eric S. 58, 175–177
Rahner, Karl 88, 125; *The Practice of Faith* 88
Rains, Claude 41
"The Rape of the Lock" (Pope) 84, 87
The Raw and the Cooked (Lévi-Strauss) 120
Raymond, Alex 107
Reagan, Ronald 63, 69
"Reality Is an Activity of the Most August Imagination" (Stevens) 160
Reason, Rex 27
"'Repent, Harlequin!' Said the Ticktockman" (Ellison) 60
Reptilicus (film) 18
Republic (Plato) 71
Return of the Jedi (film) 100
Revenge of the Creature (film) 19
Rex Morgan, M.D. (comic strip) 63
Richards, I.A. 97
Richardson, Samuel 94; *Pamela* 94
Riefenstahl, Leni 44–45
Rimbaud, Arthur 76, 77
The Ringworld Engineers (Niven) 99
Ringworld novels (Niven) 54, 95
Riverworld novels (Farmer) 95
Robbins, Amy Catherine 32–33
Robbins, Tom 67, 84; *Even Cowgirls Get the Blues* 84; *Jitterbug Perfume* 67
Robinson, Spider 174–175
Robot stories (Asimov) 151
Rodgers, Richard 106, 139; "Little Girl Blue" (with Hart) 106
Roentgen, Wilhelm 37
Rogers, Ginger 135
Rolling Stone 78
The Rolling Stones 27
Rollins, Sonny 130
Romeo and Juliet (Shakespeare) 148
Rose, Mark 177
Ross, T.J. 19
Rouse, A.L. 68
"The Royal Game" (Zweig) 87
Rudy (comic strip) 68
Ruskin, John 77
Russell, Bertrand 160
Ryan, Tom K. 68

Sagan, Carl 35, 52, 79
San Francisco Chronicle 68
Sanders, Lawrence 94, 122; *The First Deadly Sin* 122; *The Seduction of Peter S.* 94
Sandman (comic book; Gaiman) 1
Sandman: The Kindly Ones (Gaiman) 2
"Santa Claus Is Coming to Town" (Coots and Gillespie) 113–114
Sartre, Jean-Paul 83, 121; *Being and Nothingness* 121

Saussure, Ferdinand de 97, 144
Sayers, Dorothy 48–49
The Scarlet Pimpernel (Orczy) 107
Schlesinger, John 25
Schneidau, Herbert 49–50
Scholes, Robert 66–67
Schultz, Charles 63
The Science Fiction of H.G. Wells (McConnell) 166, 179
Scott, George C. 83
Scott, Ridley 126, 151
Second Foundation (Asimov) 54
The Seduction of Peter S. (Sanders) 94
Seinfeld (TV series) 5, 157
Self-Help (Smiles) 33
Seuss, Dr. 83
Shakespeare, William 22, 52, 62, 67–68, 80, 93, 98–99, 124, 135, 144, 148, 155, 161, 165; *As You Like It* 22, 52; *Hamlet* 83, 87, 93, 150, 174; *King Lear* 5, 67–68, 72–73, 85, 87, 90, 101, 124–125, 126, 128, 130, 131, 143, 158, 161, 174; *Macbeth* 98–99, 135; *A Midsummer Night's Dream* 90, 129; *Othello* 102; *Romeo and Juliet* 148; *The Tempest* 22, 80, 89–90, 129–130, 158; *The Winter's Tale* 129
The Shaman's Doorway (Larsen) 91–92
The Shape of Things to Come (Wells) 35, 43
Shaw, George Bernard 30
Sheldon, Jack 179
Shelley, Mary 5, 11, 15, 16, 17, 19–20, 128, 136–137, 150, 163; *Frankenstein* 5, 8, 11–17, 137, 150–151, 163, 170
Shelley, Percy Blythe 12, 157; *Alastor* 12; *Mont Blanc* 11
Sherlock Holmes stories (Conan Doyle) 118
Sherwood, John 19
Shuster, Jerry 107–108, 170
The Sickness Unto Death (Kierkegaard) 52
Siegel, Don 19
Siegel, Joe 107–108, 170
The Silence of the Lambs (film) 136
Silent Movie (film) 61
Simon, John 69
Sir Gawain and the Green Knight 100, 101, 162
The Six Million Dollar Man (TV series) 150
"Skunk Hour" (Lowell) 27–28
The Skylark of Space (Smith) 107
Slaughterhouse-Five (Vonnegut) 72
"Slow Dance" (Levister) 179
Slow Learner (Pynchon) 116–117, 128
Slusser, George 8, 92, 101, 149, 169, 178–179
Smiles, Samuel 33–34; *Self-Help* 34
Smith, Adam 107
Smith, Barbara Herrnstein 64
Smith, E.E. "Doc" 71, 95, 107, 170; *The Skylark of Space* 107
Smollett, Tobias 94
Sobchack, Vivian 78
Socrates 150, 153, 154
Solaris (Lem) 79
"Soldier's Home" (Hemingway) 88

Index

Some Versions of Pastoral (Empson) 86
Songs of Experience (Blake) 161
Songs of Innocence (Blake) 161
Sorel, Georges 37
Souza, John Phillip 139
The Space Merchants (Pohl and Kornbluth) 94, 122
The Space Trilogy (Lewis) 96
The Spectator 40
Spillane, Mickey 139, 159; *Kiss Me Deadly* 159
Spinrad, Norman 74, 114–115; *The Void Captain's Tale* 114–115
The Spoken Seen (McConnell) 178
Springsteen, Bruce 49, 113–114; "Born to Run" 49
Stansky, Peter 58–59
Stapledon, Olaf 54, 55–56, 147; *Last and First Men* 147; *Star Maker* 55–56
Star Maker (Stapledon) 55–56
Star Wars (film) 37, 44, 85, 157–158, 160
Stars in My Pocket Like Grains of Sand (Delany) 70
The Stars My Destination (Bester) 49, 96, 136, 159, 163
Starship Troopers (Heinlein) 48, 54
Steinem, Gloria 78
Steiner, George 62, 89, 135
Sterne, Laurence 94
Stevens, Wallace 5, 71, 76, 82–83, 115, 122–123, 127, 128, 131, 154, 156, 160, 162, 173; "Esthétique du Mal" 127; "The Man with the Blue Guitar" 76, 82–83, 122–123; "Reality Is an Activity of the Most August Imagination" 160; "Sunday Morning" 115
Stevenson, Robert Louis 151; *Dr. Jekyll and Mr. Hyde* 151
Stout, Rex 118; Nero Wolfe stories 118
Strange Wine (Ellison) 59
Stranger in a Strange Land (Heinlein) 138
Strauss, Johann 127
Stravinsky, Igor 67
Straw Dogs (film) 60
Studies in a Dying Culture (Caudwell) 181–182n
The Sturgeonodore 156
The Sun Also Rises (Hemingway) 100
Sunday, Bloody Sunday (film) 25
"Sunday Morning" (Stevens) 115
Superman (comic strip) 107–108, 170
"Surprise" symphony (Haydn) 113–114
Swayze, Patrick 127
"Sweet and Lovely" (Arnheim, LeMare, and Tobias) 179
Swift, Jonathan 70; *Gulliver's Travels* 96

Tarantula (film) 20
Tarzan of the Apes (Burroughs) 170
Teilhard de Chardin 146
The Tempest (Shakespeare) 22, 80, 89–90, 129–130, 158
Teresa, Mother 147, 151, 170
Thackeray, William Makepeace 39

Thales 156
Them! (film) 5, 20, 27
Thesinger, Ernest 14
The Thing (from Another World) (film) 19, 20
Things to Come (film) 35, 37, 39, 40, 43–44, 115, 148
This Island Earth (film) 20, 27
THX 1138 (film) 59
Tillich, Paul 122, 146
The Time Machine (film) 42
The Time Machine (Wells) 29, 30, 33, 34, 37, 38, 41, 42, 57, 97–98, 143–144, 148
Tiptree, James, Jr. [Alice Sheldon], 98
TLS 92
Todorov, Tzvetan 64, 97, 99–100, 116; *The Fantastic* 99–100
Tolkien, J.R.R. 54, 89–90, 96–97, 98; "*Beowulf*: The Monsters and the Critics" 98; *The Lord of the Rings* 54, 71, 74, 89–90, 96, 100, 102; "On Fairy Stories" 96–97
Tolstoy, Leo 101, 163; *Anna Karenina* 101, 163
Tono-Bungay (Wells) 40
The Torah 70
Townshend, Peter 106, 170
Tractacus Logico-Philosophus (Wittgenstein) 122, 156
Tracy, Spencer 115
Travels with Farley (comic strip) 68
The Trial (Kafka) 104
Trudeau, Gerry 68, 69, 70
Truffaut, François 15, 60, 169–170
Tumbleweeds (comic strip) 68
"Tutti Frutti" (Little Richard) 74
Twain, Mark 65
Twardzik, Richard 179
Twisted Sister 105–106
2001: A Space Odyssey (film) 17, 60–61, 69, 86, 126, 127, 128, 137, 157–158, 160
2010: Odyssey Two (Clarke) 54–55, 61
Tyler, Parker 18

Ubik (Dick) 79
Ulysses (Joyce) 67
"Under Which Lyre" (Auden) 137
The Universal Baseball Association, Inc., J. Henry Waugh, Prop. (Coover) 90
The Upanishads 125
Updike, John 78

V (Pynchon) 49
Valis (Dick) 79, 94
Veblen, Thorstein 153
Veeck, Bill 89
Verne, Jules 39, 51; *From the Earth to the Moon* 39
Vianney, Brother John 134
Virgil 149
The Void Captain's Tale (Spinrad) 114–115
Von Eschenbach, Wolfram 144; *Parzival* 144
Von Franz, Marie-Louise 100
Von Harbou, Thea 43; *Metropolis* 43

Vonnegut, Kurt, Jr. 32, 72; *Slaughterhouse-Five* 72
A Voyage to Arcturus (Lindsay) 89–90, 92, 100
A Voyage to the Moon (film) 37, 39, 41

Waller, Fats 108
The War in the Air (Wells) 181n
The War of the Worlds (Wells) 30, 33, 41, 42, 79
The War of the Worlds (1953 film) 42
The War of the Worlds (radio show) 42
Warhol, Andy 109, 170
Watt, Ian 95
Watt, James 51
Watterson, Bill 121–122
The Way the Future Was (Pohl) 107
Webb, Beatrice 30
Webb, Stanley 30
Weber, Max 94
Welles, Orson 42
Wells, H.G. 2, 8, 29–36, 37–45, 51, 57, 58–59, 75, 79, 96, 97–98, 114, 136–137, 147, 148, 143–144, 151, 166, 170, 179, 182n; *Ann Veronica* 40; *The Fate of Homo Sapiens* 30; *The First Men in the Moon* 30, 38, 39, 41; *The History of Mr. Polly* 40, 45; *In the Days of the Comet* 137; *The Invisible Man* 30, 39, 41–42; *The Island of Dr. Moreau* 30, 41, 151; *The King Who Was a King* 43; *Kipps* 31, 40; *Men Like Gods* 147; *Mind at the End of Its Tether* 29; *A Modern Utopia* 40–41; *The Outline of History* 35; *The Shape of Things to Come* 35, 43; *The Time Machine* 29, 30, 33, 34, 37, 38, 41, 42, 57, 97–98, 143–144, 148; *Tono-Bungay* 40; *The War in the Air* 181n; *The War of the Worlds* 30, 33, 41, 42, 79; *When the Sleeper Wakes* 36
Wells, Isabell 32
West, Rebecca 33
Westfahl, Gary 5–8
Whale, James 13, 14–15, 24, 41
What Was Literature? (Fiedler) 101
Wheel of Fortune (TV series) 112
When the Sleeper Wakes (Wells) 36

Whitehead, Alfred 130, 152
Whitman, Walt 107, 108, 150, 170; "I Sing the Body Electric" 150
Whitmore, James 27
The Who 27
Why Are We in Vietnam? (Mailer) 69
Widmark, Richard 26–27
Wilcox, Fred 22
The Wild Child (film) 15
Wilde, Oscar 108, 134–135, 139, 153; *The Picture of Dorian Gray* 108, 134–135
Williams, William Carlos 156
Wilson, Justin 116
Wilson, Woodrow 132
The Wilson Quarterly 141
The Wind in the Willows (Grahame) 91, 95
The Winter's Tale (Shakespeare) 129
Wittgenstein, Ludwig 84, 105, 122, 141, 156, 159, 160; *Tractacus Logico-Philosophicus* 122, 156
Wolfe, Gene 2
Wonder, Stevie 112, 139
Woolf, Virginia 30, 39–40
Wordsworth, William 5, 38, 131, 139, 140, 155–156, 157, 158, 160–161, 167, 178; *The Excursion* 155–156; *Lyrical Ballads* "Preface" 155; *The Prelude* 139
The World, the Flesh, and the Devil (Bernal) 146
Wray, Fay 24
Wylie, Philip 26; *Generation of Vipers* 26

Yeats, W.B. 15, 151
Young, Sean 128
Young Frankenstein (film) 14–15
Youngman, Henny 66

Zelazny, Roger 48, 70, 93; *Nine Princes in Amber* 48; *Nine Princes in Amber* series 70, 93
Zieff, Bob 179
Zosimus the Panopolitan 13
Zweig, Stefan 87; "The Royal Game" 87

www.ingramcontent.com/pod-product-compliance
Ingram Content Group UK Ltd.
Pitfield, Milton Keynes, MK11 3LW, UK
UKHW041918140426
5217IPUK00013B/208